D1522907

SUBORDINATING
INTELLIGENCE

SUBORDINATING INTELLIGENCE

The DoD/CIA Post–Cold War Relationship

David P. Oakley

UNIVERSITY PRESS OF KENTUCKY

Copyright © 2019 by The University Press of Kentucky

Scholarly publisher for the Commonwealth,
serving Bellarmine University, Berea College, Centre
College of Kentucky, Eastern Kentucky University,
The Filson Historical Society, Georgetown College,
Kentucky Historical Society, Kentucky State University,
Morehead State University, Murray State University,
Northern Kentucky University, Transylvania University,
University of Kentucky, University of Louisville,
and Western Kentucky University.

Editorial and Sales Offices: The University Press of Kentucky
663 South Limestone Street, Lexington, Kentucky 40508–4008
www.kentuckypress.com

Cataloging-in-Publication data available from the Library of Congress

ISBN 978-0-8131-7670-3 (hardcover : alk. paper)
ISBN 978-0-8131-7673-4 (pdf)
ISBN 978-0-8131-7671-0 (epub)

This book is printed on acid-free paper meeting
the requirements of the American National Standard
for Permanence in Paper for Printed Library Materials.

Manufactured in the United States of America.

 Member of the Association
of University Presses

To my wife, Kristen, and children, Taylor, Tanner, Tatum, and Tyler, whose support and love provided me the strength and motivation to research and write this book

CONTENTS

PREFACE

The research for this book began in 2012 when I was a student at the US Army's School of Advanced Military Studies (SAMS). One of the school's requirements is to write a monograph focused on an operational issue. As a military officer and former Central Intelligence Agency (CIA) officer, I decided to use the opportunity to explore the CIA and Department of Defense's (DoD) shared history since the National Security Act of 1947. This motivation stemmed from an affinity for both organizations, a curiosity regarding DoD/CIA interactions and wonderment about how each developed its distinct cultures despite shared lineage.

My research efforts began with the National Security Act of 1947, but the post–Cold War, post–Desert Storm period quickly surfaced as a key turning point in the relationship. Both the CIA and the DoD were established at the beginning of the Cold War, and the culture of each was shaped by the nearly fifty-year struggle. The collapse of the Soviet Union brought elation but also uncertainty to the CIA and the DoD. The two organizations were no longer chasing or preparing to fight Soviets but trying to understand a new world while undergoing significant budget and personnel reductions. The CIA and the DoD coordinated sporadically throughout the Cold War, but it was in the uncertain 1990s that support to military operations became the priority mission for the CIA and national intelligence. Although subsequent conflicts in Afghanistan and Iraq as well as worldwide counterterrorism operations provided a common purpose and helped develop the CIA/DoD partnership, it was policy actions and organizational changes in the 1990s that set the foundation.

My first paper, "Partners or Competitors? The Evolution of the DoD/CIA Relationship since Desert Storm and its Prospects for the Future" (2014) focused on how increased interaction in education, training, and operations resulted in tactical and operational successes.[1] This book builds upon the earlier research while delving deeper into how choices made during the late 1980s, the 1990s, and the first decade of the twenty-first century shaped the current DoD/CIA relationship. Although I still believe the evolution of this relationship provides positive benefits, the further I explore it, the more I recognize trade-offs and appreciate the risks involved. The CIA was created in 1947 to serve as an independent intelligence organization to inform policy and strategy without being unduly influenced by organizations responsible for policy implementation. Beginning in the 1990s and hastened after the events of September 11, 2001 (9/11), the demand for CIA support to military operations started to erode this separation.

After 9/11, the United States became hyperfocused on ridding the world of a terrorist threat, while issues such as a rising China and a reemerging Russia dropped in priority. The focus on identifying and targeting terrorist threats took priority over trying to understand the intentions of world leaders or informing policy and strategy development. As retired admiral William Studeman remarked during an interview, the United States dropped fundamental intelligence coverage while it focused on "Lucy and the football."[2] Although this shift toward counterterrorism and support to military operations resulted in operational successes such as the killing of Osama bin Laden and Abu Musab al Zarqawi, it has also resulted in the neglect of longer-term strategic issues.

The more I considered the evolution of the DoD/CIA relationship following Desert Storm, the more I saw linkages to and parallels with the broader militarization of US foreign policy that various authors and national security professionals have identified. The military started to emerge as the US preferred policy tool in the 1990s and then solidified that position following September 2001. The embrace of military power to transform Iraq and Afghanistan as well as the empowerment of regional combatant commanders to "shape" their environment have made the military the dominant player in foreign policy. And although Iraq, Afghanistan, Syria, and Libya have shown the limits and unpredictability of using military force, there are still loud voices arguing that military power is the solution. This imbalance has created an environment in which the DoD leads and all others support. In this regard, the evolution of the CIA/DoD relationship is both a cause and a symptom of the militarization of foreign policy. Although policy makers can recognize the benefits this partnership provides, they should also appreciate the cost the nation assumes by operationalizing its only independent intelligence organization. I hope this book helps further that understanding.

The views in this book are entirely mine and do not necessarily reflect the views, policy, or position of the US government, the Department of Defense, or the Central Intelligence Agency.

ABBREVIATIONS

ADMA	associate director of military affairs
ARCENT	Army Central Command
ASD	assistant secretary of defense
BDA	battle damage assessment
CENTCOM	Central Command
CIA	Central Intelligence Agency
CINC	commander in chief
CRS	Congressional Research Service
CTC	Counterterrorism Center
DCI	director of central intelligence
DCIA	director of the Central Intelligence Agency
DCS	Defense Clandestine Service
DDO	deputy director of operations
DDO/MA	deputy director of operations for military affairs
DDO/MS	deputy director of operations for military support
DHMO	Defense Human Management Office
DHS	Defense Human Intelligence Service
DI	Directorate of Intelligence
DIA	Defense Intelligence Agency
DMI	director of military intelligence
DNI	director of national intelligence
DO	Directorate of Operations
DoD	Department of Defense
FBI	Federal Bureau of Investigation
G2	General Staff Intelligence Section
GWOT	global war on terrorism

HASC	House Armed Services Committee
HPSCI	House Permanent Select Committee on Intelligence
HUMINT	human intelligence
IAA	Intelligence Authorization Act
IC21	Intelligence Community in the 21st Century
IRTPA	Intelligence Reform and Terrorism Prevention Act
J2	Joint Staff–Intelligence
J3	Joint Staff–Operations
J5	Joint Staff–Plans
JCS	Joint Chiefs of Staff
JIC	Joint Intelligence Center
JIOC	Joint Intelligence Operations Center
JITF-CT	Joint Intelligence Task Force–Counterterrorism
MINX	Multimedia Information Network System
MNF	multinational force
MOOTW	military operations other than war
NATO	North Atlantic Treaty Organization
NCS	National Clandestine Service
NDAA	National Defense Authorization Act
NGA	National Geospatial-Intelligence Agency
NPR	National Performance Review
NRO	National Reconnaissance Office
NSA	National Security Agency
NSC	National Security Council
NSD	National Security Directive
NSR	National Security Review
OMA	Office of Military Affairs
OSS	Office of Strategic Services
PDD	Presidential Decision Directive
PDF	Panamanian Defense Forces
RDI	Remodeling Defense Initiative
SASC	Senate Armed Services Committee
SOCOM	Special Operations Command
SOF	Special Operations Forces
SSB	Strategic Support Branch
SSCI	Senate Select Committee on Intelligence
USD	undersecretary of defense
USMLM	US Military Liaison Mission
WMD	weapons of mass destruction

INTRODUCTION

During an interview on May 3, 2011, then director of the Central Intelligence Agency (DCIA) Leon Panetta told interviewer Jim Lehrer that he was the overall commander for the Abbottabad Raid that killed Osama bin Laden.[1] Although some uniformed military officers disagreed with DCIA Panetta's assertion, Admiral William McRaven, commander, Joint Special Operations Command, who was the commander on the ground, had no issue with DCIA Panetta's role description.[2] In Admiral McRaven's opinion, arguments over who was within the chain of command were pedantic and not worthy of debate. Admiral McRaven credited the collaboration between the Department of Defense (DoD) and the Central Intelligence Agency (CIA) for the success of Operation Neptune Spear and did not believe it useful to dwell on debates about command authority. The DoD/CIA collaboration, not some outdated parochial attitude, was what brought about the demise of bin Laden. This DoD/CIA "interagency unified command" approach to locating and killing the US government's most wanted man signified the transformation of a DoD/CIA partnership from one of sporadic cooperation to one of regular integrated collaboration.

The DoD/CIA relationship expands well beyond special missions and has come to include integration during training, exercise, and operations. In the early 1990s, only a handful of military liaison officers were working with the CIA; today hundreds of uniformed personnel (active, guard, and reserve) serve in the CIA building. In addition, the agency has representatives at dozens of military commands and professional military schools.[3] There is ongoing interaction between the CIA and the DoD at multiple levels. CIA Special Activities deals directly with the theater special operations commands, and the CIA's Counterterrorism Center (CTC) deals directly with Special Operations Command (SOCOM). In addition, CIA's geographic division chiefs interact with Special Operations Forces (SOF) personnel in their region, and coordination occurs between SOF and other CIA centers such as the Counternarcotics Center. The numerous interactions between the CIA and the DoD build redundancy in the relationship, which protects against organizational stove piping and enables unity of effort.[4]

Although aspects of this relationship developed out of necessity during operations, the increased interaction during training has cultivated and institutionalized the partnership. Beyond serving as a gateway into the CIA, the CIA's associate director of military affairs (ADMA), whose origin dates back to the mid-1990s, has instituted various programs focused on increasing "support, information, and deconflicting issues between DoD/CIA" by cultivating nonparochial leaders who are familiar with both organizations and are aware of the value each brings.[5] For example, the ADMA hosts numerous military professionals during visits to CIA headquarters to build a greater familiarization of the CIA's mission. Recognizing the increased interaction between SOF and the CIA in Iraq and Afghanistan, the ADMA started bringing every newly minted special forces detachment captain to CIA headquarters to brief him or her on the CIA's mission and introduce him or her to CIA personnel.[6] The ADMA also works to educate the CIA workforce on the military mission and culture, providing predeployment briefs to CIA officers and serving as an accessible resource of information on the military or of contact information for military units.

Cross-pollination is also strengthening the relationship. A recent training class at the CIA's training facility had more than 25 percent military students, and, even more telling, a significant portion of the instructors serving at "the Farm" are from military services. Beyond the networking opportunities that joint training creates, the bond forged through shared training experience shapes the mindset of younger officers and results in organizational integration becoming a way of life and not merely a mandate. A senior CIA officer previously responsible for overseeing training throughout the organization stated in an interview that the "showcasing" of the military during training, the presence of military colleagues, and the operational experience in war zones are contributing to a more "enlightened" institution and CIA officers when it comes to working with the military.[7] This level of collaboration between the CIA and the DoD not only is unseen but also is changing institutional mindsets.[8]

Although both the CIA and the DoD originated with the National Security Act of 1947, an act that was meant to streamline national security affairs, the two organizations spent most of their first fifty years working separately toward US national security objectives. During the Cold War, they did work alongside each other in places such as Vietnam and Latin America and had established mutual-support agreements, but these previous interactions were not as consistent or integrated as their operations together after the terrorist attacks on September 11, 2001 (9/11). When the broader CIA and DoD did interact in this earlier period, it was usually contingent and in response to a significant need.[9] Although the post-9/11 collaboration involved niche and temporary elements, this book argues that the reoccurring integration of the CIA and the DoD across all facets of these organizations, in particular the ✓ CIA's increased focus on providing intelligence support to military operations and for force protection, is what sets the post-9/11 collaboration apart from these previous collaborative efforts.

Various contemporary first-person accounts describe the CIA/DoD operational relationship, often depicting a post-9/11 CIA focused on supporting the military's operational efforts and force-protection requirements. Some national security professionals argue that this increased collaboration is a direct result of the counterterrorism fight and the wars in Iraq and Afghanistan.[10] Their view is that the CIA and DoD developed a collaborative partnership in the aftermath of 9/11 to wage the global war on terrorism (GWOT). Although this viewpoint is accurate, it is incomplete because it overlooks or underestimates previous actions that set conditions for the partnership to grow.   *before?*

The GWOT gave the CIA and the DoD a common purpose, while providing an arena for iterative interaction that allowed the partnership to blossom, but the seed from which the partnership grew was planted in the late 1980s and early 1990s as the United States transitioned from the Cold War to an uncertain global environment. Beginning in the 1980s and continuing into the 1990s, policy makers and national security leaders, motivated by previous operational failures, started to focus on transforming the defense and intelligence communities for the post–Cold War world. Influenced by lessons learned during operations such as Urgent Fury, Just Cause, and Desert Storm, a major component of the transformation discussion focused on improving intelligence support to military planning, operations, and force protection. The call to improve intelligence support to military operations resulted in policy and organizational changes that altered the CIA/DoD relationship. These changes, coupled with internal changes within the DoD and the CIA motivated by the same operational failures, set the foundation for the post-9/11 partnership growth.

These organizational and policy changes were enabled by a shifting global order and technological developments that made national intelligence support to military operations both possible and necessary. The pending collapse of the Communist bloc meant the US Intelligence Community could decrease its focus on the Soviet Union and shift its gaze elsewhere. The precision-strike capability and speed of the battlefield displayed during Desert Storm increased the intelligence required for understanding, targeting, and information operations, while new computing and information technologies made it possible for soldiers on the front line to receive and disseminate national intelligence products. The "New World Order" and an accompanying regionally aligned national security strategy that was concerned with localized conflicts and with military operations other than war (MOOTW) also encouraged a shift toward increased intelligence support to military operations.[11]

Although the DoD/CIA relationship started to improve during this period, the improvement was not without cost. The increased focus on intelligence support to military operations and significant budget reductions forced the CIA and the rest of the Intelligence Community to assume risk by shifting resources away from global coverage and long-term analysis. By the late 1990s, congressional committees and independent task forces became concerned that too much focus was being placed on intelligence support to military operations and not enough on intelligence support to strategy and policy development. As this concern started to grow, the 9/11 attacks occurred, forcing the CIA to focus even more attention on immediate operations and away from global coverage and long-term analysis.[12]

Following 9/11 and with George W. Bush's declaration of a GWOT, the DoD found itself not only fighting wars in Iraq and Afghanistan but also taking a more proactive role throughout the globe. Empowered combatant commanders, embracing the concepts "shaping the environment" and "engagement" that originated in the 1990s, started devising security-cooperation plans focused on influencing their areas of operation.[13] Organized by geographic areas, enjoying large staffs and budgets, and having access to military forces and intelligence capabilities, the geographic combatant commanders' influence over foreign policy steadily increased. Along with this increased role in foreign policy came an ongoing need for greater intelligence support to the military outside traditional operations. This need, coupled with the intelligence requirements to support wars in Afghanistan and Iraq, found the Intelligence Community focused largely on supporting tactical operations rather than on long-term analysis.

Three presidents, George H. W. Bush, William J. Clinton, and George W. Bush, led the transition from the post–Cold War period to the post-9/11 period, each putting his imprint on how the CIA/DoD relationship evolved during this time. The George H. W. Bush administration was at the helm when the coalition won the Gulf War and the Soviet Union dissolved. Embracing a "peace dividend," the administration reduced national security spending and sought transformation of US national security structures.[14] Influenced by criticism of intelligence support to military operations during Desert Storm and the changing global landscape, it ordered "policy departments and agencies" to identify intelligence needs for the next thirteen years.[15] Armed with this knowledge, President Bush issued National Security Directive 67 (NSD-67), the "most dramatic reconfiguration of the Intelligence Community in decades," a major component of which was improving CIA support to military operations.[16] Yet, despite victory in Desert Storm and the Cold War, the George H. W. Bush administration could not secure a second term when a stagnant economy made international relations a secondary concern to domestic and economic issues.

Bill Clinton, the former Arkansas governor who campaigned on strengthening the economy, replaced George H. W. Bush in 1993. Two months into his administration, President Clinton directed a National Performance Review "to bring about greater efficiency and lower cost of government."[17] The review committee told the Intelligence Community it had to "improve support to ground troops during combat operations" even while it was undergoing significant budget reductions. In 1995, Clinton issued Presidential Decision Directive (PDD) 35, making support to military operations the Intelligence Community's top priority.[18] This priority was tested in Somalia and the Balkans, where an air campaign and small-scale humanitarian and peacekeeping operations provided a venue for the evolving DoD/CIA relationship.

The improved intelligence support to military operations continued into 1996, when the Commission on the Roles and Capabilities of the United States Intelligence Community and the Intelligence Community in the 21st Century study reviewed intelligence requirements in the post–Cold War world.[19] Although many civilian and military leaders testified that support to military operations deserved primacy, private organizations conducting their own reviews raised concerns regarding the dominance of military requirements over strategic intelligence needs.[20] Despite these concerns, support to military operations remained the Intelligence Community's top priority into the George W. Bush administration. The lack of intelligence support to strategic planning led former congressman Lee Hamilton to argue, "A lot of things are going to be neglected while you're providing military intelligence. Military Intelligence is important, but it is not the whole world."[21]

Eight years after George H. W. Bush lost his bid for a second term, his

son, George W. Bush, won a controversial election against Al Gore, Clinton's
vice president. Shortly after entering the White House, George W. Bush issued
National Security Decision Directive 5, becoming the third president seeking
to transform the Intelligence Community for the post–Cold War world. Part
of Bush's campaign platform criticized the Clinton administration's use of
military forces for MOOTW and promised to focus military capabilities on
strategic issues, such as an emerging China. After the terrorist attacks of September 11, 2001, the administration abandoned its promises and undertook
a global campaign against Al Qaeda and the tactic it employed. The GWOT
evolved into the US waging of counterinsurgency campaigns in Afghanistan
and Iraq that greatly surpassed any Clinton administration MOOTW effort.
These wars and global counterterrorism operations provided the CIA and the
DoD the common purpose that was lacking during small-scale MOOTW in
the 1990s. Although President George W. Bush's post-9/11 counterterrorism
and counterinsurgency operations provided the venue for DoD/CIA partnership growth, it was actions taken during all three administrations that set the
foundation.

    This book is important for its historical perspective and for an apprecia-
tion of future policy implications of this partnership. From a historical perspective, there is a lack of research that highlights how the collapse of the
Soviet Union and the end of the Cold War affected the Intelligence Community broadly and the DoD/CIA partnership particularly. Both the CIA
and the DoD were established at the beginning of the Cold War, and their
institutional identities were shaped by the nearly half-century struggle with
the Soviet Union. The end of the Cold War and the corresponding "peace
dividend" raised questions about the future of these two institutions, while
operational experiences during this same period highlighted tension in the
partnership. These questions include: Why and how did these two organizations mutually evolve from the end of the Cold War to the beginning of the
GWOT? How did this evolution shape their cultural identities and purpose?
And what are the benefits and consequences of these changes for operations
and national security?

    Exploring the evolution of the DoD/CIA relationship highlights various
contemporary implications that affect not only the two organizations but also
how the United States conducts foreign policy. The operationalization of the
CIA in support of military operations and as part of the US counterterrorism
approach limits the resources the CIA can focus on other issues. A former
intelligence leader argues that the Arab Spring in 2011 was largely unforeseen because nearly half of the CIA's resources were focused on war zones
and counterterrorism operations and not on tension in the Arab street or on

other strategic issues.[22] Although some officials argue that the CIA's focus on operations is fulfilling immediate national needs and that there will always be resource-allocation issues, others are concerned that if the CIA continues down its current path, it risks becoming a twenty-first century version of the Office of Strategic Services—an organization excellent at counterterrorism operations but lacking the ability to focus its foreign-intelligence collection capability on the world more broadly.[23]

Some academics, policy makers, and pundits argue that the CIA's focus on counterterrorism and intelligence support to military operations has resulted in the "militarization" of the CIA in the post–Cold War environment. These individuals argue that too many resources focused on supporting military operations and the counterterrorism fight results in a myopic view that neglects existential issues such as a rising China and an aggressive Russia. Of equal concern, they describe the predominance of intelligence support to military operations as a symptom of what many believe is the militarization of foreign policy.[24] From this perspective, it is the entire national security system that has been militarized, and the CIA's militarization is only a symptom of this trend. Others argue that the greatest value of intelligence is in supporting military actions by "identifying the [enemy] guy behind the door"[25] or providing information to inform a commander's decision making. Although these individuals appreciate policy makers' information needs, they believe academics and think tanks can provide the understanding necessary to formulate policy and strategy, but only intelligence organizations can provide the information necessary to enable operations.

These differing opinions highlight an important reality that goes beyond the DoD/CIA partnership and influences how leaders perceive intelligence. Even though the United States has an "Intelligence Community," there is not a consensus on the purpose of intelligence. Although some shrug off this issue and argue that the general purpose of intelligence is to inform decision making, this broad, simple definition does not capture the trade-offs incurred when determining whether to focus intelligence support on policy makers or on commanders.[26] The information required by a commander to enable decision making in war is different than information required by a policy maker to decide whether to go to war in the first place. Whereas a commander requires information to support tactical or operational action in pursuit of policy objectives, the policy maker requires information to decide whether the use of force is an appropriate policy tool. A policy maker needs to understand the benefits and limitations of the use of force in a particular situation, but he does not need to understand the tactical intelligence required to enable military operations. Finally, although the commander's understanding of the strategic situation is important for him to advise policy makers on the efficacy of the use of force and to adjust operations accordingly, he does not decide when to employ force but rather how to use force to achieve policy goals.

The "purpose of intelligence" is a discussion that extends beyond the CIA/DoD relationship, but the evolution of this partnership over the past three decades reflects broader shifts in the role of intelligence in America's national security affairs. As the US government's most significant non-DoD intelligence organization, the CIA was conceived to separate the collection of intelligence from the institutions that develop and execute policy.[27] Therefore, its increased focus on support to military operations weakens this separation, reduces its attention to strategic issues, and risks subordination to the DoD.

This book is broken down into nine chapters covering two general periods. Chapters 1–5 cover the period from 1982 to 2001, with a focus on the post–Cold War/post–Desert Storm period. Chapters 6–8 look at the post-9/11 period, with a focus on the changes to the CIA and DoD partnership spurred by the GWOT and the wars in Afghanistan and Iraq.

Chapter 1 begins in the mid-1980s, toward the end of the Cold War, when the DoD went through its most significant overhaul since its formation through the National Security Act of 1947. By taking the necessary first steps to weaken the powerful military services and establishing a unified department, the Goldwater-Nichols Department of Defense Reorganization Act of 1986 increased the DoD's influence in US foreign policy while also creating policy and structure that enabled and required future CIA/DoD collaboration.

The operational failures that motivated defense reform were the same failures that initiated discussions on greater intelligence support to military operations. Congressional and agency reviews of Operation Urgent Fury (invasion of Grenada) and the bombing of the US marine barracks in Beirut, both in 1983, which were cited as justification for defense reform, also criticized the lack of intelligence support to operational commanders. In this regard, the defense reform enacted by Congress through Goldwater-Nichols can be viewed as the initial phase of broader national security reforms that were intended to improve how the United States conducted operations. Although intelligence reform was initially not embraced to the same degree as defense reform, policy makers motivated by perceived "intelligence failures," fiscal constraints, and the changing global order started to look at ways to restructure intelligence to save money and respond in a post–Cold War environment.

Chapter 1 concludes with Operation Just Cause, the invasion of Panama in 1990 to oust General Manuel Noriega from power. Operation Just Cause served as a waypoint for the United States to measure its progress along its journey toward achieving jointness. Although the military displayed signifi- ✓ cant improvement in service interoperability during Just Cause, the operation highlighted that intelligence support to military operations had not yet attained the standard sought by the military, Congress, or the administration.

Chapters 2 and 3 look at the influence of Desert Storm on the evolution of the DoD/CIA relationship. As discussed in chapter 3, the attention given General Norman Schwarzkopf's comments on intelligence shortfalls and the concepts developed to support military operations during Desert Storm resulted in the operation being a primary catalyst for changes in the CIA/ DoD relationship in the 1990s. Although similar critiques of intelligence had been heard following Urgent Fury and Just Cause, the Desert Storm critiques received more attention and resulted in significant policy and organizational changes.

Desert Storm is also important for the introduction of technologies and concepts that became prominent following 9/11. Concepts such as "fusion center" and "operationalization of intelligence" that were later embraced during Operation Enduring Freedom and Operation Iraqi Freedom surfaced during Desert Storm. These concepts matured following 9/11, when the length and type of operations made them necessary and the increased technology made them more feasible. Desert Storm–era professionals deserve credit for strengthening the link between intelligence and operations while also weakening service and interagency parochialism. Even though intelligence support to military operations during Desert Storm was not error free, the intelligence professionals deserve credit for their effort, ingenuity, teamwork, and level of support to military operations.

Chapter 3 looks at the support for defense intelligence reform that Desert Storm generated. This momentum was in part due to the timing of the war and the celebrity status General Schwarzkopf enjoyed following the victory. With the end of the Cold War on the horizon and domestic pressure building to embrace the "peace dividend," the conditions were set for policy makers and national security organizations to be more receptive to change. General Schwarzkopf's popularity ensured that any critiques he made were taken seriously and their legitimacy little questioned. Despite his complaints being somewhat misplaced and later partially recanted, they were embraced by policy makers and were influential in building the momentum for change. In this regard, Schwarzkopf can be both criticized for his uninformed criticism of the Intelligence Community and credited for the change his comments helped generate.

Although chapters 2 and 3 focus significantly on Desert Storm military operations and the actions of DoD intelligence, these chapters are also important to gain an appreciation of the catalysts that drove debate over Intelligence Community reform and were proximate causes of CIA organizational reform to better support military operations. Despite a limited CIA role once military operations started, the push for improved interoperability between civilian agencies and the military, the calls for increased Intelligence Community support to military operations, and the friction between Schwarzkopf and the CIA over battle-damage assessments ensured that the CIA would be significantly affected in Desert Storm's aftermath.

Chapter 4 looks at how the momentum for intelligence reform within the DoD quickly expanded to the broader Intelligence Community and Congress. It considers how the executive and legislative branches worked to improve intelligence support to military operations. Although these reform measures were not initially instituted, the actions of a handful of individuals kept alive the discussion of intelligence reform and support to military operations. Over time, many of the issues that were not initially instituted found increased support as national security conditions changed and support to military operations became immediate.

Chapter 5, the final chapter covering the first period discussed, focuses on the Clinton years and how the international and domestic conditions after the Cold War drove changes within the CIA and DoD that affected their partnership. The CIA and DoD had existed only during the Cold War, and a significant amount of their energy was focused on the Soviet Union. After the Soviet fall, both organizations wrestled with their roles in a multipolar world, while policy makers slashed budgets and looked for ways to reorient the two organizations. This chapter considers the various national and institutional issues that influenced the CIA/DoD partnership and provides the context for how seemingly separate issues merged to shape the two organizations and therefore influence how their relationship evolved during the 1990s. As part of this exploration, the chapter considers how a change in administrations and the personalities of individual leaders influenced how the CIA/DoD partnership evolved.

Beginning the discussion of the second period covered, chapter 6 focuses on the arrival of the George W. Bush administration to the White House and with it the return of many old hands from previous Republican administrations. These individuals had been involved in previous efforts to reform the Intelligence Community and returned to power with the intent of furthering these efforts. Believing the previous administration had reduced intelligence funding too much, the Bush team looked for ways to increase spending and rebuild the Intelligence Community after years of reductions. Within months of taking office, the administration initiated reviews to identify where to rebuild the Intelligence Community, but their reviews were soon influenced by the necessities of war.

Chapter 7 considers the changes to defense intelligence that occurred following 9/11 to build self-sufficiency within the DoD in order to sever its perceived reliance on national intelligence support to operations. These changes were in part motivated by previous reviews of intelligence and in part by Secretary Donald Rumsfeld's desire to consolidate power and capability within the DoD. The enacted changes resulted in a significant transformation of defense intelligence and influenced how the DoD interacted with the CIA and the broader Intelligence Community. Of particular interest, this chapter shows how individual leaders shaped the DoD/CIA relationship, for better or worse, in the first five years following 9/11. It highlights how parochial and nonparochial personalities affected the relationship during the GWOT and how the nonparochial leaders' greater influence seems to have shaped the relationship in a more positive direction.

Chapter 7 also considers how the exigencies of war solidified the actions taken in the late 1980s and the 1990s to improve the DoD/CIA partnership, resulting in unprecedented collaboration between the two organizations. In addition, it looks at the increased importance of intelligence within operations. The "operationalization of intelligence" within the military is an important change in how the DoD conducts operations and explains the increased importance of national intelligence to military operations. As with the DoD/CIA partnership, the origins of the "operationalization of intelligence" can be traced back to the 1980s and 1990s.

The final chapter summarizes the evolution of the DoD/CIA partnership and considers the contemporary implications of that partnership on policy, strategy, and operations. This chapter is important for both policy makers and intelligence leaders to understand the costs and benefits incurred by the increased intelligence support of military operations. Chapter 8 also considers how the operationalization of national intelligence since 9/11 affects the purpose of intelligence and therefore influences the manner in which the United States conducts foreign policy.

1

CHANGE ON THE HORIZON

It is not sufficient to have just resources, dollars, and weapon systems.

—General David Jones, quoted in James Locher, *Victory on the Potomac*

The growth of the CIA and DoD relationship after 9/11 has much to do with internal changes that occurred within both organizations decades earlier. Many of the changes were inwardly focused and not expressively intended to improve interagency coordination and operations. Despite this fact, some of the internal organizational changes established the necessary conditions for future DoD/CIA relationship growth.

As this chapter covers, the interoperability failures during Operations Eagle Claw and Urgent Fury—the failed mission to rescue US citizens in Iran in 1979 and the invasion of Grenada in 1983, respectively—highlighted the inability of the US military services to conduct joint operations. In response to these failures, Congress looked for ways to increase interservice understanding and cooperation to enable successful joint operations. The passage of the Goldwater-Nichols Department of Defense Reorganization Act in 1986 did not completely eradicate parochial mindsets, but it did help weaken the military-service-centric attitudes. The eroding of service separation over time accustomed the services to embrace nonparochialism beyond their cloistered environments, a small yet significant step in shaping how the DoD developed relationships with nonmilitary government agencies.[1] Over time, the unification of the services through a jointness mantra empowered the DoD in relation to other national security and foreign-policy institutions. By unifying as a department and thus weakening interservice rivalry, the DoD was able to combine its efforts and increase its relative power over other departments and agencies.

Interestingly, the after-action and congressional reviews of military operations that encouraged passage of the Goldwater-Nichols Act also emphasized the breakdown of intelligence support to military operations. Although internal DoD reform was the proximate outcome of the operational failures or shortcomings, the inclusion of intelligence shortfalls in these reviews highlighted the increasing need for intelligence support to low-intensity conflicts and joint operations. The call for greater intelligence support to military operations continued after the passage of Goldwater-Nichols and, just like service jointness, was viewed as a necessary component to achieve operational success. The military and congressional reviews characterized intelligence support to military operations as such an integral part of improving operations that it could be considered a quasi–phase two of Goldwater-Nichols. Now that DoD was internally organized to conduct operations more effectively, greater external intelligence support was required to enable these operations.

It was an unseasonably warm February day in 1983 when General David C. Jones, a US Air Force aviator and the chairman of Joint Chiefs of Staff (JCS), briefed the House Armed Services Committee (HASC) for one of his last times. As General Jones sat listening to Secretary of Defense Caspar Weinberger outline "three fundamental requirements" for the US defense effort, even he probably did not fathom the coming defense transformation that his mea culpa that day would eventually result in. An intelligent, no-nonsense North Dakotan who enlisted in the Army Air Corps as a young college student during World War II, General Jones had been present for the creation of the DoD and had experienced the highs and lows of its first four decades. After eight years on the JCS, four as chief of staff of the air force and four as chairman of the JCS, Jones decided it was time to tell Congress that the DoD structure was broken.

That warm February day Jones told the HASC that the DoD structure, which had changed little since its establishment with the National Security Act of 1947, was ill designed to meet the challenges facing the military and, more importantly, the nation. Jones argued that a committee system driven by consensus was no way to run a large organization focused on action and results. In his opinion, the United States required a DoD that could operate as a unified force; the only problem was that the current system encouraged and rewarded institutional parochialism. To unify the department and resolve its issues, General Jones made four recommendations: (1) "strengthen the role of the [JCS] Chairman"; (2) "limit the role of Service Components in producing joint papers to 'input' and not 'debate'"; (3) the JCS "should receive advice from their own staff and not the service chief staffs"; and (4) "increase the role of the Combatant Commanders."[2] Jones's campaign to remold the DoD into a better-organized and unified department did not end with his testimony that day but was followed up with various articles and a continued push for change.[3] Not initially accepted by other DoD leaders, General Jones's recommendations gained momentum eight months later when Operation Urgent Fury, the invasion of Grenada, highlighted DoD's operational shortcomings.

Grenada: Joint Operations and Intelligence Support Issues

In the spring of 1983, President Ronald Reagan alerted the American public to a Soviet and Cuban buildup on the Caribbean island nation of Grenada. Although individuals closely linked to Grenada's government claimed the airport-enlargement project was part of an effort to increase tourism, Reagan argued that the project was further proof of Soviet expansionism in the Western Hemisphere.[4] During the presidential campaign in 1980, then candidate Reagan warned against Soviet inroads into the Western Hemisphere, identifying the socialist coup in Grenada in 1979 as evidence of the Soviets' intention.[5] Once in office, he proposed the Caribbean Basin Initiative, an economic development plan focused on improving the quality of life within select Caribbean countries and intertwining their interests with the United States to counter Soviet and Cuban influence in the region.[6] Although Grenada was listed as an "eligible country," its "Communist" status at the time made it ineligible to receive US benefits under the legislation.[7]

On October 12, 1983, six months after Reagan's first public mention of the airport-enlargement project in a speech, turmoil within Grenada's Marxist regime resulted in Prime Minister Maurice Bishop's overthrow, arrest, and eventual death. Bishop's Marxist New Jewel Movement regime had risen to power four years earlier when collective discontent with Prime Minister Eric Gairy's first postcolonial government led to its overthrow. Despite Bishop's Communist leanings, he followed a more pragmatic governance approach to bring economic reform to Grenada. This pragmatism, however, eventually resulted in his removal and the assumption of power by General Hudson Austin, the commander in chief (CINC) of Grenada's armed forces.[8]

On October 19, US administration officials became concerned with the safety and security of US citizens in Grenada. In response to this concern, the United States Atlantic Command under Admiral Wesley McDonald began planning for a Noncombatant Evacuation Operation of US citizens in the country.[9] Admiral McDonald, a seasoned naval aviator who had enjoyed a fascinating career that included service on Admiral Byrd's South Pole expedition and command of the first air strikes on North Vietnam following the

Tonkin Gulf incident in 1964, focused initial planning on both "opposed" and unopposed courses of action.[10] Although the evacuation planning efforts considered a range of options, McDonald's staff finally settled on an "opposed" option of a provisional joint US force led by Vice Admiral Joseph Metcalf III, commander of the US Navy's Second Fleet and comprising elements drawn from all four services.[11]

On October 25, 1983, a joint contingent of 6,500 invaded the small Caribbean nation, resulting in the evacuation of 599 American citizens, the removal of the military junta from power, and the forced departure of Cuban workers from the island.[12] Considering the multiple moving pieces involved in assembling, training, rehearsing, and executing a joint operation with an ad hoc force in less than forty-eight hours, Vice Admiral Metcalf and his subordinate commanders performed rather well.[13] Credit should also be given to other organizations because the invasion force was not only joint but also interagency. Notably, Metcalf's staff included representatives from the CIA who worked with the Defense Intelligence Agency (DIA) and military forces on the ground to help conduct sensitive-site exploitation of the Grenadian documents recovered during the invasion.[14]

Although the operation was considered a success, various questions arose on both the quality of intelligence and the perceived operational shortfalls related to communication and service interoperability. During a House Appropriations Committee hearing two weeks after the invasion, Secretary of Defense Weinberger was asked if Grenada was an intelligence failure. Although Weinberger said he did not view Grenada as an intelligence failure and downplayed any intelligence issues, the legislators questioned whether the operational commanders had taken full advantage of available intelligence and challenged the accuracy of intelligence on Cuban strength and the location of American citizens.[15]

In January 1984, the HASC conducted a "lessons learned" review focused on Operation Urgent Fury during which various congressional leaders once again questioned the lack of intelligence support to military operations. During an exchange with Undersecretary of Defense (USD) for Policy Harold Ikle, Maryland Republican congresswoman Marjorie Holt argued that intelligence issues in Grenada were the result of previous actions that "diminished our intelligence gathering capability." Although Holt did not specify, one could safely assume the previous actions she alluded to were the CIA human intelligence (HUMINT) reduction of more than eight hundred CIA case officers carried out by Stansfield Turner during the Carter administration, a culling that came to be known as the "Halloween Massacre."[16]

Holt specifically focused on the CIA, arguing that there was a contingent within the country that was "opposed to strengthening the CIA and opposed to letting them play their proper function as our intelligence agents." In Holt's opinion, it was this anti-CIA contingent that resulted in poor intelligence support to military operations during Urgent Fury. Seconding his fellow Marylander, Democrat Roy Dyson voiced his concern that the lack of quality intelligence resulted in American service members invading a country "near-blind." Citing the lack of intelligence in Lebanon preceding the bombing of the US marine barracks in Beirut that occurred a few days before the Grenada invasion, Dyson questioned why the military commander did not have a better understanding of Grenada to inform his military planning. In response to Holt and Dyson, Ikle agreed with the shortage in intelligence but also stated that resource limitations had forced the Intelligence Community to assume risk in some areas.[17]

The congressional concern over service interoperability and intelligence support to operations was reinforced in the JCS review of Urgent Fury. Although the military services believed that intelligence support required for initial planning was adequate, they identified a shortfall in intelligence support to processing captured material and a need for better "intelligence management arrangements," and they castigated intelligence organizations for "inadequate" intelligence on the locations of American citizens requiring evacuation. Regarding service interoperability, the JCS report noted the various gains made by the services in conducting joint operations but highlighted the continual shortfalls in communications, fire support, and planning.[18] Although the JCS report was more forgiving than congressional reviews regarding intelligence support to operations and more appreciative of the strides the DoD had made to improve joint operations, both Congress and the military highlighted the need for greater service interoperability and the intelligence to support it.

The HUMINT required to improve the combatant commander's understanding and to support contingency-planning efforts that Representative Holt described would largely come from the CIA. Although the military services had some capacity for tactical HUMINT interrogation and sensitive-site exploitation (the CIA also supported sensitive-site exploitation during Urgent Fury), they did not have enough clandestine capability or the long-term HUMINT collection structures in place to develop assets with the local knowledge and access necessary to achieve what Holt was describing. If military contingency planning required more in-depth knowledge of locations, and if much of this information, particularly in potential conflict areas, could not be acquired overtly, the DoD would have to depend on the CIA's clandestine collection because the DoD lacked sufficient intelligence capability.[19] What Dyson described was not a CIA surge during operations but an ongoing supporting relationship to the DoD's planning efforts.

Beirut: Intelligence to Blame?

On October 23, 1983, two days before the invasion of Grenada, a tragedy struck US Marine Corps forces in Beirut, Lebanon, where they had been deployed as part of a multinational peacekeeping mission since August 1982. The Lebanese government had requested an international peacekeeping force in June 1982 when it became concerned that fighting between the Palestinian Liberation Organization, Israel, and Syria was putting Lebanese citizens at risk. The following month, July 1982, the United Nation Security Council passed Resolution 508, which called for the departure of Israeli forces from Lebanon. Shortly after passage of the resolution, the United States became part of a multinational force (MNF) responsible for overseeing departure of foreign forces from Lebanon. The MNF eventually included contingents from France, Italy, Great Britain, and the United States.[20]

On August 24, 1982, President Reagan's notification of the deployment of US forces into Lebanon stated that the purpose of deployment was to ensure the implementation of the departure plan. The letter further stated that US forces would not become involved in "hostilities" and that the MNF would be withdrawn if a breakdown in implementing the departure plan occurred.[21] Despite the limitations Reagan initially established, the US element within the MNF eventually expanded its mission to three objectives: (1) withdrawal of foreign forces (Israeli and Syrian) from Lebanon; (2) security of Israel's northern border; and (3) an opportunity for the Lebanese government to assert its sovereignty.[22] The MNF presence in Beirut was largely accepted for the first nine months, but this attitude toward it changed in April 1983 when a suicide attack destroyed the US embassy, killing seventeen Americans and thirty-three locals.

The attack on the US embassy destroyed the CIA station, killing seven officers, including Robert Ames, the CIA's national intelligence officer for the Middle East, who was on temporary duty in Beirut at the time.[23] The bombing also severely disrupted the intelligence operations that were providing information on militias and foreign forces operating in the area.[24] In the late summer of 1983, as the intelligence network remained disrupted, a US congressional delegation arrived in Beirut. The HASC delegation was part of a broader congressional review looking at the role of US forces in Beirut and how these forces nested within the broader US strategy regarding Lebanon. Although these hearings did not result in a recommendation to remove US forces from Beirut, they did raise concerns regarding the safety of US forces in the area. More broadly, the hearings were critical of a US "involvement that some perceived to be controlled more by events than by deliberate planning and coherent policymaking on the part of US Government Officials."[25] Despite the disconnect between the use of force and policy objectives, the congressional delegation believed the presence of US forces in Beirut served America's long-term interests.

Although Congress was concerned with the safety of US ground forces in Beirut and naval forces offshore, the congressional delegation did not raise questions regarding either the quality or the quantity of intelligence support to US forces in the area. In fact, the only substantive commentary on intelligence support during the hearing came from Rear Admiral Jonathan T. Howe, then director of the Bureau of Political-Military Affairs at the Department of State. Although Howe acknowledged concerns with the evolving mission and threats to US forces in the area, he also recognized the level of force-protection awareness that commanders in the area possessed due to the significant level of intelligence support.[26] The absence of a concern over intelligence support to ground forces following the delegation's September visit is a significant oversight by the commanders and the delegates, considering the critiques that intelligence support to commanders received from both Congress and the Long Commission less than two months later, following the marine barracks bombing on October 23.

Two days after the barracks bombing, the Senate Arms Services Committee (SASC) initiated hearings to review US policy on Lebanon. The hearings were conducted over two days, on October 25 and 31, 1983, and involved testimony by Secretary of Defense Weinberger, Lieutenant General Bernard Trainor (US Marine Corps deputy chief of staff for plans, policy, and operations), Rear Admiral Almon Wilson (US Navy deputy surgeon), General P. X. Kelley (US Marine Corps commandant), and General Bernard Rogers (supreme Allied commander Europe and CINC European Command). Although the discussion touched on Lebanon policy issues, the crux of the discussion focused on the preattack preparedness actions and the postattack response. Senators questioned the measures taken by commanders on the ground to ensure force protection and whether commanders responded adequately to intelligence reports highlighting the threat of terrorist attacks.

The back and forth between senators and DoD leaders regarding preattack preparedness actions became very heated. During one exchange, Senators Sam Nunn (D–GA) and William Cohen (R–ME) excoriated General Kelley for failing to foresee the threat that suicide bombers posed to US marines even after the embassy bombing in April.[27] Even though General

Kelley's assertion that he was not in the Lebanon mission chain of command was accurate, it was not well received by the committee. Testifying alongside Kelley was General Rogers, the supreme Allied commander Europe, who told the committee that as the regional commander he was ultimately responsible for the Beirut bombing failures.

Both Rogers and Kelley argued that intelligence reporting had not pointed to the threat of a suicide attack on the marines.[28] Although the senators did not accept the generals' argument and criticized them for a lack of imagination, no congressional alarms had sounded about the terrorist threat prior to the barracks bombing. Although force protection was an issue during the HASC delegation visit to Lebanon in September 1983, the threat of a suicide bomber was not mentioned in the delegation's report. The delegation mentioned the poor tactical low ground of the marine position and the threat posed by indirect fire, but there was no discussion regarding measures required to protect against a suicide attack.[29] It is interesting and a little unnerving that congressional representatives believed themselves expert enough to comment on tactical positioning of military forces and then to critique the military for failing to assess broader terrorist threats in Lebanon. If an amateur military terrain analysis is appropriate for a congressional delegation, a terrorist threat assessment is just as appropriate, if not more so. Congress instead criticized the commanders for failing to identify a threat to US forces that its own delegation had overlooked or did not consider.[30]

Even before the testimony in late October, Secretary of Defense Weinberger, based on a recommendation by General Kelley, assigned an independent investigatory body to review the circumstances surrounding the marine barracks bombing.[31] The DoD Commission on Beirut International Airport Terrorist Act of October 23, 1983, was chaired by Admiral (ret.) Robert Long, a veteran of World War II and the Vietnam War and the recently departed CINC of the US Pacific Command. The Long Commission "examined the mission of the U.S. Marines assigned to the MNF, the rules of engagement governing their conduct, the responsiveness of the chain of command, the intelligence support, the security measures in place before and after the attack, the attack itself, and the adequacy of casualty handling procedures."[32] Echoing General Rogers's testimony, the Long Commission report identified the chain of command as those ultimately responsible for any operational failures. In addition to various issues regarding the lack of a common interpretation of the mission, convoluted chain of command, unclear rules of engagement, and medical-evacuation procedures and care, pointed to intelligence as a key issue that stymied prevention of the attack.

Although previous military leaders had praised the intelligence support to commanders in Lebanon, the Long Commission found that although there was a large quantity of threat reporting, it was of little value to the military commanders in Lebanon. Specifically, the committee report stated the one hundred intelligence reports warning of car bombs were too general and did not provide actionable information for the commanders to prevent the barracks bombing. Reaching beyond the causes of failed terrorist prevention in Beirut, the Long Commission also argued that reduction in "HUMINT collection worldwide" had contributed to Beirut and previous operational failures. "Better HUMINT to support military planning and operations" was critical to ensure the mission's success and to protect against failure. The committee provided two important recommendations regarding intelligence that dealt directly with the DoD/CIA relationship: (1) "an all-source fusion center" should be established to support US commanders during military operations, and (2) DoD/CIA should work together and take necessary actions to improve HUMINT support to operations in Lebanon and other military operations. These recommendations resembled future structural decisions made during subsequent operations.[33]

In agreement with congressional criticism made during the joint hearing on Operation Urgent Fury that occurred a month later, the Long Commission argued that "the paucity of U.S. controlled HUMINT is partly due to U.S. policy decisions to reduce HUMINT collection worldwide." Although not explicit, this statement alluded to Admiral Stansfield Turner's "Halloween Massacre" of the CIA's HUMINT capability on October 31, 1977. The Long Commission argued the HUMINT shortage had led to a "critical repetition of a long line of similar lessons during crisis situation in many other parts of the world."[34] In other words, CIA HUMINT reductions had been partially responsible for military operational failures, an interesting assessment of national intelligence capability and one that was embraced by future reviews.

In response to the Beirut bombings, Secretary of State George Shultz established the Advisory Panel on Overseas Security to review threats and security at US facilities abroad. Schultz selected recently retired navy admiral Bobby Ray Inman as chair of this panel. Admiral Inman, a former director of the National Security Agency (NSA) and deputy director of central intelligence (DCI), was the first navy intelligence officer to earn four stars. Inman, from Rhonesboro, a speck of a town in eastern Texas, joined the navy out of the University of Texas. The man once referred to as "one of the smartest people to come out of Washington or anywhere" never planned to make the navy a career. Although he initially lacked aspirations to become an admiral, his superiors realized his talent and placed him in challenging yet rewarding positions.[35] Inman remained a mentor to many rising intelligence profession-als even after his retirement to the University of Texas.

The recommendation of the Inman Panel led to the establishment of the State Department's Bureau of Diplomatic Security, which would include the Diplomatic Security Service, established to consolidate separate State Depart-ment security organizations. In addition to recommending the Bureau of Diplomatic Security and calling for "improving intelligence gathering and analysis," the panel also created the Inman Standards, which established minimum specifications for new overseas US diplomatic facilities.[36]

The congressional and DoD reviews of Operation Urgent Fury and the Beirut bombing highlighted issues regarding intelligence support to mili-tary operations. During congressional discussion of Operation Urgent Fury, elected officials from both parties argued that a reduction in HUMINT capability affected operational performance. Similarly, the Long Commis-sion report linked the lack of HUMINT support to military operations to the Beirut tragedy and other operational failures worldwide. Although historians highlight the influence of Operation Urgent Fury and the Beirut bombing on congressional action to reform the DoD, these two events also highlight the early stages of the call for increased intelligence support to military oper-ations.[37] The identification of issues related to service interoperability and intelligence support to military operations appearing together regularly in after-action reviews is evidence of the acknowledged link between joint oper-ations and the intelligence support to enable those operations.

More importantly, the recommendation that HUMINT (i.e., the CIA) tailor its collection efforts in support of military operations was an expecta-tion that would significantly affect the CIA's operational focus. Even though in the early 1980s the CIA provided threat reporting to military command-ers, this reporting was incidental to its broader collection efforts, and the suitability of a human asset was not based primarily on whether that indi-vidual could report on items of interest to military commanders. Whether congresspersons or the Long Commission report's authors realized it, increas-ing CIA HUMINT support to military operations without building up CIA HUMINT capabilities would detract from the support the CIA could pro-vide to policy makers. Many Intelligence Community leaders realized this equation years later.

Inspired by General David Jones's honesty and motivated by lessons learned during operations, both houses' Armed Services Committees tackled the controversial issue of defense reform but met resistance not only within the individual services but also among many DoD leaders. Congress did not use the Goldwater-Nichols legislation to tackle the relationship between the

CIA and the DoD regarding intelligence support to military operations, but comments made during the debate highlighted the importance of intelligence support to operations. These comments signaled that change within the DoD was only the first step in reforming how the United States conducted military operations.[38]

Goldwater-Nichols: Unifying Defense First

The call for defense reform that General Jones sent out in 1982 resulted in congressional bills and an intensifying chorus for change. The operational issues that arose during Urgent Fury and the perceived intelligence and organizational failures that were faulted for not preventing the Beirut barracks bombing provided further evidence why defense reform was needed. Despite evidence that reform was required, the introduction of a proposal sponsored by the HASC on JCS reorganization, and an increasing call for action, the SASC was slow to respond.

Following the death of Senator Scoop Jackson (D–WA), the leading Democrat on the SASC, and the announcement of Senator John Tower's (R–TX) retirement in 1983; pro-reform leaders gained influence in the Senate.[39] Beginning in late 1985, the SASC held a series of defense-reform hearings focused on previous operational issues, in particular the Urgent Fury failures, the marine barracks bombing in Beirut, and the failed hostage rescue in Iran. The senators on the committee honed in on the command-and-control and service-interoperability issues that had already been highlighted in commission reports and pursued during previous congressional inquiries.

The hearings emphasized the friction between congressional leaders intent on defense reform and defense leaders wanting to protect the institution and pursue additional resources. During questioning by Senator Jim Exon, a Democrat from Nebraska, regarding whether the failures in Iran, Beirut, and Grenada were due to command-and-control issues, Secretary of Defense Weinberger said his impression was that failures like the Iran hostage rescue had to do not with command and control but with a "complete lack of resources," something the Reagan administration was trying to remedy. Admiral James Watkins, the chief of naval operations, reinforced Weinberger's argument, saying, "We can communicate and we have demonstrated this time and time again in the last three years between Washington, D.C. and people on the ground in foreign lands. For example, while we could talk to downtown Beirut anytime we wanted to, we do not have the resources available for everybody to do that everywhere in the world at one time." In accord with Watkins, General Charles Gabriel, the US Air Force chief of staff, testified that interservice communication was strong and improving. Echoing his counterparts, US Army chief of staff General John Wickham argued that the DoD was improving interoperability by rectifying issues previously identified. Although the current crop of DoD leaders were on message, General (ret.) Edward "Shy" Meyer, the previous army chief of staff, was supporting DoD reform. General Meyer told the committee that the failure to "link our strategy and forces together" was "even more insidious" than the "hollowness" of the army he had warned against in 1979.[40]

General Meyer's decision to back General Jones's call for reform is not surprising when Meyer's own history as a reformer is considered. As army chief of staff, Meyers had striven to rebuild the "hollowed-out" post-Vietnam army. Part of this rebuilding included an army-image rebranding, which resulted in the army's memorable "Be All That You Can Be" campaign.[41] Most notably regarding the DoD/CIA partnership, General Meyers was the first service leader to consolidate special forces capability within its own command when he established the First United States Army Special Operations Command in 1982. Meyer's vision and his appreciation of the importance of special operations in future conflicts resulted in the creation of an army component that would serve as a "point of interaction with SOCOM."[42] After its creation in 1986, SOCOM in return served as a "point of interaction" with the CIA.

Although the SASC hearings focused on defense transformation, Senator Nunn highlighted the importance of intelligence support to military operations in his opening statement. Senator Nunn, a Georgia Democrat and member of the Senate Select Committee on Intelligence (SSCI), was a significant proponent of SOFs and cosponsored in 1985 the bill that established SOCOM.[43] Nunn noted the indispensable link between operations and intelligence when he complemented the DoD officials on capturing the terrorists responsible for seizing the *Achille Lauro* ocean liner, stating that "key and timely intelligence were the secrets of success, and the connectivity between the military and our intelligence community last week was superb."[44] Senator Nunn followed up this praise by saying that Senator Barry Goldwater's (R–AZ) and his goal was to take the "all-star" service teams and turn them into a "joint service all-star team" to ensure the military could meet the nation's needs. By highlighting the importance of intelligence to military operations and using it as a segue into his comments on the importance of teamwork in operations, Nunn linked DoD transformation and intelligence support to operations.

Although DoD transformation was initially driven by congressional motivation and found little support within the DoD, the executive branch entered the fray in July 1985 when President Reagan issued Executive Order 12526: President's Blue Ribbon Commission on Defense Management. The order established a commission to "study issues surrounding defense management and organization" and identified ten specific areas the president wanted the commission to tackle. These ten areas included questions surrounding the command-and-control issues and the interoperability issues that Congress was also looking to resolve.[45] President Reagan appointed David Packard, one of the cofounders of Hewlett-Packard, to lead the commission composed of fifteen members drawn from the public and private sectors. It was hoped that Packard, a prominent Republican donor and former assistant secretary of defense (ASD) during the Nixon administration, would bring a businessman's acumen to the helm of a commission chartered with improving efficiency.[46]

The Packard Commission's investigation discovered a convoluted and inefficient system and provided great sound bites for the president to push for government fiscal reform. Nearly three decades following publication of the commission's report, most people only remember the "$600 toilet seat" and "$475 hammer, " but the Packard Commission symbolizes the executive branch coming on board with the legislative branch to reform the military.[47] Among the commission's final recommendations were to strengthen the JCS chairman role by making that person the principal military adviser to the president, the national security adviser, and the secretary of defense as well as to give unified and specified commanders flexibility in structuring their commands.[48] These two changes, which were also implemented as part of Goldwater-Nichols, contributed to the reduction in service parochialism and empowered the joint combatant commanders. The empowerment of the combatant commanders was the beginning of a significant rise in their influence, an influence that eventually had great effect on the role of intelligence support to military operations.[49]

On October 1, 1986, President Reagan signed the Department of Defense Reorganization Act into law. After four long years of debate and negotiation, action to improve DoD planning and operations was finally initiated. Although the legislation focused on the DoD, the influence of Goldwater-Nichols was felt well beyond the Pentagon corridors. The structural and policy changes that came about through this act also strengthened the DoD's influence and role in foreign policy.

Structurally, by weakening the services and empowering the JCS chairman, the legislation centralized power under a joint construct. This centralization of power increased the relative power of the DoD vis-à-vis other departments and agencies. Although service parochialism remained, it was weakened to the point where service squabbles did not affect the DoD's overall strength and influence. No longer was the DoD a loose configuration of four services with limited power to reign in those organizations. Although the services retained influence and the power to man, train, and equip, military operations were now planned and executed jointly.

Structural reforms were not the only changes that increased the DoD's influence. The "increased attention to the formulation of strategy and to contingency planning" also significantly increased that influence.[50] By linking national security strategy, defense strategy, and contingency planning, Goldwater-Nichols organized DoD efforts and ensured that there was a nesting of plans to go with the nesting of structure. The centralization of both structure and plans enhanced the DoD's power, creating a system the United States could utilize not only to fight wars but also to "shape the environment" in an arguably less physically intrusive but more iterative fashion.

Part of increasing jointness and weakening the services was the authority and responsibility Goldwater-Nichols gave the combatant commanders to plan and execute operations within their areas of responsibility. The legislation made clear the combatant commanders were now the DoD point persons within their respected regions and that the service component commanders were subordinate to them. Although the National Security Act of 1947 had created the Unified Combatant Command System and the Department of Defense Reorganization Act of 1958 had "delegated full operational control over forces assigned to them," prior to 1986 the power and influence of the services had stifled any ability to plan and organize for joint operations.[51] Goldwater-Nichols changed this reality, empowering the joint combatant commands and thus initiating the rise of the combatant commanders' influence. Over time, the combatant commanders gained influence beyond the employment of forces and other military issues within their regions. Their planning efforts eventually evolved beyond contingency and warfighting to embrace "shaping" their regions in pursuit of perceived US interests. This shaping went beyond the battlefield and involved all elements of national power.[52] As the combatant commanders' authority increased, so did their influence and sway in gaining resources outside the DoD.[53]

Goldwater-Nichols did not tackle the DoD/CIA partnership directly, but it introduced policy changes that made increased DoD/CIA collaboration necessary and structural changes that made it easier. The push to link military operations to strategy and policy mandated by Goldwater-Nichols increased the requirement for better intelligence support.[54] Although the concept of policy driving operations that Goldwater-Nichols sought to establish was not novel, the legislation renewed focus on its importance. The connection between policy and operations became of particular importance as the

United States increased its participation in low-intensity conflicts that were not of an existential nature but required iterative dialogue between commanders and policy makers to determine if these conflicts continued to be in America's interest. These low-intensity conflicts for limited policy objectives required a constant coordination between policy makers, military commanders, and the Intelligence Community. As Beirut showed, when the United States deployed force for limited objectives, there had to be a constant dialogue to determine if the approach was leading to the desired condition or if the cost of action outweighed the potential benefits of action. Over time, as MOOTWs became more prominent and the combatant commanders' role and influence in foreign policy expanded beyond waging wars to include shaping the environment, the combatant commanders required constant intelligence support to increase understanding and enable operations.

Structural DoD changes created organizations that made CIA collaboration easier to conduct. As part of defense reorganization, Congress, supported by former and current defense officials, looked for ways both to strengthen and to raise the "clout" of SOFs. In pursuit of these goals, Goldwater-Nichols established SOCOM as a functional combatant command responsible for SOFs within all services. The rise of low-intensity conflicts and the failures in Iran, Beirut, and Grenada convinced policy makers of the need for a joint structure to command unconventional forces likely to fight in these environments. The centralization of SOF capabilities under a single command increased the efficiency of resource management and improved interoperability.[55] Although not an articulated justification for SOCOM's establishment, a joint SOF command gave the CIA a point of contact for its paramilitary operations, something that became important for DoD/CIA collaboration following 9/11. SOCOM now meant CIA had a direct plug-in to all DoD SOF elements, making collaboration less complex.

Around this same time and resulting from some of the same events that motivated Congress to establish SOCOM, the CIA also instituted organizational changes that affected the evolution of the DoD/CIA partnership. In the aftermath of terrorist attacks, such as the Beirut embassy and marine barracks bombings in 1983 and the kidnapping and murder of the CIA's Beirut chief of station in 1984, the CIA increased its focus on terrorism.[56] It established the CTC in response to the Reagan administration's desire to have a single entity within the US government focused on the international terrorist threat.[57] Although it is doubtful the administration could have predicted the future importance of US counterterrorism efforts, the creation of the CTC provided a venue for future DoD/CIA collaboration—a venue that became valuable during joint DoD/CIA counterterrorism operations following 9/11.

The need for greater intelligence support was identified during the reviews of Beirut and Grenada—the same reviews that identified the need for improved service interoperability. Through Goldwater-Nichols, the government had taken its first significant step toward establishing service interoperability and improving the link between policy, strategy, and military operations. Even if successful, however, Goldwater-Nichols fixed only some of the problems identified during the reviews. Not only did the need for more intelligence support to military operations remain unresolved following Goldwater-Nichols, but the legislation also instituted structural and policy changes that increased the intelligence support requirement.[58] Almost three years after passage of Goldwater-Nichols, events in Panama presented the United States an opportunity to test whether the legislation had fixed the interoperability issues that plagued the military. Panama confirmed the path initiated by Goldwater-Nichols while at the same time reaffirming the need for greater intelligence support.

Operation Just Cause: Validating Defense Reform

Three years after the Goldwater-Nichols legislation was passed, Operation Just Cause provided an opportunity to validate the changes it instituted. Panamanian dictator Manuel Noriega's support from Washington, DC, had been eroding since 1986, when Senator Jesse Helms first held hearings on the "situation in Panama."[59] A Republican senator from North Carolina, Helms had fought against the planned US turnover of the Panama Canal since 1978, so some legislators and others skeptically viewed these hearings as his attempt to use tragic events, such as the murder of Panamanian politician Dr. Hugh Spadafora, to stop the transfer of the canal.[60] For his part, Helms argued that turning over the canal to a country that was led by criminals, influenced by Communists, and lacking freedom was not in the US interest. The hearings put the Republican senator at odds with the Reagan administration, which acknowledged Panama's weakness but argued that Panama was trying to improve governance and halt criminal activity.

To bolster his case against Panama and the Panamanian Defense Forces (PDF), Helms invited Dr. Spadafora's family to the hearings and allowed a family representative to read Spadafora's sister's statement. Dr. Spadafora, a former Panamanian government official and guerrilla fighter, had been found headless after accusing Noriega of being "the drug kingpin of the region." During the hearing, Helms and others testified that Spadafora's death at the hands of the PDF showed the military regime's viciousness and that the removal of President Nicolás Barletta after he promised an independent inquiry into Spadafora's death showed the PDF's control of the country. Elliott Abrams, then assistant of inter-American affairs at the US Department of State, disputed Helms implication that Barletta had been a popular president who was removed without cause following Spadafora's death. Abrams argued that Barletta was "vehemently opposed" "by the opposition party" and viewed as an ineffectual president by many within the population.[61]

Momentum against Noriega started to build in response to articles written about his involvement in the drug trade, his nonresponsiveness to American demands, and his increased partnership with Cuba and other Communist sympathizers.[62] In February 1988, federal prosecutors indicted Noriega on drug-trafficking charges, accusing him of receiving millions in bribes from Colombian cartels and allowing Panama to serve as a major drug-transit point.[63] Following the indictment, the United States increased economic sanctions intended to drain Noriega's support in the region and within Panama to force his departure.[64] As the United States tightened its grip on Noriega, the Panamanian dictator started lashing out against US interests and holdings in Panama. Fed up with Noriega's behavior, President George H. W. Bush issued NSD-17, *US Actions in Panama,* on July 22, 1989, which "ordered military actions designed to assert U.S. treaty rights in Panama and to keep Noriega and his supporters off guard."[65]

The sanctions and other pressure tactics directed toward Noriega did not compel Noriega to cede to US demands. As the US relationship with Noriega further unraveled, his reliance on US enemies such as Libya, Nicaragua, and Cuba increased. Discouraged by the ineffectiveness of sanctions to bring down Noriega, the Bush administration tepidly supported a coup attempt by Panamanian army major Fernando Quezada in October 1989. When the coup attempt failed, the United States started to lose hope that internal pressure would bring Noriega's downfall.[66]

Panama's legislature, encouraged by Noriega's outlandish rhetoric, declared that a "state of war existed with the United States" and stepped up the PDF's aggressive behavior toward US forces in Panama.[67] On Saturday, December 16, 1989, the tension between Panama and the United States hit a boiling point when two separate PDF checkpoints fired at a group of US military officers out for dinner. The hail of bullets ended up killing First Lieutenant Robert Paz, a young marine who was born in Colombia to an American mother and Colombian father. The death of Lieutenant Paz was a catalyst that pushed the United States to an invasion.[68]

The military planning for possible operations in Panama had been occurring since February 1988 and considered different options and force packages, ranging from a minimal military footprint using forces already present in Panama to protect American citizens to a large-scale, corps-size invasion. When President Bush became frustrated with General Frederick Woerner's behavior and criticism of policy makers in Washington, he decided to replace General Woerner with General Maxwell Thurman as the Southern Command commander.[69] General Thurman, a life-long bachelor married to his work, was a hypercommitted officer that army chief of staff General Meyers had selected in the early 1980s to repair the army brand. The leader behind the "Be All You Can Be" campaign, Thurman was a well-known officer who was serving as the army training and doctrine commander when he was tapped for the Southern Command post.

The year and a half of planning and preparation for the Panama operation culminated on December 20, 1989, when 24,500 American troops initiated combat operations leading to the capture, extradition, trial, and conviction of Noriega. In Congress, the success of Operation Just Cause was celebrated and viewed as validation of the defense-transformation actions initiated through the Goldwater-Nichols legislation. Congressman Ike Skelton, a Missouri Democrat recognized for his pro-defense stances, applauded the military for avoiding repeats of the command, control, and communication issues that had plagued the Grenada operation. Congressman Skelton, whose own physical ailments had kept him out of the military, had two sons who served as career military officers, including one who had previously served in Panama.

Although the tenor of the post-Panama invasion discussion was positive, there were some stray notes regarding the operation that Congress wanted corrected. At the forefront of these concerns was the issue of intelligence support to military operations, which Goldwater-Nichols had not resolved. On February 5, 1990, during his appraisal of the "armed forces" performance in Panama, Congressman Skelton stated "we achieved our objective [defense reform] and now we have to go to the civilian side of the coin." Regarding political efforts, Skelton denounced the ill preparedness for the postinvasion conditions and the Department of State for not preparing enough for the potential of an invasion. He reserved his harshest criticism for intelligence, which, he argued, "failed us on a number of accounts." He believed that better intelligence would have resulted in the earlier capture of Noriega and awareness of the threat posed by Noriega's Dignity Battalions, which continued to fight after the PDF surrendered.[70] Although the service-interoperability issues identified in the reviews of Urgent Fury and the barracks bombing significantly improved after the passage of Goldwater-Nichols, the intelligence issues identified during the same reviews remained unresolved.

In late January 1990, barely a month after the invasion, the House Permanent Select Committee on Intelligence (HPSCI) contacted the DoD, the

CIA, and the Department of State to request their participation in a hearing on "intelligence planning and support to Operation Just Cause." The HPSCI letter to Secretary of Defense Richard Cheney requested the participation of General Thurman and top intelligence officers to gain their perspective on intelligence support during the planning and execution of Operation Just Cause. The HPSCI was "particularly" interested in "coordination among human intelligence entities and lessons learned with respect to the adequacy of organic tactical intelligence collection, processing, and dissemination systems for special operations forces in a low-intensity conflict environment."[71] It might seem odd that an HPSCI review of intelligence support was being pursued immediately following the operation, but documents reveal that concerns regarding intelligence support to operations in Panama had surfaced before the invasion even occurred.

A memo dated October 26, 1989 (nearly two months prior to the invasion) from the chairs and vice chairs of the SASC and SSCI to James Locher, then ASD for special operations and low-intensity conflicts, requested information on intelligence support to low-intensity conflicts.[72] Locher, a seasoned national security expert who had been one of the principal staffers working on the Goldwater-Nichols legislation, had been asked the previous month about his view on the importance of intelligence support during his Senate confirmation hearing. During questioning, Senator Cohen, a Republican from Maine and future secretary of defense who had cosponsored the legislation creating SOCOM and the position of ASD for special operations and low-intensity conflicts, had asked Locher his view on the "importance of intelligence in dealing with terrorism, insurgency, and related problems." Locher had responded to Cohen that "intelligence is one of our most important resources" and that he would "begin working to change some of the priorities of the intelligence community."[73]

Opinions on the importance of intelligence within the burgeoning international environment were a common theme throughout the Senate confirmation hearings of President Bush's nominees. Some of the nominees, such as Locher and Donald Atwood, seemed to link changes in intelligence to defense-transformation efforts enacted three years earlier. During his confirmation testimony to become ASD, Atwood argued that the nation's interests "will require closer coordination among those responsible for diplomatic, military, and intelligence matters."[74] In June 1990, President Bush furthered the pursuit to unify the national security organizations in the new environment when he issued *National Security Review of Low Intensity Conflict* (NSR-27).[75] The document, which directed a government-wide review of how the United States "assists in the prevention and resolution of low-intensity conflicts," focused on interagency integration and how the US government should be structured to wage low-intensity conflicts.[76] The issuance of this document acknowledged a deficiency in how the United States conducted interagency operations. Although the DoD/CIA relationship was not specifically mentioned in the document, the increased focus on low-intensity conflicts significantly affected both organizations in the future.

NSR-27 and the congressional testimony were a continuation of the nesting of policy, strategy, and plans the Goldwater-Nichols legislation had started to tackle three years earlier. The Goldwater-Nichols legislation was a necessary but not sufficient step toward improving coordination and collaboration among the US national security organizations. Congressman Skelton's remarks following Operation Just Cause highlighted the mood among many executive- and legislative-branch officials: "We achieved our objective [defense reform], and now we go to the civilian side of the coin."[77]

The 1980s began shortly after the tragic failure of Operation Eagle Claw, the Iranian hostage-rescue mission that served as a catalyst for defense-reform efforts in that decade. Although parochialism initially dominated the DoD, with services and their congressional overseers pushing against any proposals that weakened institutional powers, visionaries such as Generals Jones and Meyer as well as Senators Goldwater and William Flynt Nichols (D–AL) eventually won support for defense reform. Although the passage of Goldwater-Nichols instituted important changes within the DoD, the issues identified during reviews of Grenada and Beirut were not purely defense related. In order to fix all the operational issues, the executive and legislative branches needed to increase their aperture to include not only DoD but also the Intelligence Community. Newly appointed leaders throughout the Bush administration agreed that changes were required to posture the US national security institutions for the changing global environment and so initiated efforts to institute those changes.[78] Although these efforts began shortly after the Bush team occupied their desks, actions by another dictator nearly eight thousand miles away distracted focus from these proposed changes, while simultaneously providing evidence to bolster the case for further reform.

Less than a year after Panama, Desert Storm offered a second opportunity, on a much grander stage, to validate the effectiveness of the Goldwater-Nichols legislation. The overwhelming victory reaffirmed the increased service jointness but highlighted continued shortfalls in intelligence support to military operations. Congressional reviews of Desert Storm specifically highlighted the shortfalls in CIA support to military operations, and these reviews eventually resulted in changes to CIA structure. Although CIA HUMINT support to military operations had been an ongoing issue in the 1980s, Desert Storm served as a catalyst for change in the 1990s.

2

THE GULF WAR

If one considered the CIA's traditional role prior to the Gulf War as the basis for managing expectations of level of support it gave during Desert Storm, there should not have been much expectation that the CIA would have a significant role in supporting military operations. Its focus during the Cold War was on conducting covert action, recruiting long-term assets with access to foreign intelligence, and providing strategic analysis. Although some of the intelligence the CIA collected was useful to military commanders, without assets already in place when operations began, the asset-recruitment process was not something that could be quickly initiated to fill military commanders' immediate information needs.

Despite this reality and understanding by some military intelligence leaders that the CIA had a limited role, congressional overseers singled out the CIA for failure to support military operations in the Gulf War.[1] In addition to acknowledging the need to enhance HUMINT to understand "the morale and intentions of Iraqi forces and leaders," the SSCI took previous criticism of the CIA's failure to support planning efforts a step further by arguing that the CIA had a role in supporting military commanders during peacetime and needed to be more responsive to the DoD's requirements.[2] Expanding the CIA's role in supporting military operations to peacetime and giving regional combatant commander's peacetime control of national systems were significant steps toward subordinating national intelligence to the combatant commander.

The George H. W. Bush administration had been trying to normalize America's relationship with Iraq following the end of the eight-year Iraq-Iran War in 1988. Realizing that Saddam Hussein was a tyrant but understanding the importance of maintaining influence in the Middle East, the Bush administration hoped diplomatic engagement, military exchanges, and economic incentives could temper his behavior. On October 2, 1989, the administration published NSD-26, *U.S. Policy towards the Persian Gulf,* which stated that "normal relations between the United States and Iraq would serve our longer-term interests and promote stability in both the Gulf and the Middle East."[3] Although the administration acknowledged Saddam's brutality, it believed Iraq's economic deprivation and America's engagement could moderate the regime's behavior and allow it to serve as a counterweight to Iran. The administration's actions initially paid dividends, with Congress relenting from economic sanctions and Saddam agreeing to compensate American families who had lost loved ones when an Iraqi missile struck the USS *Stark* in 1987 during the Iran-Iraq War.[4]

Despite the efforts to normalize the US-Iraq relationship, Saddam's behavior became increasingly belligerent toward his fellow Arab League members, in particular Kuwait, which refused to forgive Iraq's debt and whom Iraq accused of exceeding oil quotas. On July 16, 1990, Tariq Aziz, the Iraqi foreign minister, sent the Arab League a letter threatening military action if Kuwait continued to ignore Iraq's concern over oil quotas, its demands for debt forgiveness, and a resolution of border disputes. A week later Iraq was moving war materiel to its border with Kuwait and, unbeknownst to the United States at the time, ordering commercial imagery of Kuwait and Saudi Arabia in preparation for an invasion. During this period, the United States was planning for and debating flexible deterrent options, including moving additional naval and airpower into the region, to convince Saddam to back down. Confidant the Arab League would resolve the situation and not wanting to escalate too far, the United States settled for deploying two KC-135 refueling aircraft and a C-131 in support of the United Arab Emirates' attempt to extend their Mirage Fighter aircraft range.

On July 25, 1990, with Iraq concerned about possible deployment of US forces in the region and with tension increasing in the Middle East, Saddam "summoned" April Glaspie, the US ambassador in Iraq, to his palace.[5] Ambassador Glaspie was later criticized for not firmly warning Saddam to halt his aggressive actions toward Kuwait, but confidence in diplomatic efforts led by Egyptian president Hosni Mubarak and Saddam's own words of restraint provided hope the Iraq–Kuwait squabble could be resolved peacefully. Despite an increase in oil prices and reassurances from Arab allies that tension was easing, Iraq continued to increase its troop strength along the Kuwait border, reaching more than 100,000 on July 31.[6] The next day, citing disagreements over territorial and financial claims, the Iraq delegation walked out of negotiations with Kuwait.[7] National Security Adviser Brent

Scowcroft notified President Bush late on the evening of August 1 that Saddam Hussein's forces had just invaded Kuwait.[8]

The United Nations Security Council immediately condemned Saddam's actions, and the United States started redirecting naval and air force capability to the region in hopes of persuading Saddam to rethink his decisions and in preparation for the possibility of military action. Over the next three days, President Bush discussed response options with North Atlantic Treaty Organization (NATO) allies and nations in the region.[9] Hoping that economic pressure would compel Saddam to depart from Kuwait so that military action would not be needed, the United Nations Security Council passed Resolution 661 on August 6, 1990, cutting off exports to and imports from Iraq.[10]

Feeling the pressure building from the coalition of odd bedfellows, Saddam became even more desperate and on August 8 started to "round up" foreign nationals in Kuwait, detaining them locally or moving them to Baghdad to serve as human shields against an attack.[11] His late-August press conference surrounded by Western children taken from their homes in Kuwait angered the world. Although Saddam intended the kidnappings to buy him time, the image of him asking a visibly shaken British five-year-old named Stuart Lockwood about his breakfast dietary preferences only hardened the United Nations' resolve.[12] By the end of December, the hostages were released, and Saddam's stay in Kuwait was running short.[13]

With Saddam ignoring warnings, Kuwait under Iraqi control, the region disrupted, and many nations fearing an attack into Saudi Arabia that would give Saddam control of 40 percent of the world's oil production, the United States and its coalition partners prepared to build combat power in the region. During Operation Desert Shield, the United States and its coalition partners amassed more than 500,000 troops in the region between August 1990 and January 1991 to compel Saddam's retreat from Kuwait and to deter an invasion of Saudi Arabia. On January 16, 1991, when the threat of force failed to compel Saddam's withdrawal, the coalition transitioned to Operation Desert Storm by initiating an air campaign focused on Iraqi leadership and military capabilities.[14]

Twenty-five years later, it is easy to forget how controversial the decision to go to war with Iraq was. In a period closer to Vietnam than to today, a powerful collection of voices warned against being drawn into a quagmire that would sap the United States of its blood and treasure. On January 12, 1991, Senator Sam Nunn, the SASC chairman whose legislation created SOCOM in 1986, and Senator George Mitchell (D–ME) offered up a resolution to give economic sanctions "more time."[15] Arguing the United States was "playing a winning hand" because economic sanctions and the Desert Shield defense were working, Nunn and Mitchell urged the Senate to restrain the dogs of war. Senator Frank Lautenberg (D), the second-term New Jersey senator and World War II veteran, had earlier warned of the terrible American casualties that could result from a ground war with Iraq. Citing a recent Pentagon order of 16,099 body bags as evidence, Lautenberg questioned whether Iraq was worth the potential cost in blood.[16] The House of Representatives was also arguing for restraint. On October 30, 1990, House Speaker Thomas Foley (D–WA) sent a letter to President Bush arguing that war with Iraq would not be a "low-intensity conflict" but could result in a "massive loss of lives" ("including 10,000 to 50,000 Americans").[17]

Those arguing for restraint and for more time for sanctions to work included not just Democratic congressmen but also two former secretaries of defense, two former chairmen of the JCS, and a former NSA director. Caspar Weinberger, the author of a doctrine that articulated the use of force as a last resort, argued for more patience. James Schlesinger, a former DCI and secretary of defense, warned that the increasingly aggressive US posture and rhetoric toward Saddam risked splintering the coalition. General David Jones (ret.) and Admiral William J. Crowe (ret.) praised President Bush for his actions to date but advised that sanctions required more time. Lieutenant General (ret.) William Odom compared the "scale" of a tank war between the United States and Iraq to the World War II Battle of Kursk between Germany and Russia and cautioned Congress not to underestimate the potential costs in blood and treasure that war with Iraq might incur.[18] Despite these voices of caution, the Senate passed a resolution authorizing the use of force against Iraq on January 13, 1991.

The campaign plan for Iraq was a four-phase operation that would begin with air and naval strikes focused on disabling Iraq's political and military communication systems, knocking out its air defense capability, and destroying ground forces to soften its defense and limit the number of coalition casualties during the ground phase. On January 17, 1991, Iraq's black sky lit up as US Air Force cruise and US Navy Tomahawk missiles rained down, smashing Iraq's communication, air defense, and nuclear, biological, and chemical capabilities.[19] Leading the war effort were two very different infantrymen, despite both being army generals.

General Colin Powell was the JCS chairman whose experience in Vietnam as a young officer framed how he viewed war's subordination to policy.[20] A native New Yorker and graduate of the City University of New York Reserve Officer Training Corps, Powell had thus far spent the majority of his general officer years advising President Reagan and senior civilian defense officials. A man universally revered for his intelligence, strategic thought, and political astuteness, he was also respected for his humility and professional-ism. Powell's effect on the military and his fellow service member's fondness for him lingered long after his retirement in 1993.

With General Powell ensuring the nesting of policy and military opera-tions from his JCS position, General Norman Schwarzkopf, Admiral Met-calf's deputy during Urgent Fury, led the fight as the Central Command (CENTCOM) commander. Schwarzkopf, a bear of a man whose father had led the New Jersey State Police during the Lindbergh kidnapping investiga-tion and later served as the US military adviser to the shah of Iran, had a mixed reputation in the military. Some viewed Schwarzkopf as a soldier's soldier whose Pattonesque mannerisms, high standards, and hard-charging personality were what made many great warriors. Other officers who worked for him or served near him viewed his motives more suspiciously, even con-temptuously. To these individuals, Schwarzkopf was a self-promoting, egotis-tical officer who berated juniors for failing to attain standards he himself did not achieve.[21] Despite many younger officers' ire toward him, Schwarzkopf continued to rise in stature, and, following Desert Storm, his public reputa-tion as one of America's greatest generals resulted in congressional legislation recommending him for a fifth star. Although the legislation never passed, the recommendation that he be placed in the pantheon of Generals of the Army underscored his reputation following Desert Storm.

On January 30, 1991, two weeks into the air war, General Schwarz-kopf swaggered up to the press podium to exhibit for the world the awesome destruction and effectiveness of the coalition's air strikes. During the press conference, the CENTCOM commander, with assistance from his lead air planner, Brigadier General Buster Glosson, displayed aerial footage of Iraqi Scuds being destroyed during air strikes.[22] This footage was intended to high-light the effectiveness of the air strikes and the precision of America's new weaponry. Although the footage was impressive, it did not, in fact, depict the destruction of mobile Iraqi Scuds. After the press conference, intelligence analysts discovered that the supposed Scud sites were actually Jordanian fuel trucks.[23] Rear Admiral Michael McConnell, the Joint Staff–Intelligence (J2) director, took the information and went to speak with General Colin Powell about the mistake. After receiving the information, General Powell picked up the phone to inform General Schwarzkopf that the Scud destruction he so proudly displayed was actually the destruction of fuel trucks.[24] The mistaken Scuds reflected a significant ongoing debate between the CIA and CENT-COM on how to assess battlefield damage.

After weeks of bombing Saddam's government facilities and military capabilities, CENTCOM was ready to initiate the ground phase of the operation. Believing that Iraq's defense was weakened to an acceptable level, Schwarzkopf argued that the coalition's ground forces should be unleashed to push the remainder of Saddam's forces from Kuwait. The debate over whether to use ground forces had been building in Washington for weeks, with Generals Powell and Schwarzkopf believing ground forces were required to remove Saddam's forces from Kuwait but air force leadership confident that, if given enough time, air power alone could bring Iraq's departure.[25]

At the time of Desert Storm, there was no standard procedure for calculating battle-damage assessments (BDA). Because the coalition's ground forces would be the ones facing off against Iraq's army, General Schwarzkopf deferred to Army Central Command (ARCENT) to determine the criteria for calculating BDA. Uncertain regarding the best approach, the army went through numerous iterations of establishing and then adjusting the assessment criteria based on intelligence derived from various sources. Initially using imagery, the army found it difficult to assess damage done to Iraqi capability based on the destruction of a few pieces of equipment, as captured in high-resolution photos. When this approach proved unsuitable, the army started to use pilot reporting to calculate BDA.[26] One of the criteria ARCENT elected to use was to count 75 percent of the "kills" A-10 pilots reported.[27] A number of intelligence agencies back in Washington, in particular the CIA, criticized ARCENT's assessment process, arguing that it greatly inflated the percentage of Iraq's military capability that was either disabled or destroyed. Based on the criticism, ARCENT reduced its percentage of declared "kills" to around 33 percent, but the Intelligence Community still claimed inflation.[28] The debate over BDA was more than an office water-cooler discussion; it had political ramifications. The administration was concerned about casualties and wanted to reduce Iraqi combat power by 50 percent before initiating the ground invasion.

The disagreement between the CIA and CENTCOM came to President Bush's attention on February 21, 1991, when DCI William H. Webster briefed him on the issue.[29] The CIA and DoD tried to work through the disagreement, but their BDA calculations were so different that they were unable to settle the dispute. Because the ground invasion was contingent on the weakening of Iraq's military capability, the BDA controversy had to be resolved before a decision to invade was made. National Security Adviser Brent Scowcroft was the individual responsible for mediating the DoD/CIA BDA disagreement and recommending to Bush if it was time for a ground invasion.[30]

Rear Admiral McConnell's phone rang on February 21, 1991; at the other end of the line was his boss, General Powell, telling him to "get your stuff, we are going to the White House." After he hung up the phone, McConnell collected his briefing "kit," which he had created for his various White House briefings on the Iraq campaign, and hurried off to a waiting car.[31] After crossing the Potomac and pulling through the White House gates, Powell and McConnell walked to Scowcroft's West Wing office for a meeting with Secretary of Defense Richard Cheney, Scowcroft, DCI Webster, and David Armstrong, a senior intelligence officer. On Scowcroft's meeting agenda that day were the CIA and DoD's divergent BDAs and whether it was time to initiate the ground phase.[32]

Scowcroft had graduated from the United States Military Academy in 1947, the same year the DoD, US Air Force, and the CIA were established through the National Security Act. An intellectual heavyweight with a PhD from Columbia University, he rose to the senior ranks of the military via a nontraditional path that included professor stints at both West Point and the Air Force Academy, along with numerous prestigious staff officer positions within the Pentagon, eventually achieving the rank of lieutenant general.[33] General Scowcroft retired from the air force in 1975, but his career as a trusted adviser continued into numerous administrations. That day in February 1991, Scowcroft the retired general had to balance his military expertise with his political judgment. The anxiety over the prospect of thousands of dead American troops concerned policy makers, in whose memories the Vietnam stalemate lingered. With this fear in the forefront, Scowcroft's job was to determine if Iraqi forces were weakened enough to limit an American body count.

Scowcroft looked at the representatives from the DoD and CIA and told them they had to come to some resolution on the BDA dispute. Armstrong admitted that Iraq's army was "highly degraded" but raised concern with the reliability of CENTCOM's evolving BDA methodology, which reported Iraqi combat units at between 42 and 72 percent strength, whereas the CIA's estimates placed them at between 75 and 85 percent strength.[34] McConnell told the group that even though the Intelligence Community had "amassed back here the best talent in the US government" to support the commander and was willing to send the "experts forward," there was a limit on how much analysts in Washington could know about conditions on the ground in Iraq. He then pointed out that "our capability to know was imagery based and the opportunity for imagery was only twice a day."[35] Supporting Cheney's and Powell's position, McConnell stated that CENTCOM had access to aircraft photography, pilot reporting, radio intercepts, and other intelligence resources that analysts in Washington could not access.[36] After listening to the two arguments, Scowcroft ended the meeting, and a few days later the ground phase began.

Whether the BDA assessments were accurate, the ineffectiveness, pliability, and lack of fight within most of the Iraqi units became apparent once the ground war kicked off on February 24, 1991.[37] In roughly one hundred hours, coalition forces swept into Kuwait and Iraq, easily defeating Iraqi forces and forcing Saddam's surrender. The fear of fighting the world's fourth-largest military quickly evaporated, and the jubilation of a decisive coalition victory quickly ensued. For the United States, the victory reaffirmed changes brought about through the Goldwater-Nichols legislation and helped exorcise some of the ghosts of Vietnam.[38]

Building a Joint Intelligence Center on the Fly

As General Schwarzkopf and his staff prepared for operations to oust Saddam from Kuwait, Rear Admiral McConnell was at the Pentagon building a coalition of his own to support the war effort. A future NSA director and director of national intelligence (DNI), McConnell was at the time a recently frocked rear admiral who had spent his career in naval intelligence. As a navy intelligence officer, he had served a significant portion of his career aboard fleets and viewed pushing intelligence to the combatant commander's corps and divisions as no different than a fleet's intelligence component "broadcasting" intelligence to its ships; the purpose of both was to enable operations by establishing a common operating picture.[39]

Understanding the importance that signals intelligence would play in the war, McConnell's fellow navy admiral and NSA director, William O. Studeman, worked with McConnell to help get the DoD Joint Intelligence Center (JIC) up and running and then to provide it with round-the-clock signals intelligence support.[40] Navy intelligence is a small, close-knit community that has produced many influential leaders within the Intelligence Community. Studeman and McConnell's relationship went back years, to include a stint together on Team Charlie, the group of top navy analysts tasked by chief of naval operations Admiral Thomas Hayward to investigate the Soviet submarine strategy.[41] Both officers also shared a common mentor in Admiral Bobby Ray Inman, the former NSA director and deputy DCI who had served as chairman of the Secretary of State's Advisory Panel on Overseas Security following the Beirut bombings.

Talented officers in their own right, Studeman and McConnell rose through the ranks of the navy and national intelligence. Following the Gulf War, Admiral Studeman, like his mentor, earned his fourth star and become the deputy DCI. Upon departing the NSA, Studeman was influential in choosing his replacement, Mike McConnell.[42]

According to McConnell, each of the services reacted differently to his request for support for military operations. The navy was supportive from the beginning and provided two of its best officers. The army was a little hesitant at first but eventually came on board and provided its best to the DoD JIC. The air force was the most resistant toward McConnell's "fusion center" project.[43] The reluctance of the Air Force Intelligence Directorate, led by then Major General Jim Clapper, a future DIA director, USD for intelligence, and DNI, was understandable. The air force would lead the air campaign, and the Intelligence Directorate had the important job of identifying Iraq's military and civilian targets. Clapper, who was consistently praised by his fellow intelligence professionals for his nonparochial leadership of the Intelligence Community as the DNI, had to have worried that air force support to the DoD JIC might decrease his directorate's focus on the air campaign. With the joint effort not building at the rate envisioned, DIA director Lieutenant General Harry Soyster called a Military Intelligence Board to ensure all the services were supportive of McConnell's efforts.[44]

With the DoD JIC functioning, the Military Intelligence Board decided in the fall of 1990 to establish a CENTCOM JIC in Riyadh to ensure that Schwarzkopf's tactical and operational intelligence needs were met.[45] In November 1990, the board sent a team to Riyadh to expand the twenty-three-member intelligence section to more than one hundred individuals two months later, in January 1991. The CENTCOM JIC served as the "single focal point for analysis as well as for collection management, production, dissemination, and tailored intelligence" within the theater and included analysts from the CIA who participated in the Tiger Team, which helped with the targeting process once Desert Storm kicked off in February 1991.[46] Early on, McConnell reached out to the CENTCOM J2, Brigadier General Jack Leide, to ensure he had the support necessary from Washington to build his intelligence apparatus.[47]

John "Jack" Leide had a rare background for an army general. A speaker of Mandarin Chinese with a Syracuse University law degree, Leide had spent more than a third of his then twenty-seven-year military career in the Far East, first serving in the Vietnam War and then as a foreign-area or intelligence officer in Taiwan, Hong Kong, Japan, and China.[48] Following his assignment at CENTCOM, Major General Leide served out the rest of his military career at the DIA, first as the director for attachés and operations and then as the director of the Defense Human Intelligence Service. During his last three years at the DIA, he oversaw HUMINT consolidation within the DoD.

During their first conversation, Leide and McConnell joked about how their experiences, one as a fleet intelligence officer and the other as a foreign-area officer in China, had prepared them for a land war in Iraq. The two flag officers hit it off, agreeing they would "have to move mountains" and conduct a "full-court press" to provide General Schwarzkopf and his subordinate commanders the intelligence necessary to wage war. Embracing the spirit of Goldwater-Nichols, McConnell and Leide were intent on building an apparatus that could exploit all of the US intelligence capability.

One of the first operators McConnell contacted was the lead planner for the air campaign. Brigadier General Glosson, an air force aviator known equally for his talent and drive, was an air-power enthusiast who wanted to prove its decisive nature.[49] A graduate of North Carolina State University, Glosson was a fighter pilot with more than a quarter-century service in the air force.[50] "A mover and a shaker," he had arrived at CENTCOM after a stint as the deputy ASD for legislative affairs and was well connected within the Pentagon and on Capitol Hill.[51] Glosson was promoted to major general five months after Desert Storm and shortly after returning to Washington as the air force liaison to Congress. Within a year, Glosson received his third star and assignment as the air force deputy chief of staff for Joint Staff–Plans (J5) and Joint Staff–Operations (J3), a prestigious position that is along a path to a fourth star. However, despite his reputation and connections, he retired in July 1994 after receiving a letter of admonishment from air force secretary Shelia Widnall for trying to influence a general officer promotion board. Even though the Pentagon and air force inspector generals concluded that Glosson lied during testimony regarding his involvement, then deputy secretary of defense John Deutch came to his defense.[52]

In early 1991, however, Glosson was an active player in determining how to provide intelligence to commanders in the war. During one of Glosson's trips to Washington, McConnell reached out to him to discuss intelligence support requirements for the air campaign. After a short conversation, Glosson and McConnell agreed to work together to ensure that General Charles Horner, the Air Force Central Command commander, had the intelligence necessary to wage the air campaign. Over the next two months, the JCS J2 and the lead planner for the air campaign became close, on the phone three to four hours a day discussing intelligence requirements.[53] The personal relationship gave Glosson direct access to the intelligence required for targeting when the transmission through normal intelligence channels was not quick enough.[54]

Two to three weeks after the effort to build an intelligence fusion center began, McConnell, Studeman, and others brought together two to three hundred people into the Pentagon to establish the DoD JIC.[55] The motivation to build the DoD JIC was a belief that operational requirements should drive intelligence. If the DoD JIC was going to be relevant, the intelligence professionals had to understand the military's intelligence requirements and to focus their collection efforts accordingly. This meant that setting up a "fusion center" was useless unless the Intelligence Community understood the commander's information requirements, was able to collect the intelligence to answer those requirements, and had the means to distribute its products to the troops on the ground.

McConnell understood that when the ground war kicked off, the divisions, brigades, and other military units had to have access to the latest intelligence on Iraq's military disposition and status. Although the DoD JIC and the CENTCOM JIC were built to bring together the resources of the Intelligence Community, dissemination of intelligence was constrained due to the limited communication architecture possessed by forces on the ground. Because there was neither the time nor the resources to build a new system for dissemination, the DoD JIC and the CENTCOM JIC had to exploit the organic capabilities within the units. Although not a perfect solution, the Multimedia Information Network System (MINX) provided a means to broadcast the intelligence.[56]

In 1972, Datapoint Corporation introduced MINX, the first "desktop videoconferencing system."[57] MINX resembled a personal computer but provided "point-to-point and multipoint" imagery and data-transmission capability.[58] The system was compact enough that it was deployable, and its encryption capability enabled it to disseminate classified intelligence to the troops on the ground. McConnell's plan was to "broadcast" intelligence reports using MINX so the commanders on the ground could have the most up-to-date intelligence the JICs possessed.[59]

McConnell's "broadcasting" approach was based on his experience as an intelligence officer in the navy, where it was standard practice to push intelligence out to all the fleet's ships. Not appreciating the difference in how services operated, McConnell assumed that if he made the intelligence available, the units' intelligence officers would know how to gain access. After the war, McConnell found out that some of the ground forces had not received much of the tactical intelligence on the disposition of Iraqi forces. Although the broadcasts were not heard by all, at least one resourceful division intelligence officer was tuning in. Lieutenant Colonel Keith Alexander, a highly intelligent officer with graduate degrees in physics, electronic warfare, and business, was the First Armored Division's assistant chief of staff for General Staff Intelligence Section (G2). According to McConnell, some divisions complained about the level of intelligence support, and their commanders were unaware that the DoD JIC was pushing intelligence down to the troops on the ground, but Alexander found the broadcasts and utilized them to his commander's advantage.[60] Following Desert Storm, Alexander rose through the ranks, eventually attaining a fourth star, becoming the longest -serving NSA director, and serving as the first commander of US Cyber Command.

The CIA's Contribution to the Gulf War Effort

Admiral McConnell did not see much of a role for the CIA once the war kicked off but wanted to ensure complete Intelligence Community support to the combatant commander. Early on in his effort to build the DoD JIC, McConnell reached out to DCI William Webster's office. President Reagan had tapped Webster, a former judge and Federal Bureau of Investigation (FBI) director, following Bill Casey's death, the Iran-Contra scandal, and withdrawal of the nomination of Robert Gates as DCI. Not an intelligence professional, Judge Webster was selected more for his unimpeachable character and righteous reputation than for his intelligence expertise. McConnell's first call to the DCI's office was answered by one of Webster's assistants, who promised to discuss CIA participation in the DoD JIC with DCI Webster. Despite the assistant's promise, his "don't call us, we'll call you" attitude belied his guarantee.[61] When McConnell did not hear back from the DCI's office, he reached out to air force lieutenant general Michael Carns, the director of the Joint Staff, for assistance. Carns informed the chairman of the JCS, General Powell, of the issue, and Powell contacted DCI Webster. Following Powell and Webster's conversation, the CIA assigned a senior intelligence officer to serve as McConnell's liaison to the agency.[62]

Despite the DCI office's slow response and the later criticism that the CIA did not support the military because it failed to "fully incorporate" its Iraq analysts into the DoD JIC, the CIA in fact committed significant resources to supporting the US military in Iraq.[63] A week prior to Iraq's invasion and up until the Iraqi army crossed Kuwait's border, it was Charlie Allen, a CIA analyst and national intelligence officer, who had warned that Iraq was going to invade.[64] Following the invasion, the CIA established task forces within both the Directorate of Intelligence (DI) and the Directorate of Operations (DO), while it surged the number of CIA officers worldwide focused on the Iraq mission.

The DI sent analysts to work in the DoD JIC and the CENTCOM JIC as part of the national intelligence surge to provide reach back into the CIA, and a senior analyst traveled to Saudi Arabia to prepare Schwarzkopf for his August meeting with Saudi government officials. The DI not only sent personnel to the intelligence centers and to brief senior defense and military leaders but also provided Iraq-centric briefs to deploying units and military professional schools to assist those service members preparing to deploy. CIA analysts serving in the CENTCOM JIC participated in the targeting process, and CIA analysts at headquarters and in the field supported the military planning efforts for the ground invasion by providing information on locations of weapons of mass destruction (WMD) in Iraq, Iraq ground force "order of battle" and unit position, minefield locations, and Iraqi infrastructure, including road networks.

The most significant commitment the CIA made was to provide a number of liaison officers to the Pentagon and CENTCOM. Compared to the Pentagon, the CIA is a small organization with little surge capacity. Realigning officers to support Gulf War operations and calling up to active duty a number of reservists within the CIA affected the CIA's ability to collect on other intelligence requirements. The CIA also deployed joint intelligence liaison elements to CENTCOM headquarters in Saudi Arabia. These teams of "operations officers, analysts, and communication specialists" served as conduits to the CIA's resources and expertise to support CENTCOM's operational requirements.[65] Yet despite these efforts to support the military, controversies rose regarding intelligence support to the operation. These controversies and the subsequent congressional reaction increased the CIA's focus on supporting military operations, thus risking the agency's subordination to DoD.

Through the support of the services and national intelligence agencies, the JCS J2 and CENTCOM J2 built a novel intelligence apparatus whose primary focus was supporting the CENTCOM commander. The DoD JIC that was built to support the operational commander served as a blueprint for the establishment of the National Military Joint Intelligence Center in March 1992. The center included representatives from the NSA and the CIA, while at the same time consolidating the DoD's intelligence as well as indications and warning production "into a single, jointly manned center."[66]

3

THE GULF WAR'S AFTERMATH

From Victory to Vitriol

No combat commander has ever had as full and complete a view of his adversary as did our field commander. Intelligence support to Operations Desert Shield and Desert Storm was a success story.

—General Colin Powell, in CIA, Gulf War Task Force, "CIA Support to the US Military during the Persian Gulf War," June 16, 1997

Preparing for Blowback

On the afternoon of March 3, 1991, the same day General Schwarzkopf and the victorious coalition military leaders stood with their conquered Iraqi foes, Secretary of Defense Richard Cheney was already thinking about the intelligence lessons learned from the conflict. That day he gave Richard Haver, his special assistant for intelligence, a month to research and write an analysis on the performance of intelligence leading up to and during the war. As Haver stood wondering what drove the rush to review following such a lopsided victory, Cheney explained that the celebration would soon end, and then questions would arise regarding why elected officials and former military professionals had overestimated casualties. According to Haver, Cheney believed there was a significant pushback against war based on casualty estimates, and "when people are that wrong in Washington, it had to be intel."[1] That March day, Haver departed Cheney's office with his marching orders to limit each issue to one page but to investigate everything that had gone well and wrong throughout the lead-up and execution of the war.[2]

Cheney's concern over congressional reaction was justified. The vote to go to war was the closest since 1812, and many congresspersons claimed they were influenced by the Intelligence Community's briefs on Iraqi capability.[3]

According to L. Britt Snider, a former SSCI staff member and CIA inspector general, SSCI staffers recalled Intelligence Community testimony that "the Iraqi military was the most advanced in that part of the world, battle-tested by eight years of war with Iran. . . . The Iraqis would use chemical and biological weapons against the coalition forces. . . . In all likelihood, the United States was in for a prolonged conflict of at least six months' duration involving many casualties." Based on these "dire predictions," many congresspersons voted against the authorization for the use of force.[4] Senator David L. Boren (D–OK), the SSCI chairman, was angry, believing the Intelligence Community had "sandbagged" him with their intelligence assessment, and Senator Sam Nunn believed his vote had "impaired his credibility as chairman of the SASC."[5] According to Bruce Riedel, however, a senior CIA Middle East analyst at the time, the CIA analysts were just trying to explain the quality and effectiveness of the Iraqi military in relation to their Arab neighbors and had left it up to the US military and others to put the Iraqi capability in context with the coalition forces' capability.[6]

Rich Haver is somewhat of a legend in the Intelligence Community, known for effectiveness but sometimes ruffling feathers in the process. He has a deep intellect and a remarkable recall, which he credits his undergraduate history professor Stephen Ambrose for helping him develop.[7] Haver served in the uniformed navy during the Vietnam War but gained his reputation largely as a civilian analyst and leader within navy intelligence.[8] He was also a mentee of Admiral Bobby Ray Inman, who selected him and future admiral Bill Studeman in 1976 to determine what was driving Russian "activity towards the US Navy." Haver and Studeman's investigation pointed to Russia "reading the navy's mail" and to the compromise of the navy's crypto machines. Supporting the findings, Inman sent Haver around the world to speak with navy forces about the compromise. Evidence the Soviets were reading the US Navy's mail was "paper thin," and most of the navy was reluctant to accept Studeman and Haver's findings until the John Walker case surfaced.[9]

John Walker, who had retired from the navy in 1976, had been spying for the Soviets since October 1967, when he walked into the Soviet embassy in the United States to offer his services and information on the KL-47 crypto machines. Over the next eighteen years, Walker expanded his spy ring and compromised the crypto machines the navy used to secure communications. He evaded FBI scrutiny until 1984, when his wife came forward and recounted his treachery.[10] The navy then finally accepted Studeman and Haver's conclusions.

Knowing that navy leaders would not warmly receive news of the compromise and valuing officers willing to go against the grain, Inman promised to take care of Studeman and Haver. A decade later Studeman sat in Inman's chair as DNI, and Haver resided down the hall as his deputy. As Studeman's deputy, he conducted the damage assessment on the Walker spy case and then, following his stint as Cheney's special assistant, served as DCI Gate's and then DCI R. James Woolsey Jr.'s director of community affairs, a position from which he handled the Ames spy case damage assessment. Temporarily leaving government after his CIA stint, Haver returned to defense intelligence during the early years of the George W. Bush administration.

Haver's investigation into intelligence support during the Gulf War had him journeying throughout the Intelligence Community, to the various military commands, and into policy makers' offices, including the Oval Office. The highly classified report Haver wrote for Secretary Cheney considered not only the performance of intelligence during the war but also why the Intelligence Community had failed to accurately predict Saddam's behavior. It identified twenty-three issues for intelligence support leading up to and during the Gulf War. Among the issues was the need to further exploit and expand technology to ensure persistent collection and to "get information the last mile" to the troops on the ground. To accomplish persistence, the report highlighted the value of the burgeoning unmanned aerial vehicle (drone) technology. The CIA and the military pursued this technology in the years to come, an investment that paid dividends in the Balkans, before becoming one of the Intelligence Community's and America's most visible—and controversial—assets after 9/11.

Regarding national intelligence collection, the report gave signals intelligence positive reviews, stating that it was "centrally [run] and responsive." The report said imagery was unresponsive because there was no central NSA-like organization ensuring that commanders' imagery needs were met. Finally, the report said that HUMINT was "a mess" and "a day late and dollar short," failing to take advantage of the numerous defector debriefings leading to the ground invasion. According to Haver, the issue with HUMINT reflected a lack of attention given to it by the military services. He argued that the navy and air force had shuttered their HUMINT capabilities years earlier, and although the army and marines retained theirs, they never "exercised" the capability. In Haver's opinion, the "entire HUMINT enterprise was unprepared," and efforts had to be made to ensure preparedness in the future. Because the HUMINT capability required for war could not be grown overnight, the DoD had to find a way to build and exercise that capability during peacetime. DoD did not possess the expertise, so it needed the DCI's and CIA's assistance.[11]

Both the CIA and DoD have HUMINT collectors, but the DoD's HUMINT capability has not traditionally held a position of prominence within the department.[12] According to Major General (ret.) Michael Ennis, US Marine Corps, a former DIA deputy director for HUMINT and a former deputy director of community HUMINT for the National Clandestine Service (NCS), there is a "real negative bias towards HUMINT" within DoD, where it is the "least understood, least supported, and least trusted" of the intelligence collection disciplines. According to Ennis, "this lack of understanding, trust, and support for HUMINT within all of DoD resulted in service HUMINT, with the exception of the army's Great Skills Program being a poorly managed career field with little upward mobility, and in defense HUMINT (which relies heavily on augmentation from the services), an organization who's capabilities are hampered by insufficient logistic support, a risk-adverse leadership, and an excessively bureaucratic approval process"—a reality recognized by both DCI George Tenet and Congress.[13]

The DIA does possess clandestine HUMINT collectors, and the military services have tactical HUMINT collectors, such as interrogators and counterintelligence HUMINT professionals, but DoD's clandestine capability has always been controversial, and its interrogators and counterintelligence capability have often been the first casualties when the budget axe has been swung.[14] Ennis described how "in the mid-1990s the army made significant ✓ cuts to its tactical HUMINT force (which had been largely unused since the end of the Vietnam War), to provide structure for a new weapons initiative."[15]

Cheney's prediction that policy makers' attention would soon shift toward perceived intelligence shortcomings was perceptive. In April 1991, the Congressional Research Service (CRS) published the report *Desert Shield and Desert Storm: Implications for Future U.S. Force Requirements*. With the looming budget reductions, the shift away from the Cold War, and the transition to a more regionally focused strategy, the US Congress was looking at Desert Storm to inform future force reductions.[16] Regarding intelligence, the CRS report highlighted the need to "fuse" all source intelligence at the tactical and strategic intelligence levels. It emphasized the benefits that new technical collection systems had provided commanders during Desert Storm but argued that these systems had severe limitations in providing commanders with greater battlefield awareness. It asserted that the "strategic and tactical intelligence failures" that plagued Desert Storm could not be remedied with more technology but required greater HUMINT. HUMINT shortfalls, it contended, were not new and had been the root of past intelligence failures. The report specifically noted the "lack of HUMINT professionals able to furnish otherwise unavailable information from high-priority areas has been obvious for many years" and that "indigenous networks" needed to be developed during peacetime; a responsibility that would certainly fall upon the CIA.[17]

In *Desert Shield and Desert Storm,* the critiques regarding HUMINT shortfalls not only were in line with elements of Haver's report and concerns raised by the chairmen of the HPSCI and the SSCI but echoed comments made following the Beirut bombing and Operation Urgent Fury. In the aftermath of these events, representatives from both political parties argued that slashing HUMINT in previous years and the lack of investment in HUMINT to rebuild the capability were largely to blame for intelligence shortfalls during military operations.[18] Although some of the issues, such as shortage of interrogators, were service related, the larger issues with HUMINT were directed to the CIA. The military units could expand the language skills necessary for debriefings and interrogations, but they did not have the ability or resources to generate and sustain the type of clandestine networks described in the CRS report and during SSCI hearings. If HUMINT were required to enable planning before operations and to ensure force protection during operations, the networks had to be established and developed during peacetime, long before any combat boots hit the ground. Establishing networks in peacetime to support possible future military operations would place a significant burden on the CIA while also risking its subordination to geographic combatant commanders.

Despite the fact that HUMINT support to military commanders was a reoccurring issue, not enough had been done during the decade between Beirut and Desert Storm to remedy the problem; there simply was no urgency to introduce the changes required to increase intelligence support to military operations. Part of the issue was that more pressing Cold War requirements had taken precedence over the analysis necessary to reform the Intelligence Community. This prioritization was understandable because there were (and are) legitimate questions regarding whether the emphasis on support to the military was appropriate for the nation's only independent intelligence agency. With the Soviet Union still around, it was difficult to reallocate intelligence resources, but with the Soviet Union weakened it became easier.

Desert Storm not only confirmed ongoing issues with intelligence support to military operations in the minds of many legislators but also proved a boon to the military's public image. From a publicity standpoint, the overwhelming victory in the Gulf War transformed General Norman Schwarzkopf into a celebrity with a bully pulpit and a receptive audience.

Schwarzkopf's Triumph and Stoking the Intelligence Debate

General Schwarzkopf and other Desert Storm veterans enjoyed a hero's welcome when they returned to the United States. Ticker tape parades in New York, Washington, DC, and Hollywood drew millions of revelers celebrating the victory and praising the troops. A relatively unknown civil servant to the majority of Americans before the Gulf War, Schwarzkopf enjoyed celebrity status upon his return. Salivating Madison Avenue advertising firms wanted to cash in on his hero status, and brands were reaching out to Schwarzkopf doppelgängers to market their goods. Schwarzkopf's image and story were so lucrative that Bantam Books paid him $5 million for his story in June 1991, less than six months after his return from the Middle East.[19] His hero reputation accompanied him when he took his seat before the SASC on June 12, 1991.[20]

General Schwarzkopf had been critical of CIA support during the planning and execution phases of the Gulf War. When Saddam took Western hostages in August 1990 to deter a military response to his invasion of Kuwait, Schwarzkopf claimed the lack of HUMINT sources limited US options.[21] He criticized the CIA and other national intelligence agencies for providing contradictory analysis and not distilling intelligence to enable his decision making.[22] His frustration with what he viewed as the CIA's unwillingness to assume a supporting role lingered even after his congressional testimony, and he noted in his biography that "the CIA was the only agency to dissent: on the eve of the ground war, it was still telling the President that we were grossly exaggerating the damage inflicted on the Iraqis. If we'd waited to convince the CIA, we'd still be in Saudi Arabia."[23] In a telling response to Schwarzkopf's frustration with the CIA over BDA, in 1993 the Gulf Air Power Survey and an HASC subcommittee found that Schwarzkopf's own BDA estimates had been greatly inflated.[24]

His criticism received publicity and was noticed by Senator John Warner (R–VA), a member of both the SASC and the SSCI. According to McConnell, Senator Warner's office had reached out to General Schwarzkopf to get his insight on intelligence support to the military during the war. The senator's office was informed that the general's schedule was currently too hectic, and he could not make himself available. Dissatisfied with this response, Senator Warner contacted Cheney, who reached out to Schwarzkopf and told him that white space had just opened on his calendar.

Although Schwarzkopf made clear his concerns with intelligence, there was less certainty regarding his awareness of what support intelligence had actually provided him. To overcome this shortfall, Brigadier General Leide,

Schwarzkopf's intelligence chief spent a week reviewing with Schwarzkopf the support intelligence provided during Desert Storm prior to his testimony. According to McConnell, this education changed Schwarzkopf's perspective on intelligence support, and he partially recanted his previous critiques during an interchange with Senator Warner. When Warner asked why Schwarzkopf's earlier comments regarding intelligence had been more critical, Schwarzkopf supposedly said that at that point he had not had time to reconsider the support intelligence provided, which he did later. Warner asked Schwarzkopf to let the press know that he had reconsidered intelligence performance and had changed his opinion about the support he received during Desert Storm. Although Schwarzkopf agreed to Warner's request, McConnell spent the next few weeks eyeing press reports for signs of Schwarzkopf's recant. It never came.[25]

Despite what Schwarzkopf said prior to June 12, 1991, his testimony that day regarding intelligence support was pretty balanced. He testified that "intelligence support" was excellent, but, in addition to the BDA issues, he identified the need for the Intelligence Community to develop a capability that would provide commanders "near real-time" information. As later critiques by Congress depicted, this support could not merely be left up to technical systems that could fail during war but had to include HUMINT elements to meet the commander's expectations. Because HUMINT systems necessary to support the wartime commanders had to be developed over time, the CIA had to work on this development during peacetime.[26]

Even though Schwarzkopf's testimony included compliments of intelligence support, the *Washington Post* and *New York Time* headlines the next day focused on his critiques. Both newspapers highlighted the CENTCOM commander's frustration with "caveated, disagreed with, footnoted and watered down" intelligence reports that did not enable his battlefield decision-making ability.[27] Congressional criticism of the "duplicative and contradictory" intelligence provided to the military commander during Desert Storm echoed Schwarzkopf's complaints.[28] Although understandable, this critique highlights a tension between a military commander who wants certainty to make decisions and an Intelligence Community that appreciates the uncertainty of the situation it is analyzing.

Twelve years later another report on the failure of the Intelligence Community in Iraq cited "groupthink" as an issue in the analysis of Iraq's WMD programs.[29] These two reports, separated by more than a decade, seem to be at odds with each other—the Gulf War–era report striving for greater analytical consensus to enable command decision making and the WMD report embracing analytical friction to protect against groupthink. Although both policy makers and commanders appreciate agreement on intelligence analysis to support decision making, the pursuit of consensus raises the prospect of groupthink within the Intelligence Community. Contradictory analysis might make it difficult to decide courses of action, but there is goodness in analytical friction for better understanding of the possibilities present within any operational environment.

In response to Schwarzkopf's criticism and subsequent concerns surfacing from Gulf War illness or syndrome, numerous reviews of intelligence performance during Desert Storm were done. These reviews, conducted by various elements within the executive and legislative branches, considered the performance of both tactical and strategic intelligence. The reviews were typically balanced, but over time the critiques of intelligence were embraced, and significant changes were implemented in response.

The military services' after-action reviews of intelligence support were mixed regarding CIA support. The then classified *Annual Historical Review* for fiscal year 1991 by the Department of the Army's Office of the Deputy Chief of Staff for Intelligence highlighted the CIA, army, and other DoD intelligence agencies' collaboration in support of CENTCOM operations and the use of overt HUMINT in the targeting process to "nominate, target, and destroy" Iraq's capabilities.[30] Whereas the report praised overt HUMINT (i.e., military), the Third Army and ARCENT G2's after-action review criticized clandestine HUMINT (i.e., CIA) for being "critically short" and contributing little to the operation."[31] This criticism echoed the CRS report, which argued that "strategic and tactical intelligence failures can be traced directly to the shortage of well-qualified, area-oriented HUMINT specialists."[32]

The report on the US Air Force Gulf War Air Power Survey mentioned the CIA liaisons sent to work with military planners focused on the air war and described how informal relationships between air force planners and CIA and DIA officers furthered planning efforts and concealed some of the air force's internal failures. The report also described how Schwarzkopf viewed the CIA as a "supporting agency," explaining that Schwarzkopf, "as the supported commander," "was given the authority to designate targets or objectives, set the timing and duration of supporting actions, and establish other instructions necessary for coordination and efficiency of operations."[33] Although many CIA officers and leaders agreed they were supporting military operations during Desert Storm, their definition of the term *support* probably more closely resembled that of *Webster's Dictionary* and not the command-relationship "support" that Schwarzkopf had in mind.

The CIA also conducted internal reviews to determine how to improve its support to military operations. Deputy DCI Richard Kerr, a career CIA analyst, selected Dan Childs and Charlie Allen to conduct the CIA's own review of its support to military operations during Desert Storm. Dan Childs had served in the Intelligence Community since 1957, moving back and forth between the SSCI and the CIA.[34] Charlie Allen, a legend within the Intelligence Community and the analyst who had predicted the Iraq invasion of Kuwait, had joined the CIA in 1958 and eventually served as the first chief of intelligence for the CIA's CTC, the first assistant secretary for intelligence and then undersecretary for intelligence in the Department of Homeland Security. Child and Allen's report highlighted differing views between the CIA and the DIA regarding intelligence support. The CIA perspective was that the entire national security apparatus should come together for "a national war effort," whereas the DIA viewpoint was that the Intelligence Community should "integrate into DoD systems when war loomed."[35] This distinction was important: the CIA viewed wartime operations as a partnership, but the DoD viewed the DoD/CIA relationship as one of subordination—differing viewpoints that became even more relevant during the GWOT, when the United States embraced perpetual and preemptive war.

The DoD's *Final Report to Congress on the Conduct of the Persian Gulf War,* issued in April 1992, captured the significant effort and resources the Intelligence Community had in fact contributed to the war effort. The report argued that intelligence support to General Schwarzkopf was "one of the larger efforts in the history of the U.S. Intelligence Community," which "reflected the investment of billions of dollars in technology and training and the contribution of thousands of intelligence professionals, both military and civilian, from a variety of agencies and staff."[36] Yet despite how the Intelligence Community had provided the combatant commander a previously unsurpassed level of intelligence support, the increasing appetite for such support could not be satiated. The jointness introduced by Goldwater-Nichols and the burgeoning battlefield technology increased the intelligence "calories" necessary for operational success.

SSCI discussions in the spring and summer of 1991 were particularly critical of the CIA's level of support, arguing that Desert Shield and Desert Storm "highlighted enduring problems in ensuring CIA understanding of and responsiveness to military requests." To alleviate these issues, the SSCI told the CIA to establish a new position, assistant deputy director of operations (DDO), who would "ensure that military requirements are fairly represented within CIA and to advocate an earlier and more effective interaction by CIA with DoD operational planners." The SSCI specifically noted that the assistant DDO would be responsible for "receipt of tasking to satisfy military requirements," a significant subordination of CIA capabilities to operational commanders.[37] Coordination of intelligence capabilities in support of military commanders through a "unity of effort" was one thing, but the mention of "taskings" created the perception that military commanders have command authority over national intelligence capabilities.[38]

Removing any doubt regarding the power the SSCI wanted to give military commanders during operations, the SSCI report authorizing fiscal appropriations for 1992 stated, "Shortcomings in intelligence support relate not only to gaps in collection, but also to the ability of military commanders to task available assets to collect the right information at the right time as well as the capability subsequently to transmit collected information—from both national and tactical sources—in sufficient quality and with adequate speed." To ensure that the CIA was responsive to these taskings, the SSCI "mandated" that the CIA DI and DO not only integrate into combatant commanders' JICs but also report to the JCS and CINC J2s.[39]

The SSCI and SASC's reviews of Desert Storm operations in the spring and summer of 1991 were not the end of congressional criticism of intelligence support. Over the next decade, policy makers pointed to intelligence shortfalls during Desert Storm as evidence of the need to prioritize intelligence support to the military. In August 1993, the HASC's Subcommittee on Oversight and Investigations published *Intelligence Successes and Failures in Operations Desert Storm/Shield*. This report credited the Intelligence Community for its creativity and proactivity in trying to provide General Schwarzkopf the information he needed to make decisions. It also highlighted the performance and intelligence value of burgeoning technologies such as the Joint Surveillance and Target Attack Radar Systems, Advanced Synthetic Aperture Radar System, and unmanned aerial vehicles.[40] According to a memo by the DoD, although "information and intelligence provided the decisive edge," and new technologies allowed the military to "pierce the fog of war," the technologies also "exponentially increased demand for information."[41] It seemed that the better intelligence performed and the increased coverage technologies provided, the more intelligence was required. Instead of satisfying commanders, intelligence improvements and technology developments were only increasing expectations.

The combatant commanders, empowered by Goldwater-Nichols, were encouraged by legislators who criticized the Intelligence Community for failing to support military operations. *Intelligence Successes and Failures in Operations Desert Storm/Shield* criticized the absence of a unified intelligence structure in support of the combatant commander. The report was particularly harsh of the CIA, arguing that it took a "hands off attitude toward the concept of joining in the organized support given the combat commander" and thus should not remain outside the JIC during future operations.[42] This critique clearly articulated the subcommittee's view that all national intelligence capabilities, including the independent CIA, should be subordinated to the military commander during wartime. This perspective arguably runs counter to the very reason an independent central intelligence organization was created. Even more burdensome, the HASC seemed to believe the CIA should be developing HUMINT networks in peacetime that can be used by military commanders during war.[43] No one at the time seemed to realize that relying on the CIA to develop networks throughout the world in anticipation of future military operations would be a significant burden on the agency and necessarily detract from its strategic intelligence mission.

Appreciating the potential value of integrated intelligence to combatant commanders, the HASC report identified the importance of a unity of effort in support of the combatant commander during wartime. Because understanding the capabilities, needs, and requirements of the partner organization could not occur overnight, it was argued, construction of the DoD/Intelligence Community relationship needed to begin in peacetime. It is not surprising that some commanders viewed the Intelligence Community as an extension of their staff as the military began to conduct more humanitarian and peacekeeping operations and the distinction between war and peace became blurred.

The HASC chairman who approved *Intelligence Successes and Failures in Operations Desert Storm/Shield* was California congressman Ronald Dellums (D), an experienced legislator with stints on both the HASC and the HPSCI. Despite his service on these two committees, Dellums was not viewed as a protector of either defense or intelligence. In fact, his history with the CIA was rather contentious. In the mid-1970s, in the aftermath of Watergate and following DCI William Colby's release of the "Family Jewels" (a collection of internal CIA documents that listed past CIA misdeeds and actions that might not be looked upon favorably by Congress and that had been put together at the request of DCI James Schlesinger, who wanted to get a better handle on what had occurred in the past, and then turned over to Congress by DCI William Colby), Dellums served on the House Select Committee on Intelligence (Pike Committee), which "investigated whether intelligence activities threatened the rights of American citizens."[44] During the Pike hearings, Dellums skewered DCI Colby about the CIA's operations and its abuse of citizens' rights. During one particularly heated exchange when Colby refused to discuss classified information in open session, an angry Dellums asked Colby, "What makes you believe that you can play God?"[45] Although Congressman Dellums's argument regarding the role of Congress in "checks in balances" was fair, his forcefulness displayed a distrust, if not a seething dislike, of a clandestine intelligence organization within a democracy.

The investigation of intelligence shortfalls in support of Desert Storm military operations continued into 1997–1998 with the Gulf War illness investigations. Concern over Saddam Hussein's use of chemical and biological weapons had been around since the invasion, but when Desert Storm veterans started displaying unexplained symptoms of an illness, these concerns increased. In 1997, the Senate Committee on Veteran's Affairs established the Special Investigation Unit to identify failures preceding, during, and following the war that contributed to or exaggerated the Gulf War illness problem. In support of the Gulf War illness reviews, the CIA established the DCI Persian Gulf War Illnesses Task Force in March 1997 to ensure the investigations had access to the appropriate intelligence and to assist investigators in analyzing the information.[46] Although the purpose of the Gulf War illness investigations was to understand the government's response when Gulf War veterans started displaying symptoms, the investigators also considered intelligence on WMD locations in relation to force protection and support to military operations during the war.

The Special Investigation Unit argued that the CIA did not provide adequate support to military operations. Its report stated that intelligence operations were not integrated and that the CIA's unwillingness to be part of the intelligence team was one of the main issues. The Investigation Unit believed that, despite establishing the joint intelligence liaison element, the CIA remained outside the team. The report recommended establishing "a single focal point in unified commands to gather, analyze, and report all intelligence information in support of any military operations in order to avoid the information sharing and communication failures that occurred during the Gulf War" and stated that the DCI "must fully coordinate and cooperate in ensuring this unified effort."[47] Echoing the HASC report from five years earlier, the Gulf War illness Special Investigation Unit recommended increasing CIA support to military commanders during wartime. This report's questioning of the CIA in relation to the exposure of service members to WMD was reminiscent of the critiques of the CIA support during the Beirut bombing in 1983;[48] both reports considered the CIA responsible for collecting tactical intelligence related to force protection.

The DoD Initiates Reform Efforts

Two months prior to Schwarzkopf's SASC testimony, the DoD published *Plan for Restructuring Defense Intelligence.*[49] Although the plan was focused on DoD reform, the changes it implemented also affected the CIA. With the defense budget being slashed and intelligence support to the military an increasing priority, there was concern about the Intelligence Community's relationship with the military. Bud Shuster (R–PA), nine-term congressman and HPSCI cochair, reflected this concern when he announced during a joint session of the HPSCI and SSCI that the "committees are going to watch very carefully . . . Secretary Cheney's conduct of his reorganization particularly because of the cost-free support the Intelligence Community receives from the military."[50] Shuster's statement reflected the general tone of the HPSCI hearings, which were focused largely on increasing intelligence support to the military. This focus and the cuts in defense spending should instead have made the HPSCI cochair concerned with the "cost-free support" the CIA would provide the military, not vice versa.

The development of the DoD's plan had started in December 1989, when Secretary Cheney requested a review of defense intelligence to ensure it was adapting to the changing international environment with the collapse of the Soviet Union and domestic fiscal conditions while still providing the capabilities that combatant commanders required. The history of this effort goes back to the Reagan-era Packard Commission, which had focused on restructuring defense management and procurement processes and was supposed to be in line with the principles and objectives identified in the Defense Management Review of July 1989. Accepting the significant budget cuts on the horizon, the plan sought ways to increase "jointness" while cutting expenditures and reducing duplication.

In cooperation with the executive branch, Congress was also trying to "bring defense intelligence in line with the organizational structure established by Goldwater-Nichols."[51] In the National Defense Authorization Act (NDAA) of 1991, Congress mandated that the secretary of defense and the DCI conduct a review of all intelligence capabilities, revise priorities, reorganize efforts, and reduce personnel. The NDAA's objective was to eliminate redundancy, streamline intelligence efforts, and cut personnel costs. Most notably, the NDAA instructed the secretary of defense and the DCI to "strengthen joint intelligence functions, operations, and organizations" and to "improve the responsiveness and utility of national intelligence systems and organizations to the needs of the combatant commanders."[52] A tall order for the DCI and secretary of defense: they were being asked to consolidate

intelligence resources and increase support directed toward combatant commanders even while undergoing a 25 percent reduction in personnel between
fiscal year 1992 and fiscal year 1996.

Informed by the Defense Management Review and the NDAA, the
twenty-eight-page restructuring plan gave precise implementation guidance to the NSA, the DIA, and the military services on how to reduce and
consolidate intelligence capabilities to achieve the goals of increased service
interoperability, decreased expenditures, and empowerment of the combatant commander. The restructuring plan required each service to consolidate
its intelligence capabilities into one headquarters. This reduction in "management overhead" was intended to streamline operations and reduce costs.
The plan also called for the combatant commands' regional components to
"eliminate" their intelligence production capabilities and consolidate them at
the combatant-commander-level JICs. Although the Desert Storm experience
highlighted the value of the JICs, the push toward them was as much about
reduced costs as it was about focusing intelligence support toward the combatant commander and away from the services. Under the restructuring plan,
service components retained only minimal intelligence capability required
for current operations and planning.[53]

The US Pacific Command was one of the first organizations to consolidate its analysis capabilities. In the early 1990s, Captain Lowell "Jake" Jacoby
took over as the US Pacific Fleet intelligence chief. Jacoby soon realized the
"peace dividend" meant the Pacific Fleet could not afford to retain the command's Fleet Intelligence Center, and so he reached out to his boss, Admiral
Chuck Larson, the fleet commander, to propose a solution. Jacoby argued that
money could be saved by consolidating the three analysis centers at Pacific
Command, Pacific Fleet, and Pacific Air Force into one centralized analysis
center. Admiral Larson supported Jacoby's proposal and, unbeknownst to
Jacoby at the time, would become the Pacific Command commander in 1991.

One of Jacoby's "politically astute" subordinates recommended contact-
ing Marty Hurwitz, the General Defense Intelligence Program manager at
the DIA, about his proposal. Jacoby told Hurwitz that if Hurwitz "endorsed
the concept" and provided a few million in "startup money," Jacoby could
"consolidate" the analysis centers and save DoD "30 percent annually." Hurwitz liked the idea, and after Jacoby won support from the initially reluctant
Pacific Command J2 and the Air Force Pacific Command G2, the decision
to consolidate the analysis centers moved forward. The plan to reorganize
defense intelligence highlighted Pacific Command's efforts to establish a JIC
and tasked other combatant commands to follow suit. While in Hawaii, Captain Jacoby was promoted to rear admiral and served as both the JIC com-

mander and the Pacific Command J2 before departing to become the JCS J2. Jacoby rose up the navy ranks to vice admiral, serving as the director of naval intelligence and then as the DIA director during the early phases of the wars in Afghanistan and Iraq.[54]

In June 1991, Lieutenant General Harry Soyster, the soon-to-be retiring director of the DIA, submitted a plan to the ASD for command, control, communications, and intelligence, Duane Andrews, that proposed "centralizing" defense HUMINT to streamline operations and taskings and to gain efficiencies. Andrews accepted the recommendation in August 1991 and tasked Soyster with producing an implementation plan for HUMINT consolidation.[55] Although portions of Andrews's memo to Soyster are redacted, his guidance to Soyster included giving the DoD HUMINT manager (i.e., the DIA) "HUMINT operational tasking authority over all elements of the DoD HUMINT system" and considering an organization where the HUMINT manager controlled all DoD "HUMINT resources and operations."[56] DoD HUMINT consolidation began during the last months of the Bush administration and carried over into the Clinton administration.

During Desert Storm, the Intelligence Community worked assiduously to develop a joint/interagency infrastructure responsive to the combatant commander's requirements. Leaders such as Rear Admiral McConnell reached out to units preparing to fight the war to identify their needs. Unfortunately, no amount of hard work in that short period could completely make up for the shortfalls that existed in the system when the conflict began. As both Congress's and the DoD's post mortem reviews acknowledged, the Intelligence Community had been built to focus on a Soviet threat, not on a regional threat from Iraq. Thus, based on the nation's priorities, the Intelligence Community had focused its resources on the Soviet Union and had taken risks in smaller regions. Considering this focus and the lack of an interagency intelligence structure to support the military, it is not surprising that intelligence failed to meet the combatant commander's expectations during the Gulf War.

The US military was on the cusp of a "Revolution in Military Affairs" that introduced technology that gave the commander the ability to access intelligence not previously possible. At the same time, new weapon systems were introduced that required more intelligence to employ. As the CRS report *Desert Shield and Desert Storm* argued in 1991, the technological intelligence collection systems had "severe limitations,"[57] and as Desert Storm highlighted, the United States needed HUMINT in place to make up for these shortfalls in supporting the new weapon technologies. These technological capabilities and intelligence requirements enabled operationalization of intelligence but required greater synchronization and collaboration between national intelligence and military operations. The intelligence requirements, coupled with the feasibility of intelligence provision, raised the combatant commanders' expectations regarding intelligence. With Goldwater-Nichols empowering the combatant commander, the commanders were now in a position to demand greater intelligence support.

As Michael Warner points out in *The Rise and Fall of Intelligence,* the increasing dedication of national intelligence resources to military operations during Desert Storm became "the minimum expected of [the Intelligence Community] in future conflicts—and the military leaders did not shrink from demanding the resources of the CIA and other agencies to sustain it." As Warner goes on to explain, the prioritization of support to the military, coupled with the cuts in defense intelligence capabilities driven by budget reductions, resulted in a significant focus of national intelligence resources on military operations.[58]

The burgeoning DoD intelligence consolidation and reform efforts were influenced by the lessons learned during Desert Storm as well as by ongoing domestic and international political changes. The reduction and streamlining efforts were not merely internal DoD maneuvers but also an interagency effort that affected the Intelligence Community's structure, increased its focus on military operations, and altered the purpose of national intelligence. The perceived intelligence failures and shortfalls during Desert Storm as well as the changing strategic and domestic landscape resulted in numerous intelligence reviews in the 1990s.

4

END OF THE COLD WAR AND THE CONTINUATION OF REFORM

The year following Desert Storm was a busy year for intelligence reviews. From February 1991 to April 1992, both the executive and legislative branches of the federal government conducted reviews of the Intelligence Community and either took executive action or proposed legislation. The year began with Secretary of Defense Richard Cheney's review of the DoD in February and March 1991 and ended in April 1992 with Robert Gates testifying before the first joint SSCI/HPSCI conference on the Gates Task Force findings and proposed reform measures. During this period, the SSCI initiated a review of the Intelligence Community (March 1991–April 1992); Gates's nomination as DCI and confirmation hearings occurred (September–November 1991); President Bush issued NSR-29 focused on intelligence reform (November 1991); the Gates Task Force review of the Intelligence Community occurred (November 1991–April 1992); Senate and House bills on intelligence reform were introduced (February 1992); and NSD-67 was issued (March 1992).

National Security Review 29: Call for Intelligence Reform from the Top

In November 1991, sensing the final collapse of the Soviet Union and realizing the significance of that collapse on the "changing international landscape," President George H. W. Bush ordered the executive-branch agencies to identify what those changes meant for the US national security apparatus.[1] Domestic fiscal concerns regarding an ongoing recession threatening America's economic health partially drove President Bush's review. After the fall of the Berlin Wall, the president called for national security spending cuts amounting to approximately 25 percent. He and other national leaders believed the global standing of the United States was contingent not only on a strong defense but also on its economic health. The reunification of Germany and the weakening of the Soviet Union provided the United States an opportunity to embrace the "peace dividend" and put America's fiscal house in order.[2]

If there was ever a modern president who entered office understanding the Intelligence Community, it was George H. W. Bush.[3] President Bush had served as Gerald Ford's director of central intelligence during a contentious period following Watergate and the Church and Pike Committees. Although serving as DCI for only a short period, Bush carried the CIA through a tumultuous time and became beloved by most of the CIA's workforce.[4] In 1999, CIA Headquarters in Langley, Virginia, was renamed the George Bush Center for Intelligence in Bush's honor.[5] Understanding Bush's tenure as DCI and his relationship with the secretary of defense is important and informative to understanding subsequent developments in the DoD/CIA relationship.

In 1976, DCI Bush was not particularly close with Ford's secretary of defense, Donald Rumsfeld, who assumed his Pentagon position two months prior to Bush's appointment as DCI. Rumsfeld and DCI Bush had previously served together in Congress and in the Nixon administration. Both had presidential political aspirations and the type of pedigree necessary to propel them into that position. They had never been close, and the feud between them gained momentum during the Ford administration when some officials told Bush that Rumsfeld had recommended him for the DCI position just to ruin his potential for the vice presidential nomination in 1976. Although the exact origin of the tension is unknown, Bush confirmed his low opinion of Rumsfeld in his biography, telling his biographer, Jon Meacham, "I don't like what he did [referring to Rumsfeld's service in the George W. Bush administration], and I think it hurt the President, having his [Rumsfeld's] iron-ass view of everything. I've never been that close to him anyway. There's a lack of humility, a lack of seeing what the other guy thinks. He's more kick ass and take names, take number. I think he paid a price for that."[6] Many who worked for Secretary of Defense Rumsfeld in 2001 would agree with these sentiments.

DCI Bush looked to salvage Americans' trust in their intelligence organizations and bring the different elements of the Intelligence Community closer together in the aftermath of the Church and Pike Committee hearings. One of the initiatives during Bush's tenure as DCI was the creation of the Committee on Foreign Intelligence to bring a "policy-level focus to intelligence problems" and to work through "DoD and DCI" equities.[7] Although Bush believed the DCI should focus on strategic intelligence and leave tactical intelligence to the DoD, he and Rumsfeld bumped heads over the DCI's objectives. As Ford's secretary of defense, Rumsfeld was concerned that Bush was trying to gain control over DoD intelligence resources. Therefore, to centralize his authority and improve intelligence support to military operations, he undertook his own efforts to restructure defense intelligence.[8] This effort included the creation of the position of director of defense intelligence, with authority "over assigned DoD intelligence programs and activities," and the establishment of a Defense Intelligence Board to "improve the interaction between intelligence users and producers, to improve the coordination between various elements of the Department of Defense, and to improve intelligence-related planning and decision-making."[9]

Similar to his perspective during the George W. Bush administration nearly three decades later, Rumsfeld was determined to build a strong defense intelligence apparatus focused internally on support to operations. This focus caused friction at times with the broader Intelligence Community and its leader, DCI Bush. Rumsfeld argued that the majority of the intelligence budget was focused on supporting military operations, and he was unwilling to cede control to the DCI. The prescient Richard Lehman, a career CIA analyst and adviser to DCI Bush, encouraged him to stand against Rumsfeld's campaign to gain greater control over systems that were increasingly being used for both tactical and strategic collection.[10] The collapsing of strategic intelligence and tactical intelligence intensified over the next forty years, with many losing sight of any differences between them.

Bush's and Rumsfeld's reorganization efforts occurred following a congressional push to reform how the United States conducted foreign policy. In 1972, Congress established the Commission on the Organization of the Government for the Conduct of Foreign Policy, informally referred to as the Murphy Commission. The Murphy Commission grew from concern by members of Congress that the United States conducted foreign policy in a disjointed manner driven more by organizational interests than by common purpose. The report the commission produced highlighted the importance of subordinating defense and intelligence to policy, arguing that defense and intelligence, as foreign-policy tools, should be focused on achieving policy objectives and not on promoting institutional interests.[11] Although Rumsfeld and Bush might have disagreed about control and influence over intelligence, DCI Bush's reform objective on improving intelligence support to policy was in line with the congressional push to streamline the US national security processes. Despite the Murphy Commission's warnings, however, defense gained a greater influence over foreign policy in the coming decades as national intelligence increased its support to military operations.

In November 1991, when President Bush issued *National Security Review 29: Intelligence Capabilities 1992–2005,* he probably reflected on his earlier reform efforts in 1976. Although markedly different periods for the United States, with the fall of 1991 being a time of jubilation following victory in the Gulf War and the Cold War victory and 1976 being a time of post-Vietnam and post-Watergate doldrums, both marked the beginning of uncertainty for the Intelligence Community. In 1976, the Intelligence Community was trying to recover and reclaim America's confidence in the aftermath of the Church and Pike Committee hearings. In 1991, the Intelligence Community was celebrating its contribution to the victory over Iraq and the Soviet Union while also coping with the Gulf War intelligence critiques and trying to understand what came after Cold War victory. NSR-29 was Bush's second opportunity to help the Intelligence Community cope with uncertainty and adapt to a changing environment.

Echoing aspects of the Murphy Commission, NSR-29 stated that policy requirements should drive intelligence resources and required a "comprehensive identification by policy departments and agencies of their anticipated intelligence information and support need to the year 2005," before the Intelligence Community developed its resource wish list. NSR-29 stated that policy makers had in the past shirked their responsibility "in setting intelligence priorities and requirements," and NSR-29 was being published to fix this flaw in a post–Cold War world. NSR-29 told policy makers to focus beyond typical foreign-policy issues and consider how "global problems" such as "health," "natural resource scarcity," and the "environment" should influence intelligence capabilities.[12] Among the issues President Bush wanted policy makers to focus on was intelligence support to the military.

In line with his perspective as DCI, President Bush viewed intelligence as a community effort and understood that resource-allocation issues had to be based on policy requirements, not on organizational interests. This perspective was shared by others in his administration, and their actions equally focused on building a unified intelligence organization, not one dominated by any policy department or agency. One of these individuals was the new DCI, Robert Gates, who authored NSR-29, was a driving force behind its publication, and was largely responsible for implementing its findings.

Gates Task Force and Intelligence Reform

On November 12, 1991, President Bush swore in Robert Gates as the fifteenth DCI. As Bush, the eleventh DCI, reminisced about his year at the helm of the CIA and the Intelligence Community, he described the enormous challenges facing Gates. Signaling the guidance he would give three days later with the issuance of NSR-29, Bush spoke of the need for intelligence reform to adapt to the post–Cold War world. Gates was a close adviser of President Bush, serving as his deputy national security adviser under Brent Scowcroft since 1989. In this position, he had been the driving force behind Bush's intelligence reform, essentially developing the idea he later implemented. Gates's experience as an intelligence professional, coupled with his knowledge of policy and political maneuvering, made him an ideal candidate to implement the NSR-29 objectives.[13]

A Kansan with a PhD in Russian history and a tremendous intellect, Gates had served in the Intelligence Community for twenty-three years when he was selected as DCI. He had been a key adviser to five administrations and, beginning with Richard Nixon, had worked on the National Security Council (NSC) for four of them.[14] Influential officials had recognized Gates's intellect and talent throughout his career, resulting in his meteoric rise within the national security establishment. One of these individuals was Admiral Bobby Ray Inman, who as deputy DCI in 1981 had recommended the thirty-eight-year-old Gates to Bill Casey as someone who should be groomed as a future DCI.[15] Despite Gates's young age, DCI Casey had promoted him to the position of deputy director of intelligence after John McMahon moved into the executive director position.[16] Gates eventually replaced McMahon, who had previously replaced Inman, as the deputy DCI. Following Casey's death, Reagan nominated Bob Gates as his DCI, but controversy surrounding the Iran-Contra scandal derailed Gates's initial nomination.[17] When Gates withdrew his name from consideration, Reagan nominated then FBI director William Webster. The Iran-Contra scandal did not slow Gates's rise for long, however. Following Webster's tenure as DCI, Bush renominated Gates for that position.

The SSCI hearing on Bob Gates's nomination occurred over multiple days in late September and early October 1991. Nearly twenty-five years after these nomination hearings and with his image as a sage senior statesman established, it is easy to forget how contentious the confirmation hearings were. During the hearings, the SSCI heard testimonials regarding Gates's intellect and leadership from former colleagues such as Bobby Ray Inman and John McMahon. Gates also heard his reputation excoriated over issues ranging from allegations that he was involved in "slanting" analysis to allegations that he played a role in the October Surprise. As expected, the crux of the testimony and questioning centered around the Iran-Contra scandal, in particular regarding what Gates knew and when he knew it. Although the Iran-Contra discussion was significant and a mixture of pro and con testimonials were heard, Gates's second nomination as DCI passed the SSCI by an 11–4 vote and the full Senate by a 61–31 vote.[18]

During his testimony, Gates described his vision for the Intelligence Community and identified issues he would tackle during his tenure. Among these issues were improving the responsiveness of intelligence collection to policy makers' requirements and increasing the investment in both HUMINT and technology. Regarding intelligence support to the military, Gates highlighted two issues. First, he argued, "the relationship between our national and tactical intelligence programs must be dramatically improved." This issue had to do with strengthening individual organizational relationships to solidify the Intelligence Community. Because tactical intelligence programs resided in the military, strengthening the relationship between tactical and national intelligence was a euphemism for strengthening the relationship between the military and nonmilitary intelligence. Gates did not stop with a broad generalization of tactical and national programs but specifically argued that the "CIA's relationship to and support for the U.S. military must be improved."[19] This nod toward improving intelligence support to military operations was in line with comments made by the SSCI chairman, Senator David Boren. Although both Gates and Boren argued for increased intelligence support to military operations, the consistency of their words through the years show that neither wanted a subordination of national intelligence to DoD but rather an equal partnership, with organizational responsibilities clearly defined.[20]

On November 9, 1991, three days before his swearing-in ceremony at CIA Headquarters, Bob Gates reached out to Rich Haver to request a meeting with Secretary of Defense Cheney for the afternoon of the ceremony. Uncertain about the agenda for the meeting, Cheney asked Haver for a point paper to prepare him for the discussion. Knowing Bobby Ray Inman was involved in Gates's confirmation, Haver reached out to the retired admiral. Admiral Inman, who had helped further both Haver's and Gates's careers, provided a "terse rundown of what Gates's big ideas were with the Intelligence Community." Haver used Inman's input "as the framework" and rounded out the point paper with insight he derived from Gates's testimony and from previous conversations between them. On the morning of November 12, Haver dropped by Cheney's office to give him the paper, and, after a quick look, Cheney said, "Thanks, about what I figured." Haver departed from Cheney's office and went about his day. That afternoon, following the Cheney/Gates meeting, the secretary of defense summoned Haver back to his office to pick up the point paper. When Haver arrived, Cheney handed him the point paper, which was now covered in scribbled notes. Cheney was not a note taker, at least in public, and receiving a paper back from him was not normal. Cheney told Haver the paper was "very helpful" in informing his discussion with DCI Gates and that Haver's job description had just changed.[21]

When Haver had first started working as Cheney's intelligence adviser, the secretary of defense had told him to "be a thorn in Judge Webster's ass for DoD." Cheney said that DCI Webster and the rest of the CIA "were fine guys," but to ensure that DoD interests were protected, the DoD was going to have to "push him [Webster]." Now that Bob Gates, an experienced intelligence official and confidant of President Bush, was DCI, Cheney's guidance flipped. Cheney rescinded Haver's earlier marching orders, telling him, "Now your job is to make sure Bob Gates succeeds because DoD does everything it can to make him succeed." Cheney understood the military services would not be happy with some of the reforms and wanted Haver to keep him apprised of who within DoD was not supporting the new DCI. According to Haver, Cheney understood the Intelligence Community's flaws and wanted to improve intelligence support.[22]

Although Cheney's attitude toward the CIA mellowed after Gates became DCI, his desire to protect the DoD's interests probably drove this change. It is hard to believe that Cheney suddenly embraced a more benevolent approach to bureaucratic interaction. It is more likely he saw an opportunity to use resources outside the DoD to alleviate some of the budgetary strain. The days of plentiful defense spending were coming to an end, and the military services could no longer afford an autarkic approach. The DoD's own intelligence reform efforts, initiated six months earlier, were driven by an economic environment that assailed duplication. As the DoD's leader, Cheney was concerned with providing intelligence support to the war fighters and with rectifying the issues that had plagued past operations. Although autarky makes operations easier, there was no way to remain autonomous during these anemic times.

DCI Gates also appreciated the coming fiscal constraints and understood he had to fix the flaws of the Intelligence Community while navigating an uncertain and tumultuous time; fighting change and budget reductions would be futile. As the first post–Cold War DCI, Gates had to bring the different factions of the Intelligence Community together, identify responsibilities, and reduce duplication. This approach was the only way the community could survive reductions and at the same time continue to support its diverse customers. Gates also heard rumblings about the need to improve CIA support to military operations since Operations Urgent Fury and was motivated to resolve these issues when he took over as the DCI.

One of the most important and "hardest" actions Gates took to improve the DoD/CIA partnership was to ask his close friend Dick Kerr to resign as deputy DCI and to replace Kerr with Vice Admiral William Studeman. Gates and Kerr had a close relationship, and there was mutual respect and admiration between the two career CIA officers, but Gates thought it was important to give the military a significant voice in the CIA leadership in order to improve intelligence support to military operations.[23]

The same month Gates became DCI, he established fourteen task forces to determine how the Intelligence Community needed to transform to ensure relevance in a post–Cold War world. These reviews were in support of NSR-29 and were consistent with Cheney's post–Desert Storm intelligence review.[24] The focus of the fourteen task forces was split equally between internal CIA and broader Intelligence Community issues. The seven CIA task forces focused on intelligence support to policy makers, the issue of politicization of intelligence, future methods of communicating with policy makers, the improvement of HUMINT collection, the handling of information pertaining to law violations, internal CIA communications, and CIA openness. Gates's intent with the internal CIA task forces was to "revolutionize both the culture and the intelligence processes at the CIA."[25] He had identified many of these issues during his confirmation testimony, and improving CIA HUMINT collection had been an issue of concern for Congress since previous military operations. Of particular concern was CIA clandestine HUMINT support to the military, which, following Desert Storm and other operations, was identified as a significant shortfall.

During his nomination hearings testimony, Gates had described the CIA role as evolving from one that was historically separate from the military to one that was more intertwined because of the rise of low-intensity conflicts and the growing difficulty in distinguishing between war and peace. He told Congress,

> CIA has basically been considered a fundamentally peacetime organization. . . . But war . . . was defined as something like global thermonuclear war. . . . What the Gulf War showed, unlike Vietnam . . . was that in this intense, very large conventional war, we had something in between . . . peace and full-scale war. We really didn't have, I think, very good procedures particularly for CIA support for military opera-

tions of that scale. I think that is one of the areas we need to look at. . . .
We discovered some real problems there during the course of the war
. . . in terms of the transmission of our information to local commanders, to the commanders on the ground.[26]

Gates understood that the end of the Cold War had changed the DoD/CIA
partnership and that he, as DCI, had to ensure that this changed partnership
evolved in the right direction. Part of this evolution involved increased CIA
support to military operations while still maintaining the CIA's support of
the policy makers.

The final seven task forces focused on changes to the Intelligence Community. In April 1992, Gates told the SSCI and the HPSCI that his intent
was to improve coordination within the Intelligence Community while
maintaining its decentralization to ensure that consumers' "diverse needs"
were met, an important acknowledgment by Gates.[27] Although the various
intelligence organizations could assist each other through collaboration, they
all existed for different purposes and had to retain that individual identity
and mission focus. To strengthen how the community functioned, Gates
made various changes to its management and collective analysis processes.
According to Rich Haver, who served on three of the task forces, Gates knew
ahead of time what he wanted the task forces to produce and selected individuals who were aware of his desires and would recommend those changes.
He also gave them only three weeks to produce the task force reports. With
only a year left in Bush's first term, time was of the essence for any meaning-
ful intelligence reform to occur.[28]

On April 1, 1992, Bob Gates sat before a joint session of the two congressional intelligence oversight committees to brief them on the findings of
the task forces and his initiatives for the Intelligence Community. According
to Gates, Intelligence Community reform efforts should focus on four areas:
community management, community analysis, integration of the collection
disciplines, and the strengthening of support to the military.[29]

The post–Cold War environment, defined by certain budget reductions
and uncertain requirements, mandated a community approach to intelligence. Gates and other leaders understood that the "diverse" requirements
of the various consumers necessitated a decentralized intelligence approach.
The only problem was that fiscal constraints made duplication unsustainable,
and the Intelligence Community had to streamline to ensure all customers' needs were met. The streamlined-community approach did not mean
subordination or blurring mission lines; it meant defining the requirements,
identifying responsibilities, and then reducing duplication. Gates realized

the dynamic environment meant that initial allocation decisions were probably wrong and that community leadership needed the flexibility to realign resources. To achieve this flexibility, he replaced the Intelligence Community staff with the DCI community staff and made Rich Haver the first director of community affairs. Haver and his staff focused on streamlining the Intelligence Community to reduce costs while maintaining its capabilities to support a varied customer base.[30]

Part of streamlining Intelligence Community efforts involved strengthening "an independent community analytical and estimative capability" while reducing overall intelligence costs. To achieve these goals, Gates increased the size of the National Intelligence Council and moved it and the national intelligence officers out of the CIA to highlight their independence from any one intelligence organization. He then empowered the National Intelligence Council chair and the national intelligence officers within the community to make it clear they were the leads for community estimates. Regarding alternative analysis, he increased emphasis on "red teams" and "Team A vs. Team B" approaches, while also looking to nongovernmental organizations to support analytical efforts.[31] The Intelligence Community could benefit from the alternative views and expertise provided by university and think-tank scholars without having to maintain this resource in house. Although budget reductions might have influenced Gates, he truly valued the potential capability within nongovernment organizations to tackle difficult problems. When Gates became secretary of defense in 2006, he once again turned to universities and other nongovernmental organizations to "engage their expertise."[32]

The third part of Gates's reform effort was improving the "management, direction, and coordination" of collection efforts.[33] The idea was to designate a lead for each collection discipline that would establish standards and oversee the development of each individual discipline, while ensuring that the discipline was providing the collection required to feed comprehensive analysis. Gates still appreciated the differing intelligence requirements of various agencies but also understood the value in having a lead for each discipline that could maintain standards and develop the discipline. For example, Gates established the National Human Intelligence Tasking Center and made it a responsibility of the CIA's DDO. As the lead for HUMINT, the center was responsible for establishing and enforcing HUMINT standards, "managing and tasking" requirements, and charting the future of the discipline.[34] As Christopher Andrew points out in his book *For the President's Eyes Only,* the creation of the National Human Intelligence Tasking Center was directly related to the failure of the United States to understand Saddam Hussein's "political and military aims." This increased HUMINT was required to penetrate the inner circles of other "third world leaders anxious to acquire chemical, biological, or nuclear weapons" in a post–Cold War world where proliferation was a growing concern.[35]

Gates also worked to remedy organizational issues linked to the BDA controversies that had surfaced during the Gulf War. Since Desert Storm, there had been a push to consolidate imagery within a single organization, as the NSA had done for signals intelligence. Although various reviews recommended this unification and DCI Gates was willing to place this new organization within the DoD, General Powell's concern over consolidation negatively affecting DoD's mapping capability postponed the consolidation for about four years. Although Powell agreed that imagery capability was "broken," he did not believe defense mapping was broken, and so he could not support an action that subsumed the Defense Mapping Agency into a centralized imagery organization.[36] Not able to establish a truly centralized imagery organization, Gates settled for a loose confederation known as the Central Imagery Office.[37] Although the establishment of the Central Imagery Office was the initial step toward consolidating imagery, its director lacked any real authority or ability to compel cooperation from the Defense Mapping Agency, the National Photographic Imagery Center, the CIA, or the DIA.[38] This problem was rectified following the second round of intelligence reform in the mid-1990s.

Not publicly debated but associated with the Desert Storm BDA controversy and the increased requirement for military support was consolidation of programs in the National Reconnaissance Office (NRO). During the Gulf War, Schwarzkopf had complained about the conflicting BDA, which was determined largely through satellite imagery. After the war, he had complained of not receiving timely and adequate imagery intelligence to enable his decision making and had argued that the Intelligence Community had to remedy this shortfall because the future of warfare required it.[39] On March 5, 1992, DCI Gates established a task force to determine how the NRO should evolve in the post–Cold War world.[40] He asked Robert Fuhrman, the former president of Lockheed Martin to chair the task force, whose members had a diverse background within both the Intelligence Community and the commercial sector.

The NRO had been established through a joint agreement between the CIA and the DoD in September 1961, one year before Kennedy's space-race speech, but its existence had remained classified until 1992. And even though the NRO wasn't formally established until 1961, reconnaissance programs had been developing in the CIA and the services since the Eisenhower administration initiated the U2 Spy Program in 1954. The military services had been using reconnaissance aircraft for years, but the technology and secrecy involved in the U2 Program significantly raised the bar and brought the CIA into the mission. Over time, both the DoD and the CIA had assumed leadership roles within the NRO, but their programs had remained largely separated and focused on individual organizational needs. From 1974 to 1992, the NRO consisted of three separate programs: (1) the Air Force Satellite Reconnaissance Program (Program A), (2) the CIA Satellite Reconnaissance Program (Program B), and (3) the Navy Program (Program C).[41]

The Fuhrman Task Force concluded that a centralized NRO was still required, but the separate "alphabet programs" had led to parochialism and made it "difficult to foster loyalty and maintain focus on the NRO mission." The task force recommended combining the individual programs into "intelligence discipline lines" to increase efficiency, eliminate duplication, and instill a common NRO culture.[42] Its recommendations were implemented through NSD-67, which established three functional directorates: (1) the Signals Intelligence Directorate, (2) the Imagery Intelligence Directorate, and (3) the Communications Directorate. These directorates were eventually located together at new NRO headquarters in the Washington, DC, suburbs,[43] the funding of which became a major controversy within the legislative oversight committees.[44]

Gates's fourth area for intelligence reform focused specifically on improving the DoD/CIA relationship by establishing the associate DDO for military affairs (DDO/MA) and the CIA Office of Military Affairs (OMA). Gates explained that this new position and organization were "responsible for improving CIA's support to military planning, exercises, and operations. More specifically, this office would be responsible for coordinating military and CIA planning, strengthening the role of DCI representatives at major commands and at the Pentagon, developing procedures so that CIA is regularly informed of military needs for intelligence support, developing plans for CIA support in nation, theater and deployed Joint Intelligence Centers during crises, and the availability of CIA officers for participation with the military on selected exercises."[45] Gates believed the CIA support to the military was important enough that he made the associate DDO/MA position the number three position in the DO.

DCI Gates wanted the associate DDO/MA to be "a real snake eater" and asked General Powell to send him a guy who fit that description. The first name Powell sent did not fit the "snake eater" criterion, so Gates asked for another name. When the second name did not fit the criterion either, Gates contacted Powell to request a third name. Powell asked Gates if he thought an operator or a guy that had the "credibility" and "could walk right into his [Powell's] office" was more important. Gates then accepted the second nominee, Major General Ronald Lajoie, a guy with credibility who could walk into Powell's office.[46]

Lajoie came to the CIA from the JCS, where he served in the J5 as the deputy director for international negotiations. He had spent his early career as a transportation officer and then an intelligence officer, during which time he served in Vietnam with the Twenty-Fifth Infantry Division. After Vietnam, he spent the rest of his career as a foreign-area officer in Russia, which included a three-year stint as the chief of the US Military Liaison Mission (USMLM) and two tours at the US embassy in Moscow.

The USMLM is a little-known but fascinating piece of Soviet-US relations during the Cold War. Established in 1947 to serve as a liaison between the supreme Allied commander Europe and the chief of the Group of Soviet Forces in Germany, the USMLM was a fourteen-man organization stationed in Potsdam, East Germany. Its mission was to serve as liaison between Soviet military units and US military units in Germany, but its "classified primary responsibility" was to collect intelligence on Soviet capability it observed in East Germany.[47] According to Major General Lajoie, the Soviet-US agreement allowed the USMLM's personnel free movement throughout East Germany, but it never envisioned them snooping around at Soviet "deployment sites." The personnel's ability to observe Soviet equipment that had previously been observed only via satellite provided valuable information to American forces that might have to face off against Soviet divisions.[48] A colonel at the time, Lajoie was chief of USMLM in 1985 when a Soviet sentry killed an unarmed American officer while he was "conducting reconnaissance on a Soviet training installation in an area not officially restricted." The death of Major Arthur Nicholson angered Washington, DC, and increased tension between the Soviets and the Americans. Three months after this incident, Lajoie's vehicle was followed and rammed by a Soviet vehicle during a nighttime deployment. Fearing increased tension on the heels of the Nicholson killing, the Soviets quickly apologized for the Lajoie incident.[49] After his stint in charge of the USMLM, Lajoie was promoted and sent to Paris as the defense attaché before moving back to Washington, DC, to establish the On Site Inspection Agency as part of the Intermediate Range Nuclear Forces Treaty implementation measures; in this position, he was responsible for inspecting the East German missile installations, and on one occasion armed guards chased him and his men away. Following service with this agency, Lajoie served on the JCS, where in 1992 Lieutenant General Jim

Clapper, the DIA director, reached out and asked him to serve as the first associate DDO/MA.[50]

The creation of the associate DDO/MA position and the OMA was a direct result of Schwarzkopf's post–Gulf War tour in Washington, DC, when he complained about intelligence support and not having control of all operations within his theater. The CIA did not like Schwarzkopf's quest to acquire power over entities outside DoD, but CIA officials' desire to get Schwarzkopf "off their back" trumped their concern over his power grab. Although they did not accept Schwarzkopf's argument that they should be his subordinates, they were receptive to improving the DoD/CIA partnership. Because the purpose of Lajoie's new organization was to support military operations, it was placed within the DO, the CIA's HUMINT collection arm. The DO was led by Tom Twetten, who had been the DDO for about a year when Lajoie arrived. A former army intelligence officer and Iowa State graduate, Twetten was a career Middle East case officer who had served as the Near East–South Asian Division chief. As it was with Gates, Twetten's assignment as the DDO was mired in political controversy due to his service on the NSC staff with Lieutenant Colonel Oliver North during the Iran-Contra scandal.[51]

Lajoie started pulling in military officers, and Twetten provided him CIA DO and DI personnel to build an OMA of around forty officers. After building the OMA structure, Lajoie focused on three initial goals: (1) increase the CIA's focus and military access to collection efforts that would support military planning; (2) "demystify the CIA" so military leaders could have a better understanding of the CIA's role, capabilities, and limitations; and (3) help professionalize DoD HUMINT so the military clandestine effort could better collect on its own requirements and not depend on the CIA.

Lajoie "came to appreciate" that CIA representatives at the combatant commands were an important tool in providing quality support and managing expectations. At the time, CIA employees did not consider an assignment as a CIA representative to the military "career enhancing." To move past this stigma and to ensure the best candidates were selected to represent the CIA, Lajoie started chairing a selection committee. He also understood there was a need to educate both the CIA and the military to demystify the CIA and overcome the mutual ignorance that often resulted in friction. In pursuit of this goal, the OMA started hosting future flag officers, War College classes, and combatant command J2s at CIA headquarters to increase military understanding of CIA operations. Lajoie also worked with Twetten to increase the level of CIA support to exercises, a move intended to educate both military and CIA officers.[52]

Lajoie found the CIA, in particular the DO, always willing to support the military. Fondly remembering his experience twenty years later, he said in 2015, "I always had a good feeling about the CIA, especially the DO, which has a gung ho attitude and is always willing to rush to the sound of the guns. . . . [T]hey have the money, cover, and forward-deployed resources, which allows them to react quickly and get people on the ground to support whatever military operation ensues."[53] Lajoie's and others' efforts strengthened the DoD/CIA partnership, but concern remained over whether requests for support of DoD would consume CIA resources.

The push for intelligence reform spurred by Desert Storm and the Cold War was not limited to the executive branch. At the same time, the DoD and Dick Cheney were restructuring defense intelligence, Bob Gates's task forces were looking for ways to transform the entire community, and the HPSCI and the SSCI were debating intelligence reform legislation. There was a significant issue overlap in the debate occurring within the executive and legislative branches, particularly with regard to management and intelligence support to military operations. Although the legislation never made it into law, the congressional input helped inform discussion and encourage reform. Leading the legislative debate were two congressmen from Oklahoma, Senator David Boren and Representative David McCurdy (D–OK).

Sooner Born, Sooner Bred:
Boren, McCurdy, and Congressional Reform

The initial congressional push for broader Intelligence Community reform began with the Intelligence Authorization Act (IAA) of 1991.[54] The IAA noted that both the HASC and SSCI intended to conduct studies, to hold hearings, "and, if necessary, to draft legislation to achieve these objectives."[55] Regarding intelligence support to military operations, the IAA raised concern over separation of "tactical and national intelligence communities" and described the growth of defense intelligence as an understandable response by commanders who questioned national intelligence support to operations. This interesting perspective appeared to insinuate that the CIA's mission had always included support to military operations and thus to conclude that the CIA had been neglecting this mission. Although redundancy had been okay, the lean times increased concern over intelligence expenditures. In conjunction with SASC efforts, the IAA also directed the secretary of defense and the DCI to review DoD intelligence "with the objective of consolidating redundant functions, programs, and entities, and strengthening joint intelligence organizations and operations." Interestingly, the IAA was introduced on

August 3, 1990, one day after Saddam invaded Kuwait and before Schwarz-kopf's Gulf War intelligence critiques caught the attention of the HASC and the SSCI.

The SSCI hearings on the Intelligence Community began on March 21, 1991, nearly a month after Desert Storm and while Haver's review of intel-ligence during the war was wrapping up. Although intelligence performance during Desert Storm shaped the discussion, Pennsylvania senator Arlen Spec-ter (R) had introduced legislation the previous month that informed it. Sen-ate Bill 421, the National Intelligence Reorganization Act, proposed creating an independent director of national intelligence who would oversee and have budgetary authority over the entire Intelligence Community.[56] Although most senators agreed that some form of intelligence reform was required, they all were not convinced that reform had to be congressionally mandated. This was the third time Specter had introduced DNI legislation, but this time he hoped to ride the post–Desert Storm euphoria to convince his colleagues that intelligence reform, like defense reform, required legislative action.[57]

In his opening statement for the hearings, SSCI chairman Senator David Boren explained that the Intelligence Community, which had been estab-lished nearly forty-four years earlier, had to evolve beyond its Cold War focus. He explained that the transition would occur during a period of fiscal auster-ity and required a streamlining of intelligence capabilities and a slashing of redundancy throughout the community. One of the areas Boren focused on during his statement was the relationship between intelligence and defense. He explained that the SSCI was concerned that "despite a sizeable growth in development in intelligence," intelligence was not meeting the commanders' intelligence requirements. In addition, there was a growing concern that "two separate empires," "one on the military side and one on the civilian side," were becoming unmanageable and that actions had to be taken to ensure tactical and national intelligence were integrated to reduce cost. Boren men-tioned specifically the need to increase investment in human intelligence to "rebuild some of the strength" previously cut from HUMINT.[58] The opening comments on increasing HUMINT and improving support to the military revealed SSCI's objective of strengthening the DoD/CIA partnership as an element of reform.

The SSCI had been focusing specifically on enhancing HUMINT since 1989, and the Desert Storm critiques only increased the committee members' drive for HUMINT reform. The committee acknowledged that access to enemy intentions might require additional HUMINT capabilities, but they were also focused on increasing CIA support to the operational commander. Although the CIA's supposed failure to support the military during Desert

Storm is what roused the debate in 1991, the SSCI was looking beyond war-time and wanted to improve the CIA's HUMINT support to DoD during peacetime. The concern was that the HUMINT sources necessary to sup-port the wartime commander had to be developed during peacetime and that identifying the sources with access required CIA involvement in DoD plan-ning efforts. If pursued, CIA support to DoD planning efforts could put a significant strain on CIA resources and shift it from an organization focused mainly on supporting the policy maker to one focused largely on supporting the military. This would be a fundamental change for the CIA.[59]

The witnesses that March day in 1991 reflected the influence of the Gulf War critiques and the importance the SSCI placed on intelligence support to military operations. Admiral (ret.) Bobby Ray Inman, Lieutenant General (ret.) William Odom, and Donald Latham were all former defense intelligence officials with tremendous knowledge of both operations and intelligence. The discussion focused on two issues: (1) What are the US intelligence needs in a post–Cold War world? (2) Considering the intelligence needs and the fiscal environment, how should the Intelligence Community be structured?

The first witness to testify was Bobby Ray Inman, the retired admiral and mentor to Bob Gates, Rich Haver, Mike McConnell, and Bill Stude-man. The chairman of the President's Foreign Intelligence Advisory Board, Inman argued for a bottom-up assessment of national security requirements before pursuing any structural reform of the Intelligence Community. Cau-tioning against salami-slicing capability, Inman argued that the future course of the Intelligence Community could not be identified without knowing the "needs" of the NSC and departments. According to Inman, this knowledge had to be generated without the involvement of the Intelligence Community, whose agencies had their own parochial interests.[60]

After arguing that intelligence needs should drive focus and structure, Inman turned to the question of organizational reform. The admiral had long been a supporter of competitive analysis to encourage rigor in review, chal-lenge assumptions, and reduce groupthink. Despite the value he placed in competitive analysis, he understood the budget environment required trade-offs and recommended dividing up analytical responsibility between the separate agencies to ensure broader coverage. Regarding community man-agement and leadership, Inman argued that an independent DNI would be the best solution if resources were not an issue, but this option was not fea-sible in the current fiscal environment, so he argued instead for strengthen-ing community management by establishing an executive director in the CIA to manage the community staff.[61] Nine months later his recommendation to conduct a bottom-up review without the Intelligence Community's initial involvement was implemented when President Bush issued NSR-29. A year later Gates established a new director of the community staff position at the CIA.

Like Admiral Inman, Lieutenant General Odom had served as the director of the NSA and was a respected national security professional. Odom had a long and illustrious military career, moving between military and scholarly assignments. During his career, he had served on the USMLM in Potsdam, as an army attaché in Moscow, as a professor at West Point and Columbia University, as a participant in the Civil Operations and Revolutionary Development program in Vietnam, as National Security Adviser Zbigniew Brzezinski's military adviser, and as the head of Army Intelligence. A man of deep intellect, Odom was the rare army officer who had pursued a nontraditional path to the pinnacle of his profession. A prolific author, he blended his military experience with his academic training, publishing books on topics such as US foreign policy, counterinsurgency, and the Soviet military. Influenced by his Vietnam experience and his willingness to speak out against what he perceived as poor policy decisions, Odom became a notable critic of the George W. Bush administration's decision to invade Iraq in 2003 and its subsequent surge.[62] Distancing himself from the counterinsurgency hype that swelled within the US Army ranks during the Iraq surge, he argued that this approach was nothing new and that a similar approach had failed before in Vietnam. Referring to the surge in Iraq as merely a "new tactic" with "no serious prospect for success," he continuously pushed against policy makers, and up until he passed away in May 2008, he argued that American troops should leave Iraq.[63] Although policy makers largely ignored his sage advice in 2008, one could argue the conditions in Iraq ten years later underscore his accuracy.

Demonstrating the same independence of thought he showed regarding Iraq a decade later, Odom told the SSCI in March 1991 that the Intelligence Community required a DNI. The DNI would serve in a commander-like position, prioritizing requirements and managing resources. Underneath the DNI should reside separate collection "disciplines," which, similar to Admiral Inman's recommendation, would be centrally managed. Regarding analysis, Odom argued that policy makers and commanders required tailored analysis focused on their individual requirements. Although collection could be consolidated and centrally managed, each commander and policy maker had to retain his or her own analytical capability.[64]

Donald Latham, a former ASD for command, control, communications, and intelligence under President Reagan, was the final witness. Like Inman and Odom, Latham believed the DNI provided value in centrally managing resources. Latham, however, did not agree with Odom that centrally managing each collection discipline with separate analytical capabilities was the right approach. He believed that separating by collection discipline created unnecessary stovepipes that would further divide the community and weaken support to the consumer. He also believed new technologies offered the ability to fuse collection disciplines to enable the user to view the intelligence picture in real-time.[65]

It is clear from Latham's testimony that he viewed intelligence primarily from a support-to-the-military perspective. Although his argument to centralize all collection under one agency and create a DNI with budgetary power might weaken the secretary of defense's authority on paper, his approach focused intelligence largely on the needs of the military. From his argument that DoD had to have some control over national intelligence to his description of a "single console" displaying all source intelligence, Latham believed intelligence was primarily a commander's tool.[66] This view highlighted an issue that Odom mentioned at the beginning of his testimony: "We shall only talk nonsense about organization and structure unless we have a commonly accepted paradigm of what intelligence is supposed to do, for whom, and how it is supposed to do it."[67] SSCI testimony that day and on subsequent days over the next year highlighted the lack of an "intelligence paradigm" among elected officials and national security professionals.

In 1991, when Representative Dave McCurdy assumed the chairmanship of the HPSCI, it was the first time two congresspersons from the same state simultaneously chaired their respective intelligence committees in the two houses. The hometowns of Senator Boren and Congressman McCurdy, both graduates of the University of Oklahoma School of Law, are separated by only seventy-six miles. Senator Boren, whose father, Congressman Lyle Boren, once represented the same district as McCurdy, spent his childhood between Oklahoma and the Washington, DC, area. He returned to Oklahoma after graduating from Yale and Oxford Universities; following law school, he began a professional career that included stints as a professor, lawyer, state representative, and governor. In 1978, he returned to Washington, DC, to represent his state in the US Senate. Boren served in the Senate for sixteen years, as the chairman of the SSCI for roughly six of those years. A leading member of the Democratic Party in the 1990s, he was influential in the rise of his former SSCI aide, George Tenet, to the position of DCI under Presidents Bill Clinton and George W. Bush.

When Boren was Oklahoma's governor, Dave McCurdy was a young assistant state attorney in Oklahoma. A graduate of the University of Oklahoma, McCurdy was elected to the US Congress when he was only thirty years old and served six terms in the House of Representatives. A one-time ally of Bill Clinton, he gave the seconding speech awarding Clinton the Democratic Party's nomination for president during the party's convention in 1992.[68] The Clinton/McCurdy alliance publicly splintered less than two years later when McCurdy questioned Clinton's policies and referred to him as an "old Democrat."[69] Representative McCurdy left Congress in 1995 after he lost the race for the Senate seat vacated by Boren when Boren retired from Congress to become president of the University of Oklahoma.[70] These two Oklahomans, with help from others such as Senator Arlen Specter, took the congressional lead on intelligence reform in the early 1990s. By 1995, both Boren and McCurdy were retired from Congress, and others were picking up the legislative lead on intelligence reform.

On February 5, 1992, Senator Boren and Congressman McCurdy introduced intelligence reform bills in their respective chambers. On introducing the bills, both legislators cited their desire to spur discussion on how the Intelligence Community needed to transform in the post–Cold War world. Acknowledging the Bush administration's actions, they perceived their legislation as contributing to the ongoing debate and did not expect it to be wholly adopted.

The Intelligence Reorganization Act of 1992 could be considered part of a proposed second phase of reform to ensure that US national security structures were better organized to achieve US foreign-policy objectives. Goldwater-Nichols had achieved two important goals: (1) unified the services and centralized power under a joint construct and (2) established a system or process where the National Security Strategy would drive military strategy development and planning efforts. The Intelligence Reorganization Act sought to establish a unified intelligence structure that supported the DoD and the efforts of other departments while also assisting strategy development and planning efforts in pursuit of policy objectives.

To unify the Intelligence Community, the legislation recommended a DNI who would serve as the president's principle adviser and head of the Intelligence Community. As head of the Intelligence Community, the DNI would have such responsibilities as "developing" the National Foreign Intelligence Program budget, "managing collection capabilities," and "eliminating waste and unnecessary duplication." To improve the Intelligence Community's responsiveness to consumers' needs, the legislation established the Committee on Foreign Intelligence within the NSC. As in the committee proposed during the Ford Administration, the president's national security adviser would chair the Committee on Foreign Intelligence, and its members would include the DNI, the secretary of defense, the secretary of state, the secretary of commerce, their deputies, and other members the "President designates." The committee would be responsible for ensuring that intelligence priorities were nested with the president's "policy and objectives."[71]

Because improving intelligence support to military operations was one of the driving forces behind intelligence reform, numerous elements focused on improving the defense/intelligence partnership, particularly with regard to the DoD/CIA relationship. First, the legislation mandated that either the DNI or the deputy DNI be a commissioned military officer to ensure that DoD equities were understood and considered by the Intelligence Community leadership. The Intelligence Community had been led by active-duty military officers in the past, but never before had it been mandated that one of the top two Intelligence Community leaders be a current serving military officer.[72]

To replace the DCI as manager of the CIA, the legislation established the position of director of the Central Intelligence Agency (DCIA), who would not only be responsible for the CIA but also oversee HUMINT collection for the entire Intelligence Community. This would place the responsibility on the CIA for remedying all shortfalls in HUMINT support to military operations that every congressional review of military operations had identified since Grenada. To ensure that the CIA responded to DoD HUMINT needs, the legislation established an assistant DDO for military support (DDO/MS). The assistant DDO/MS would be a two-star flag officer and serve as the DoD's "principal liaison" to the CIA, responsible for facilitating the DoD/CIA partnership.

To unify the Intelligence Community in support of military operations, the sponsors of the legislation believed they needed to strengthen the management of defense intelligence. To help accomplish this goal, the Intelligence Reorganization Act created an ASD for intelligence whose responsibilities included integrating tactical intelligence and national intelligence and ensuring that the Intelligence Community supported DoD operations. In the ASD for intelligence, there would be one person responsible for the "development of policy, resource allocation, and oversight" of DoD intelligence while also ensuring that the remainder of the Intelligence Community was providing adequate support to military operations.[73] Finally, the legislation looked to rectify the Gulf War BDA controversy and consolidate imagery under a National Imagery Agency that would fall underneath the DoD.

Congressman McCurdy's National Security Act of 1992 shared numerous similarities with Boren's legislation. Both bills established a DNI position that would have enhanced budgetary and management authorities over the current DCI. Unlike Boren's bill, McCurdy's legislation did not allow the DNI to be an active-duty military officer. This did not mean McCurdy was not focused on improving intelligence support to the military. His act made intelligence support to military operations one of the DNI's primary responsibilities and ensured that military equities were considered by mandating that the deputy DNI be an active-duty flag officer.[74]

With the recommended establishment of the DNI, both bills did away with the DCI and created the DCIA. The DCIA would be in charge of an organization that was significantly reduced in comparison to the current CIA. Like the Senate bill, the House bill focused the CIA on HUMINT collection and had the CIA assuming responsibility for directing the Intelligence Community's HUMINT activities, while a new Office of Intelligence Analysis would integrate analysts from throughout the community. Unlike the Senate bill, McCurdy's legislation did not focus on strengthening the DoD/CIA partnership specifically by establishing an assistant DDO/MS within the CIA or creating an ASD for intelligence.[75]

The introduction of the intelligence reform bills in early February 1992 was followed by numerous hearings with expert testimony throughout February and March. Over the course of a month, the SSCI pulled together a group of national security experts to testify on the proposed intelligence reform. Admiral Inman and Lieutenant General Odom testified for a second time since the committee had started to pursue intelligence reform the previous year. In addition to Inman and Odom, James R. Schlesinger (former secretary of defense and DCI), Ambassador Frank Carlucci (former deputy DCI and deputy secretary of defense), General (ret.) Paul Gorman (former Southern Command CINC), General (ret.) Alfred Gray (former commandant of the US Marine Corps), Dr. Richard Betts (professor and former SSCI and NSC staff member), Harold P. Ford (former senior CIA analyst and National Intelligence Council deputy), Ambassador Morton Abramowitz (former ambassador to Turkey and Thailand), and Senator Arlen Specter testified before the SSCI.

Boren made it clear early on during the hearings that the United States could not sustain "separate civilian and military intelligence empires" and that a significant focus of intelligence reform was going to consist of consolidating these two kingdoms into one.[76] He understood that intelligence was a vital element of military operations and argued there was "no more important consumer" than the "military commander." Because budget reductions were certain, Boren believed that the DoD required an intelligence czar to streamline defense intelligence and to ensure that adequate intelligence support from the broader community was forthcoming during operations. Large-scale military operations were infrequent, so the United States could accept risk by shifting support away from policy makers toward the military during these periods. Of course, this discussion occurred before the rise of low-intensity conflicts and the introduction of continuous war after 9/11.

The first hearing on February 20, 1992, brought Lieutenant General Odom back to testify regarding the reform bills. His background in the Intelligence Community during the Cold War and his academic research interests made him an ideal witness to testify on intelligence reform in the new operational environment. In November 1991, his book *On Internal War: American and Soviet Approaches to Third World Clients and Insurgents* had been published.[77] The book considered the difference between Soviet and American approaches to Third World conflicts during the Cold War. Odom's ultimate recommendation was that the United States should "eschew involvement in internal war entirely," but he believed America's push for "involvement" in the 1990s meant this suggestion would fall on deaf ears. Accepting this reality, he offered some suggestions for a new strategy in waging low-intensity conflicts.[78]

In his book, Odom described the significant intelligence resources required to wage the low-intensity conflicts he saw America pursuing in the future. He argued that waging low-intensity conflicts required information on the social, economic, and military factors, not just the on the opposing forces' orders of battle.[79] During his testimony in February 1992, he described how the end of the Cold War, the rise of low-intensity conflicts, and the increasing technology were going to increase "intelligence tasks" in the future. He believed that many officials were underestimating how taxing these new military operations were going to be and that the United States needed to focus analytical resources on supporting these military efforts.[80] Odom was not the only witness to testify about how low-intensity conflicts would increase the requirement for intelligence support to operations.

General (ret.) Paul Gorman was a former Southern Command CINC who had served as the national intelligence officer for General Purpose Forces. Gorman became the Southern Command chief five months after the Grenada invasion and during a period of increased focus on insurgencies and drug wars in Latin America. His experiences shaped his view that the United States had to rethink "the traditional dichotomy of war vs peace, with which this Republic was formed and [with] which it has lived for so many years, [and] may have to . . . set [it] aside in order to deal adequately with the problems of the present."[81] Gorman described a United States constantly engaged in some form of low-intensity conflict. Whether the United States was assisting in a counterinsurgency, waging a drug war, or combating terrorism, it was irrelevant whether the United States viewed its actions as war if those it was countering viewed themselves as being at war with the

United States. In articles Gorman wrote after retirement, he described the increased role combatant commanders must play in this new "strategically amorphous" environment and the importance of intelligence in supporting their new responsibilities.

Gorman's testimony to the SSCI reflected his writings about the increasing number of low-intensity conflicts, the CINCs' role, and the importance of intelligence in this new environment. Gorman did not support the intelligence reform legislation because he "feared that the changes would strengthen the 'Beltway Barrier' between the US Combatant Commands and the intelligence centers in the Washington D.C. region." Gorman believed that the "intelligence apparatus in Washington ought to be focused outward, to those who must collect the information and act on the intelligence rather than upward to hierarchy." In a dynamic world, where the United States is always engaged in some degree of conflict, Gorman believed it best to decentralize intelligence so it could support those on the ground. To accomplish this decentralization, Gorman argued for an increased influence of the military over intelligence, going as far as to recommend a military operator and not an intelligence professional as the deputy of national intelligence.[82] If adopted, Gorman's recommendation would significantly increase the CINCs' influence in foreign policy. Placing the intelligence apparatus in direct support of the CINCs would not only increase their intelligence capability but largely enable them to shape US foreign policy toward the region they commanded. If the CINCs controlled where intelligence focused in their regions, they could largely determine the important issues to focus on, thus shaping how policy makers viewed those issues.

The other military officer testifying that day, General (ret.) Alfred Gray, a former US Marine Corps commandant, recommended less-invasive changes to increase intelligence support to military operations. Gray, whom the NSA inducted into its hall of fame in 2008 for his work operationalizing signals intelligence in support of military operations, opined that the Intelligence Community had served the United States well throughout its history. Although he applauded the SSCI's efforts in encouraging this important debate, he favored allowing the secretary of defense and the DCI to move forward with their plans before legislating change. Notably, Gray indicated that the DoD/CIA relationship required improvement and recommended that the DoD increase the number of exchange officers it sent to the CIA. These exchange officers would not be intelligence professionals but rather "young combined arms warriors" who could use their knowledge of CIA operations when they commanded battalions and other units in the future.[83]

Congress wanted to improve the support that tactical intelligence and strategic intelligence provided each other, but the intelligence reform discussions focused mainly on national intelligence support to military operations. This focus is understandable: the Gulf War intelligence debate had been going on for more than a year, and intelligence support to military operations had been an issue for more than a decade. Without the Soviet Union as a main adversary, and with the increased focus on low-intensity conflicts becoming the "normal form of conflict in the 1990s," it was an easy decision to focus so much attention on improving intelligence support to the military.[84] Congressional reformers understood that the Intelligence Community had to support the military but cautioned against its subordination to the military commander. Boren, McCurdy, and the other supporters of the intelligence community were trying to find an optimal structure to ensure that all consumers' needs were met while also eliminating duplication. Although improving intelligence and decreasing expenditures is an admirable pursuit, it is difficult to achieve in an environment where eliminating duplication results in winners and losers.

The intelligence reform discussions in February–March 1992 not only displayed broad support for increasing intelligence support to the military but also reflected a difference of opinion on the purpose of intelligence. The spectrum of witness testimony highlights the varying opinions. James Schlesinger—former DCI, secretary of defense, and first secretary of energy who had served in the Nixon, Ford, and Carter administrations—argued for decentralized intelligence. Schlesinger believed that the varied consumers, from the battalion commander on the battlefield to the president in the White House, required different intelligence to perform their jobs. Although centralization sounded attractive, he argued that the Intelligence Community had evolved to its current decentralized structure because that is what the different consumers required. Centralizing the Intelligence Community might save money, but it could create a structure that provided less value to its customers. Schlesinger stated, "Only if intelligence assets are widely distributed and marbled throughout the user communities, will the ultimate task of policy best be achieved."[85] In Schlesinger's view, the definition and purpose of intelligence were delineated by the organization that intelligence served.

General Gorman also argued for decentralization, but with a different view of why it was important. Whereas Schlesinger argued for decentralization because he believed all organizations have unique intelligence requirements, Gorman argued for it because he believed the CINCs needed more capability to support their role in the new environment. He viewed intelligence from an operator's perspective, believing it should be "pushed out" from Washington to commanders in the field. This stance reflected a certain view of the purpose of intelligence that was biased more toward enabling operations and less toward informing strategy or policy. This view was shared by General Odom, who argued that analytical support to policy makers often did not provide any valuable insight or help determining policy actions, whereas analytic support to the military at all levels provided the commander more clarity and understanding. Although Odom's main analytical argument focused on the importance of decentralization of analysis, his opinion of tactical analysis compared to strategic analysis highlighted where he thought intelligence provided the most value: at the policy-implementation level (i.e., military operations).[86]

On March 17, 1992, two days before the final SSCI hearing on the intelligence reform bills, the DoD formally addressed its nonsupport of the legislation. In a six-page letter signed by Secretary of Defense Cheney and the department's general counsel, the DoD argued that the "bills are unnecessary and so severely flawed that selective amendments would not make either of them acceptable." Reiterating witness statements made during testimony over the previous month, the letter argued that the Intelligence Community had evolved over the years in response to the needs of the individual departments and agencies and through lessons learned. Individual organizations had specific intelligence requirements geared toward their mission, and consolidating them would negatively affect those organizations.[87]

The creation of a DNI who "would manage all collection activities" was the greatest concern to DoD because it believed this change would weaken intelligence support to the military. Similar to Gorman's testimony, the letter described the necessity of keeping intelligence linked to operations and argued that centralization significantly inhibited the secretary of defense's ability to ensure that link was not severed. The letter tried to reassure Congress that the DoD understood the need for reform and highlighted the department's cooperative efforts with the DCI to incorporate change based on lessons learned during operations.[88]

The letter belied a recommendation made by General Schwarzkopf during his SASC testimony in June 1991 regarding the standardization of analysis. Frustrated with conflicting analysis, Schwarzkopf had suggested developing "standardized methodology within the Intelligence Community" so the "guy in the field" would not receive "caveated" reports that disagreed with each other.[89] The DoD's stance, as the letter explained, was that a "centralized analytic structure to produce government-wide intelligence would inhibit competitive analysis and, then, threaten the integrity of the intelligence product and prevent competing analytical views from coming to the attention of senior decision makers."[90] This contradiction represents a disconnect between the reverent status Schwarzkopf enjoyed with respect to the public and the more balanced perspective of those in his own institution. Whereas Congress showed deference to the war hero and took his critiques at face value, DoD leadership, who had observed the Intelligence Community's performance during the war and knew Schwarzkopf personally, questioned his accuracy. The disagreement between Schwarzkopf and DoD leadership was not widely known, but the letter hints at the disharmony regarding the intelligence reform debate, of which Schwarzkopf's critique was a proximate cause.[91]

Like many myths, the claim of poor intelligence support during Desert Storm started to develop the semblance of reality. Three years after victory in Desert Storm, Admiral Studeman participated in a symposium on the war that included former commanders, many whom complained about the intelligence support they had received. Unwilling to accept this perspective, Admiral Studeman, who was NSA director during Desert Storm, went "through a list of twenty-five to thirty things" that identified all the support intelligence provided military operations. Later on, during the reception, fellow panelists acknowledged to Studeman that after further consideration they thought they might have exaggerated the lack of intelligence support.[92] Yet, despite evidence to the contrary and a partial recant, Schwarzkopf's initial intelligence critique became an accepted reality.

On March 30, 1992, President George H. W. Bush issued *National Security Directive 67: Intelligence Capabilities: 1992–2005*.[93] NSD-67 was a follow-up to NSR-29's assessment of the intelligence capabilities required by consumers in the post–Cold War environment. It approved both NSR-29's findings and DCI Gates's recommended realignment of resources to posture the Intelligence Community to serve the consumers.[94] Two days after Bush issued his directive, DCI Gates briefed the joint SSCI/HPSCI session on the Intelligence Community reform measures he was implementing. Following the joint hearing, the HPSCI and SSCI intelligence reform bills did not progress further, and congressional discussion on intelligence reform quieted down for a while. Boren and McCurdy were not successful in establishing a DNI, but their congressional actions helped encourage change driven by executive fiat. In a city not known for responsiveness, the speed at which reform was proposed and initiated in this case is remarkable. Less than three months after NSR-29 was published, the Gates Task Forces formed and reported their findings, and the associate DDO/MA was established at CIA.

Implementing Partial Reform and Preparing for a Loss

Gates's strategy for implementing the task force recommendations had three phases. The first phase focused on implementing changes that were widely accepted throughout the Intelligence Community. These changes had "no entrenched efforts" and so could be easily implemented. Once the first phase was complete and sufficient "momentum" for change was generated, transition to the second phase could occur. The second phase required realignment of resources, where there would be winners and losers. This phase involved a "base-capability study" that considered the minimal resources necessary to support consumer requirements. The third phase was the most difficult; it looked to rectify the Intelligence Community's "fundamental flaws." The changes this rectification required were going to be contentious because they affected groups of people with entrenched interests and "political clout." According to Haver, phases two and three reform objectives were never fully achieved.[95]

In the summer of 1992, Bob Gates mentioned to Dick Cheney and Rich Haver that he thought Bush was going to lose the presidential election that year.[96] At that time, some polls showed Ross Perot (39 percent) leading Bush (31 percent) and Bill Clinton (25 percent),[97] but Cheney scoffed at the notion of predicting election results that early.[98] Although Cheney brushed off Gates's comments, Gates's prediction proved accurate five months later. With intelligence reform phases two and three not yet implemented, Gates told Haver to get rid of the remaining intelligence reform recommendations. According to Haver, phases two and three could occur only in the second term of an administration because they involved reallocating resources. With a second term for Bush not looking promising, Gates feared only the budget cuts would make it to a new administration and not the understanding of why resource-realignment decisions were made. Although Gates understood budget cuts were necessary, he intended to do all he could to strengthen the community while reducing duplication. Informed by his three decades in the Intelligence Community, he considered the "winners and losers" during resource allocation. When the new administration assumed the helm, he feared the thoughtful analysis would be lost and only reductions would remain.[99]

President Bush's four years in office saw significant turmoil at home and abroad. In just two years, the Berlin Wall had collapsed, and the Soviet Union had disintegrated. In 1990–1991, the United States suffered through a recession, but the poor economic conditions lingered even longer. Although

Bush initially stood fast to his campaign promise of "no new taxes," the significant budget deficit and congressional pressure led him to support tax increases along with budget reductions in an attempt to correct the course of America's economic vessel. Budget cuts were significant, with roughly a 15 percent reduction in defense between 1990 and 1993.[100] The intelligence budget, which had grown by 125 percent between 1980 and 1989, was reduced by roughly 12 percent by 1993 and was continuing on a downward trend.[101]

The changing world required a reassessment of US strategic interests, which provided the administration an opportunity to reduce national security expenditures and benefit from the "peace dividend." The shift to a regionally focused strategy provided the DoD an opportunity to reduce structure and realign forces for the "New World Order." Always a visionary, General Colin Powell, the JCS chairman, initiated the Base Force Concept to determine the appropriate mixture of forces to respond to a new military strategy focused on regional threats. Along with the new force structure came a new defense strategy focused on regional engagements through "forward presence" and "crisis" response. Now that the threat of Soviet tanks rolling through the Fulda Gap was gone, the US military had to posture and prepare for low-intensity conflicts that could arise in various regions throughout the world. Most importantly, the DoD had to do its part to ensure that the United States would retain its dominance in the world and be able to bring former Communist nations into the democratic fold.

The nearly 90 percent approval ratings Bush enjoyed following the Gulf War soon dissipated, with the staggering economy and the broken promise not to raise taxes sinking his approval rating below 40 percent by the time voters went to the polls in November 1992.[102] Bush's defeat brought to power the charismatic Arkansas governor, whose campaign platform focused largely on domestic issues and recovering America's economic health. The desire to reduce national security expenditures to strengthen the sickly American economy did not end with the George H. W. Bush presidency, however. Running on the memorable quip "It's the economy, stupid," Bill Clinton entered the White House with an electoral mandate to strengthen the economy. Part of the Clinton administration's strategy to revitalize the economy was a determined focus to make federal government more effective and efficient. Sharing the Bush administration's belief that a new unipolar world presented an opportunity to cut national security significantly, the Clinton administration continued the trend of reduced defense spending initiated by its predecessor. Part of this reduction meant looking for opportunities to use existing capabilities to cover requirements, and the intelligence needs of the post–Desert Storm military constituted one of those identified requirements.

5

"IT'S THE ECONOMY, STUPID"

The Clinton Years and Intelligence Reform

Bill Clinton's 1992 presidential campaign's focus on domestic policy, the economy, and the 7.8 percent unemployment rate brought him to the White House with just more than 43 percent of the popular vote.[1] During the campaign, Clinton adviser James Carville hung a sign at Clinton's campaign headquarters reminding the volunteers what issue was most important to the electorate: "It's the economy, stupid." This mantra for the Clinton campaign emphasized that the sagging economy meant people were more concerned with their pocketbook than with national security issues.

Although Clinton honed in on the economy and is often associated with initiating the national security drawdown in the 1990s, the "peace dividend" reductions had started before his inauguration on January 23, 1993, and enjoyed bipartisan support. On August 1, 1990, the same day Iraq invaded Kuwait, President George H. W. Bush stood before an Aspen Institute audience proposing a 25 percent reduction in active-duty military forces, reaffirming a figure that Secretary of Defense Richard Cheney had proposed to Congress in June 1990.[2] Between 1990 and 1993, the defense budget was reduced roughly 8 percent a year, with an average yearly reduction of 5.7 percent. The Bush administration's final budget proposal in January 1993 recommended active-duty force reductions through 1999, when the number of active-duty personnel would be 1.568 million, a reduction of 28 percent from fiscal year 1987.[3] From 1989 to 1996, the military slashed its officer ranks by a staggering 23 percent, and the Intelligence Community reduced its ranks by 17.5 percent between 1993 and 1997.[4] The CIA was hit particularly hard, with DO personnel reductions reaching 20 percent and budget reductions going up to 30 percent in the 1990s.[5]

The end of the Cold War and the poor economic health of the United States necessitated national security reductions, but these reductions came at a time of transition that brought confusion and change to both the DoD and the CIA. It was in the midst of this fluid environment that the United States took its second attempt at intelligence reform in less than five years. As in 1992, little intelligence reform legislation resulted from these efforts, but actions were taken that improved the DoD/CIA partnership while increasing the CIA's focus on supporting military operations. Although an improved DoD/CIA relationship was a positive result, the pressure to increase CIA support to military operations not only affected the CIA's support to policy makers but also risked its subordination to the DoD.

DoD Intelligence Reform Continues

As Congress was complaining about HUMINT support to military operations and telling the CIA to increase its support to the military during both peacetime and wartime, the DIA was undergoing significant cuts, forcing it to consolidate DoD's HUMINT capability. If the DoD lacked the HUMINT capability to inform contingency planning during Desert Storm, further reductions made it more necessary to turn to the CIA for support. With the CIA also experiencing reductions, however, increased military support requirements forced it to reprioritize and shift resources away from long-term analysis, thus affecting its ability to provide intelligence support to policy makers.

Lieutenant General James Clapper, who served as the air force assistant chief of staff for intelligence during Desert Storm, became the DIA director in November 1991. Clapper, a graduate of the University of Maryland's Air Force Reserve Officer Training Program in 1963, had spent his early career as a signals intelligence officer and his general officer time within geographic combatant commands and at US Air Force Headquarters. Clapper retired in 1995 after serving as DIA director but returned to government service in 2001 as the director of the National Imagery and Mapping Agency until 2006, when his willingness to work for the DNI as the head of a national intelligence organization earned him Donald Rumsfeld's ire and he was forced to resign.[6] In 2007, Secretary of Defense Robert Gates made Clapper the second USD for intelligence, and in 2010 President Obama made him the fourth DNI.[7]

When Clapper took over the DIA, he had to focus his efforts on reducing the DIA workforce by 20 percent while at the same time ensuring that this reduced capability could support the new operational environment. To accomplish these goals, Clapper reduced the number of DIA director- ates from nine to four and then consolidated the five former directorates and other various offices into three centers: the National Military Intelligence Collection Center to manage DoD's HUMINT as well as measurement and signals intelligence collection capabilities; the National Military Intel- ligence Production Center to focus on the development and dissemination of finished analysis; and the National Military Intelligence Systems Center to better organize DoD's imagery efforts.[8] Closely linked to the National Military Intelligence Collection Center and most significant in regard to the DoD/CIA relationship, Clapper continued the DIA HUMINT consolida- tion that was initiated under Lieutenant General Harry Soyster's tenure as DIA director.

The HUMINT restructuring plan that Lieutenant General Soyster sub- mitted to Duane Andrews, the ASD for command, control, communica- tions, and intelligence, in June 1991 was eventually codified in Department of Defense Directive 5200-37, *Centralized Management of Department of Defense Human Intelligence (HUMINT) Operations.* This directive identified the DIA director as the DoD HUMINT manager and "centralized the decisionmaking process under" him. It authorized operating bases around the world where the DIA, individual services, and the combatant commands would work together. With decreasing budgets, the military could not afford the cost of redundant HUMINT collection efforts or the multiple support systems within the mil- itary services. To streamline HUMINT efforts, the DoD established joint operating bases where the services and DIA maintained separate HUMINT capabilities but worked together by portioning the collection requirements and sharing a common "HUMINT support service."[9]

There initially was confusion over what centralization meant. The US Department of the Army G2 argued that the operating base concept allowed the services to retain "responsibility for the conduct of intelligence opera- tions," while the DIA managed the collection requirements. As the army G2 History Office's *Annual Historical Review* stated at the time, "DIA would tell us what to collect—we'd figure out how to do it and be responsible for the results."[10] According to the army G2, the DIA looked at the operating base concept differently and believed it gave DIA day-to-day control over HUMINT operations.

By 1993, the ongoing reductions were continuing to take a toll on the DoD, and the focus on centralizing the DIA's and the military services' HUMINT resources and personnel evolved into the consolidation of the

DoD's HUMINT capabilities. That year the DoD established the Defense Human Intelligence Service (DHS), placing the military services' HUMINT personnel directly under the DIA and consolidating the DIA, army, navy, and air force HUMINT programs into a "single DoD HUMINT budget." The transfer of personnel and money from the military departments to the DHS was intended to reduce expenditures and carry forward the jointness introduced with Goldwater-Nichols.[11] The plan was driven by guidance provided by both the secretary of defense and the DCI that mandated cuts between fiscal year 1995 and fiscal year 1999. Development of the DHS plan was an interagency effort, with groups from the "military departments, the Joint Staff, the DIA and the CIA" working together to establish a way forward for defense HUMINT consolidation.[12]

On November 3, 1993, Deputy Secretary of Defense William Perry, who three months later became secretary of defense, signed the memorandum directing consolidation of defense HUMINT. The memorandum established the DHS and created a consolidated defense HUMINT budget within the General Defense Intelligence Program. Establishing the new DHS as a "joint field operating activity" and creating joint duty positions ensured the DIA control beyond merely apportioning collection requirements to the different services. Perry did allow the services to maintain "a small, carefully focused HUMINT capability, designed to meet specific overt non-sensitive needs which cannot efficiently be met by the DHS," but the consolidation memorandum made it clear the DIA was responsible for the bulk of DoD HUMINT operations.[13]

Major General Jack Leide, Schwarzkopf's J2 director during the Gulf War who had worked closely with the DoD JIC, was assigned as the first director of the DHS and the National Military Intelligence Collection Center in June 1993. The previous summer, a year after his CENTCOM boss's complaints regarding intelligence revitalized the decade-long effort to improve intelligence support to operations, Leide arrived at the DIA as the director for attachés and operations (an element that fell under the DHS and National Military Intelligence Collection Center when established). In his role as the new DHS boss, Leide was responsible for ensuring that DoD HUMINT was reduced by 350 personnel and simultaneously for trying to build an organization that could meet the Pentagon's, the military services', and the combatant commands' HUMINT intelligence needs.[14] This was a hefty task, but Leide was not alone in trying to reform an organization in a new environment characterized by significant cuts.

Reforming Government and Prioritizing Support to Military Operations

The establishment of the DHS and the resulting streamlining of DoD HUMINT operations was in line with the Clinton administration's efforts to reduce the size of the federal government. On March 3, 1993, six weeks after Clinton was inaugurated as the forty-second president of the United States, he stood before a crowd at the Old Executive Office Building adjacent to the White House to announce a new effort to "bring about greater efficiency and lower cost of government."[15] President Clinton charged Vice President Al Gore with leading the National Performance Review (NPR) and gave him six months to assemble a team, review government organizations, and present a report. Gore not only contributed his name and power of position to the review but also embraced an integral role in the NPR's operations. Although the initial review lasted only six months, it operated throughout Clinton's term in office.[16]

The NPR had similar objectives to the Reagan administration's President's Blue Ribbon Commission on Defense Management (Packard Commission), with both the NPR and the Packard Commission seeking to bring greater efficiency and transparency to how the federal government operated.[17] Although similar in objectives, the NPR's aspirations were much larger and looked to "make the entire federal government less expensive and more efficient, and to change the culture of our national bureaucracy away from complacency and entitlement toward initiative and empowerment."[18]

During its existence, the NPR reviewed the operations of the Intelligence Community and, like congressional and executive reviews since the late 1980s, focused significant attention on improving intelligence support to military operations. Of the seven Intelligence Community recommendations, three focused specifically on integrating the thirteen separate intelligence organizations into a community, and three focused on improving support to the Intelligence Community's customers.[19] Although the recommendations acknowledged the Intelligence Community's diverse customer base, the military was the only customer that received a recommendation focused purely on improving the support it received.

The NPR's seventh recommendation, "Improve Support to Ground Troops during Combat Operations," argued that it was the Intelligence Community's responsibility to support the individual "shooter" on the ground with a tailored product that was relevant and useable. Although improving intelligence support to troops on the ground is an admirable goal, placing responsibility for this support on the entire Intelligence Community and not just on the DoD risked burdening an Intelligence Community that was already undergoing significant budget cuts. Collaboration is a good thing, but the integrated approach the NPR recommended paid scant attention to the fact that each intelligence organization evolved over time to provide intelligence support to a distinct customer base, something former DCI James Schlesinger had identified as an issue in 1992.[20] This neglect, coupled with the NPR's signaling to the Intelligence Community that the military enjoyed primacy among the community's various customers, risked subordinating national intelligence to the military.

In March 1995, six months after the NPR Commission published the seven Intelligence Community objectives, President Clinton confirmed the primacy of the intelligence consumer when he issued *Presidential Decision Directive 35: Intelligence Requirements* and identified intelligence support to military operations as the top Intelligence Community priority.[21] Removing any doubt from CIA employees regarding where their efforts should be focused, President Clinton told them during a headquarters visit a few months after issuing PDD-35 that providing "prompt, thorough intelligence to fully inform their [commanders'] decisions and maximize security of our troops" during operations was the first priority for the Intelligence Community. As Michael Warner argues, PDD-35 resulted in a "diversion of shrinking national, strategic intelligence resources to growing, tactical missions."[22] This diversion only hastened following September 11, 2001, when the Intelligence Community became even more focused on tactical problems.

As Al Gore's committee pursued ways to "reinvent" government, Secretary of Defense Les Aspin was leading the DoD through its own review. The Bottom-Up Review focused on how to restructure and reduce the US military to save money while maintaining its ability to wage two regional wars. For the Intelligence Community, the NPR and Bottom-Up Review were inextricably linked. The NPR was trying to organize the Intelligence Community to support the military during planning and operations, and whatever force structure and defense strategy came out of the Bottom-Up Review, the Intelligence Community had to be organized to support it.

Les Aspin rolled out the Bottom-Up Review in October 1993, the same month of the tragic Black Hawk incident in Somalia and two months before Clinton accepted Aspin's resignation as secretary of defense. Aspin, the intellectual former congressman who had served as one of Secretary of Defense Robert McNamara's whiz kids, looked forward to remaking the post–Cold

War DoD, but early controversy over the "don't ask, don't tell" policy, Bosnia, and Haiti made his first eight months in office bumpy. The tragedy in Somalia, especially controversy over Aspin's denial of the mission commander's request for armored vehicles, sealed his fate, ensuring he did not remain Clinton's secretary of defense.[23] Aspin's forced resignation was a blemish on his impressive record as a policy maker and national security leader. As a consolation, Clinton made Aspin the chair of the President's Foreign Intelligence Advisory Board and gave him a new mission: to review the Intelligence Community and reorganize it for the twenty-first century.[24]

The Commission on the Roles and Capabilities of the United States Intelligence Community (Aspin-Brown Commission) was mandated in the IAA of 1995.[25] Dissatisfied with previous reform efforts, the commission was another post–Cold War attempt to institute intelligence reform. Although Congress had deferred to the executive branch two years earlier to implement change, events such as the Somalia tragedy, the Ames spy case, and controversy over the funding for the NRO building caused some congresspersons to call for reform through legislation. The commission was a joint executive and legislative endeavor focused on how the Intelligence Community should transition in the post–Cold War environment. On one side of the reform debate were congresspersons such as Senator John Warner (R–VA), who was a supporter of the Intelligence Community and had come to its defense when Schwarzkopf was complaining after Desert Storm. Warner was suspicious of congresspersons "advocating slash and burn of the intelligence budget" and even proposing legislation to disband the agency.[26] The Clinton administration's placement of Aspin, who was not known as being pro-CIA, in charge of a review did not "sit well" with some members of Congress and added to the tension.

Les Aspin had been a member of the House Select Committee on Intelligence led by Representative Otis Pike (D–NY) in the mid-1970s. The Pike Committee was the House version of the Church Committee, which had investigated the Intelligence Community after Watergate and the release of the "Family Jewels." The Pike Committee hearings were particularly contentious as Republicans and Democrats continuously butted heads over the simplest of issues, with leaks to media and other outsiders constantly occurring.[27] Aspin followed up his service on the Pike Committee with service on early forms of the HPSCI.[28] He passed away before the Aspin-Brown Commission completed its work and was replaced by Harold Brown, secretary of defense during the Carter administration.

Similar to the intelligence reform legislation of 1992, the Aspin-Brown

Commission sought to consolidate intelligence capabilities by streamlining the community and eliminating redundancy. The commission recommended that the DCI retain responsibility for serving as the president's main intelligence adviser and leader of both the Intelligence Community and the CIA. To alleviate some of the DCI's management responsibility, the commission recommended breaking the current deputy DCI position into two presidentially appointed and Senate-confirmed deputy positions, a deputy director of the Intelligence Community and a deputy DCIA. Although the DCI would still be responsible for leading both the Intelligence Community and the CIA, the deputy director of the Intelligence Community would have no direct CIA management role, and the deputy DCIA would lack a community-management role. The commission argued that two presidentially appointed deputies would give the DCI two "senior managers of stature" who could speak "authoritatively" on their respective organizations, thus providing the DCI "greater freedom to choose where to devote his energy."[29] By identifying the deputy director of the Intelligence Community as the acting DCI whenever the DCI was absent, the commission essentially made that person the primary deputy and placed Intelligence Community interests over CIA interests.

The commission also pursued budget reductions by increasing the coordination between the secretary of defense and the DCI and restructuring the budget by intelligence disciplines. The commission hoped this would help eliminate redundancy within the community. To improve the dialogue between policy makers and the Intelligence Community, the commission once again recommended the NSC establish a Committee on Foreign Intelligence chaired by the national security adviser and composed of the NSA director, the DCI, the deputy secretary of defense, and the deputy secretary of state. This new committee would be responsible for providing iterative guidance on where the Intelligence Community should focus its collection and analysis efforts based on national priorities.[30]

Although the Aspin-Brown Commission's recommendations on the Intelligence Community's leadership, structure, and budget authorities were not novel, the commission had one recommendation that, if enacted, would fundamentally alter the DoD partnership. Citing the "costs and difficulties involved in maintaining a separate infrastructure within the DoD for the conduct of clandestine HUMINT operations," the commission recommended folding DHS clandestine operations into the CIA and making one clandestine service that would handle both military and national HUMINT collection requirements. The idea was to establish one organization that understood how to manage, develop, and direct clandestine HUMINT operations to ensure effective employment while also consolidating resources and deconflicting operations. The military would still retain certain HUMINT capabilities such as interrogators and counterintelligence HUMINT, but their clandestine capabilities would be consolidated under CIA. This proposal was not supported by Chairman Brown, who believed consolidation would "make the DIA's assets too civilian from the CINC point of view," or by Lieutenant General Clapper, who believed the proposal would result in the loss of HUMINT support to the military.

The HPSCI did not rest while waiting for the Aspin-Brown Commission to report back. As the commission was conducting its investigation, the HPSCI was holding its own hearings to discuss the future of the Intelligence Community. Senator Warner and Aspin had worked together to ensure there were not two competing hearings debating the Intelligence Community's future, thus making a political spectacle of intelligence reform. Larry Combest (R), the HPSCI chairman from West Texas, had a different perspective on the intelligence reform discussion and believed there was value in "proposing radical intelligence reform" to force a suitable compromise between the different reform perspectives.[31] Between May and December 1995, the HPSCI held six separate hearings involving a diverse number of national security leaders and discussing a wide range of intelligence topics—from technology's effect on intelligence to the role of intelligence in policy making—as part of the HPSCI's Intelligence Community in the 21st Century (IC21) effort. In Congressman Combest's view, the only discussion topic that was off the table was whether the United States required an Intelligence Community; "beyond that, everything else is on the table for examination and debate."[32]

A major point of discussion during the House hearings in the second half of 1995 was the role of intelligence, in particular the increased importance of intelligence support to military operations. The witnesses argued that technology was providing military commanders more capability to wage war but requiring more intelligence to enable the capability. Technological developments were also increasing the intelligence consumer base, with the mantra "from the sensor to the shooter" highlighting the push to get intelligence into the hands of the individual soldier on the ground.

DCI John Deutch testified that integration of intelligence and military operations would only increase the intelligence support DoD required. He believed the combatant commanders would become the main consumer of intelligence, stating "that over time the CINCs are going to become the key to the demand side of the intelligence future. I think it is starting now."[33] Richard Kerr, the former deputy DCI, alluded to the trade-offs that increasing military support incurs, pointing out that although intelligence support to military operations is important, the CIA had other support requirements. Regarding the DoD/CIA partnership, Kerr and John McMahon, Kerr's predecessor as deputy DCI, acknowledged that the CIA was not meeting the military's HUMINT support requirements, but Kerr cautioned that the military's "insatiable appetite" for intelligence made doing so nearly impossible. Paul Kaminski, the USD for acquisition and technology, articulated this cost when he argued that national intelligence was no longer focused primarily on Washington but also on the "day-to-day real-time operations."[34] Kaminski's enthusiasm in noting this evolution highlighted the disconnect that existed between many CIA and DoD leaders regarding the purpose of the CIA.

The witnesses were not the only ones acknowledging the primacy of the military need for intelligence support and its flourishing hunger for information. Congressman Combest stated that the "primary objective of intelligence is to provide for the military user" and argued that "intelligence is becoming an even more integral part of the modern battlefield. We talk about support to military operations as an important mission of U.S. intelligence, but we may not fully grasp the ramifications of how new technology will ensure a seamless web of intelligence, command, control, and communications to the warfighter." Combest also acknowledged that the United States did not have "unlimited resources" to direct toward intelligence and that decisions had to be made on how to apportion the limited resources.[35]

Congressman Combest sent the IC21 Staff Study to Speaker of the House Newt Gingrich on April 6, 1995. The 379-page report covered a wide range of topics—from restructuring the HPSCI and the Intelligence Community to reassessing collection requirements. Similar to discussions that occurred during the eight months of hearings, the IC21 Staff Study considered the trade-offs of increasing support to military operations. Echoing some of the Intelligence Community and DoD leaders, the report described how increasing technology and the push to have intelligence flow to the individual soldier were placing a significant burden on the Intelligence Community. This burden was only going to increase as the DoD pursued new operational concepts such as Dominant Battlefield Awareness that provided the false hope of "piercing the fog of war" but required significant multidiscipline intelligence resources to achieve.[36]

The report argued that these military demands made it difficult for the "Intelligence Community to meet the broader national security challenges of the 21st Century" and that military requirements were already sapping resources away from "maintaining the necessary intelligence base" that was "critical in addressing future national security needs." Although the report argued that both supporting military operations and "maintaining the necessary intelligence base" had to be considered, it described an Intelligence Community already subordinated to the DoD.[37]

The IC21 Staff Study supported the Aspin-Brown Commission's recommendations to reestablish the Committee on Foreign Intelligence and to create a separate clandestine service composed of both national resources and military resources. It also pursued a similar path to establishing "corporateness" within the Intelligence Community by establishing two deputy DCI positions, one responsible for the day-to-day operations of the CIA and the other for managing the Intelligence Community. The IC21 report departed from the Aspin-Brown Commission recommendations in a few areas. Two areas of particular note were its calls to give the DIA director new responsibility as the director of military intelligence (DMI) and the establishment of a new Technical Collection Agency to consolidate all technical collection capabilities.[38]

Regarding the consolidation of all clandestine HUMINT, the IC21 report acknowledged that clandestine operations must develop over time, forcing a reassessment of the CIA's earlier decision to reduce its number of stations globally. The IC21 report called for a "global presence" of CIA clandestine capability throughout the world that could assist the US military in its planning efforts. Because clandestine HUMINT operations could not be established overnight, and because clandestine operations had provided commanders some of the best intelligence during operations due to the "limitations of technical collection capabilities in environments largely devoid of signals," CIA clandestine operations would have to be in place and conducting operations in support of the military during peacetime. Although the IC21 report acknowledged the importance of CIA HUMINT support to policy makers and warned about spreading the Intelligence Community too thin, its assessment that the clandestine service "must accept its responsibility to support the requirements of the military not only for strategic intelligence—something in which it can excel—but also for appropriate tactical intelligence support in times and places of military engagement—a responsibility that often falls to it only by default," reflected its true preference. The IC21 might have been paying lip service to the importance of CIA HUMINT support to policy makers, but its recommendation to reestablish a global presence and build during peacetime the networks necessary to support military operations showed that CIA support to military operations was the priority.[39]

In 1993, the DIA director, Lieutenant General Clapper, assumed the title of DMI to help solidify his leadership role within the DoD's Intelligence Community. Although DoD intelligence was dispersed, the DIA director's leadership role increased as the Military Intelligence Board gained more influence in managing support to military operations. As both chair of the MIB and DIA director, Clapper wanted to differentiate between his two roles. He also believed the title *director of military intelligence* gave him more clout in dealing with the diverse elements of the defense intelligence community even though he lacked any "command authorities."[40] James Woolsey, the DCI at the time, did not support the DMI title, believing it weakened his authority as the DCI and resulted in more, not less, confusion. The decision was made not to alienate DCI Woolsey by "formalizing" the title, and the issue was temporarily dropped. The recommendation to establish a DMI who was a uniformed military intelligence professional was not adopted, but the position of USD for intelligence was established during the George W. Bush administration. Although the concepts were slightly different, the USD for intelligence would help centralize intelligence within DoD, and so many of the concerns Woolsey voiced in 1993 resurfaced.[41]

Although Congressman Combest agreed the military was the most important intelligence consumer, he also understood that others required intelligence support, and he wanted to ensure an independent Intelligence Community not under DoD control. This push for independence is why the IC21 recommended a "corporate approach" that would allow the Intelligence Community not only to realign resources and reprioritize when required but also to build an independent culture that would separate it from the agencies it supported. The recommendation to establish a Technical Collection Agency was part of this "corporate approach," consolidating technical collection and maintaining a separate identity from the organizations it supported.[42]

According to Loch Johnson, the Aspin-Brown Commission and the IC21 recommendations were stifled by the DoD and its "congressional allies" who feared the proposals would weaken the DoD. The leadership of the oversight committees, Senator Arlen Specter and Congressman Combest, sought a revolution in intelligence by establishing a truly independent Intelligence Community. The revolution did not occur, but evolutionary change did take place. The NDAA of 1997 established the National Imagery and Mapping Agency, consolidating the DoD's Defense Mapping Agency, the Central Imagery Office, and other DoD imagery elements with the National Photographic Intelligence Center and other CIA imagery elements. When President Clinton signed the NDAA on September 23, 1996,[43] the five-year debate on how to consolidate imagery finally concluded. The United States now had a centralized imagery intelligence organization, and the DoD had a more effective combat support agency for enabling military operations, once again highlighting that support to military operations was the Intelligence Community's first priority.

The CIA under Attack and the Arrival of John Deutch

The HPSCI IC21 hearings witness list encompassed an impressive array of individuals drawn from both the government and the private sector, including seven of the past ten DCIs stretching back to 1966. The tenures of the testifying former DCIs had been tumultuous, with many serving in the 1970s, when the existence of the Intelligence Community, in particular the CIA, was questioned. Richard Helms, James Schlesinger, and William Colby had been DCI during the Nixon years and were affected by the Family Jewels disclosure. Schlesinger had ordered the investigation of the Family Jewels; Colby had released these documents to Congress; and Helms had pled guilty to misleading Congress based on evidence that surfaced within them. Stansfield Turner became DCI shortly after the release of the Church Committee Report and the leaking of the Pike Committee Report. Turner's teetotaler and moralizing personality alienated many in the clandestine service, and his direct assault on their colleagues did not win him any allies. Judge William Webster took over the CIA following the death of Bill Casey and the Iran-Contra scandal, when some top CIA leaders were being prosecuted. Webster came to the job as DCI after Bob Gates, Reagan's first choice, became a casualty to Iran-Contra, and Webster's appointment was intended to signify a cleanup of the agency. These DCIs served at the helm of the CIA during some of its darkest days.

The testimonies of the former DCIs depicted an Intelligence Community that was in defilade against outside attack in the 1990s. Victory in the Cold War should have brought ticker-tape parades and speeches but instead brought questioning of existence, reduced budgets, and second-guessing. As is often the case with the passage of time, the end of the Cold War erased much of the memory of the existential threat the Soviet Union once posed. The fear that brought about the domino theory and the Red Scare was replaced with a belief that the world was moving inextricably toward democracy.

Bill Colby, the quintessential Cold Warrior whose death near his southern Maryland home less than a year after he testified was as mysterious as his career, warned against erring like their post–World War I and World War II predecessors.[44] As Colby pointed out, the confluence of the end of the Cold War, the uncovering of CIA agent turned KGB mole Aldrich Ames, and questions over the character of American assets had resulted in a cacophony of voices encouraging changes ranging from budget reductions to the closing of the CIA. Although the Intelligence Community had already been reduced between 15 and 17 percent since 1990, individuals such as Senator Pat Moynihan (D–NY) argued that the end of the Cold War should result in the end of the agency. A writer, professor, and former ambassador to the United Nations, Moynihan proposed legislation to dissolve the CIA in 1991 and again in 1995.[45]

Introducing his legislation, Moynihan argued that the CIA had contributed little to victory in the Cold War and claimed that the CIA's analysis on the fall of the Soviet Union was inaccurate. Although his position was on the extreme edge of the spectrum, the recent capture of Soviet spy Aldrich Ames threw additional fuel on the fire and provided CIA detractors more ammunition. The Ames case prompted criticism of the CIA from the chairs of both the HPSCI and the SSCI and put the agency on the defensive. As Michael Sulick, former director of the NCS, details in his book *American Spies: Espionage against the United States from the Cold War to the Present*, SSCI chairman Senator Dennis DeConcini (D–AZ) actually conducted a jailhouse interview of Ames.[46] Although it is understandable that the SSCI chair wanted to learn from an espionage case, DeConcini asking Ames his opinion of Moynihan's legislation and the CIA's management practices went a little too far.[47] The Ames case, controversy over the funding for the NRO building, and a less than ideal relationship with President Clinton resulted in DCI Woolsey's departure from the CIA in January 1995, the same month Moynihan introduced his legislation.[48] *Amen*

John Deutch, the man Clinton picked to replace Woolsey, did not instill confidence or reassure the CIA workforce about their future. Before Deutch even arrived at the CIA, he was telling Congress that he was going to "redesign" the DO "from the ground up" to prepare it for "operations in the current times." His call to "change the culture" of the DO before he was even confirmed to sit behind the DCI's seventh-floor desk alienated many in the CIA who had served in intelligence for years.[49]

Deutch came to the CIA from the DoD, where he had served as the deputy secretary of defense and had developed a preference for the uniformed services. He believed the CIA's most important mission was supporting military operations and argued that the roughly 90 percent of the intelligence budget that the DoD already received was not enough. Deutch told Loch Johnson, the noted intelligence expert, that "the [Intelligence] [C]ommunity's effort is really to support military operations, to be ready to tell a commander: 'We know where the Iraqi position is' . . . submarines . . . a lot of very valuable stuff. . . . What a huge difference that can make. In Bosnia, providing technical and human intelligence has worked great. . . . It prevents casualties."[50] Although Deutch's sentiments echoed other calls for increased intelligence support to military operations, as the head of the CIA Deutch had a responsibility to balance the agency's military and policy maker support requirements and, most importantly, to maintain its independence. It appeared that if it were up to Deutch, the CIA would become another combat support agency, similar to the NSA or the National Geospatial Intelligence Agency (NGA), thus depriving the nation of its only independent intelligence organization.

During his first all-hands inside the CIA's auditorium, known as the "Bubble," Deutch tried to convince CIA leaders that he had "harbored a secret desire to be the Director of Central Intelligence," but they knew he did not plan to be at the CIA for long and hoped to depart to lead his beloved DoD.[51] It was bad enough that CIA employees knew that Deutch considered the CIA directorship a rest stop on his journey to becoming secretary of defense, but the new CIA executive director Nora Slatkin's stated doubt that CIA officers were as good as military officers was even worse.[52] Slatkin, who had served as an assistant secretary of the navy, was not the only one who had made the move with Deutch from the Pentagon. Deutch also brought over former deputy assistant secretary for intelligence Keith Hall to replace Rich Haver as the executive director for community affairs and Brigadier General Michael Hagee as his personal assistant.[53]

The attention Deutch placed on the military went beyond installing DoD colleagues in positions of power in the CIA. Understanding the increasing importance of operational support to the military, Deutch moved the associate DDO/MA out of the DO and created the position of associate DCI for military support.[54] This meant a flag officer responsible for ensuring the DoD/CIA partnership would report directly to the DCI and not through the DDO.[55] It also meant an increase in rank from a two-star billet to a three-star billet. After 9/11, the CIA consolidated the associate DCI for military support and the OMA into the office of the ADMA.[56]

To fill the associate DCI for military support position, Deutch brought over Rear Admiral Dennis Blair. Blair, who had retired from the military as the Pacific Command CINC, was a navy surface warfare officer and Rhodes scholar. In 2009, President Barack Obama selected Blair to replace Vice Admiral (ret.) Mike McConnell as DNI. Blair's tenure as DNI lasted less than two years, but that was long enough for him to bump heads with DCIA Leon Panetta over who should select the senior intelligence officer in each country.[57]

On March 22, 1995, about a month before Deutch arrived at Langley, New Jersey representative Robert Torricelli (D) sent President Clinton and the *New York Times* a letter accusing the CIA of involvement in the murders of Michael Devine, an American citizen, and Efrain Bamaca Velasquez, a Guatemalan leftist guerrilla and husband of Jennifer Hardbury, an American citizen. In the letter, Torricelli, then a member of the HPSCI, identified

Guatemalan army colonel Julio Roberto Alpirez as a CIA asset and accused him of murdering the two men. Making public this information violated Torricelli's responsibility as a member of the HPSCI and was investigated by a House Ethics Committee. Although Torricelli was not punished because the committee said the rules governing classified material were not clear and subsequently clarified them, it said that Torricelli would have been "guilty" under the clarified rules.[58]

Devine and his wife, who was also an American citizen, lived in Guatemala for nearly three decades running a restaurant in Poptun and a hotel nearby.[59] In June 1990, a group of Guatemalan officers detained Devine for questioning, and his decapitated body was later found next to his vehicle along a rural highway not too far from his home. Bamaca, also known by the nom de guerre "Commander Everardo," was a leader of a leftist guerrilla group battling the Guatemalan government when he disappeared following a firefight in March 1992. Initial reports claiming he committed suicide on the battlefield to avoid capture were later found to be false. Bamaca had been captured by Guatemalan forces, held in captivity, tortured for a period, and then killed.

Admiral Bill Studeman, the highly respected navy intelligence officer, had been serving as the acting DCI for about three months when he walked into an ambush on April 5, 1995.[60] The open SSCI hearing that spring day on the CIA's "alleged improprieties" in Guatemala included testimony from the widows of Bamaca and Devine and brought the debate over the character of CIA assets to the forefront. Subsequent investigations by the CIA's inspector general and Clinton's Presidential Intelligence Advisory Board determined that evidence against Colonel Alpirez was "unreliable" and that there was "no indication that U.S. government officials were involved in or had prior knowledge of the death, torture or disappearance of U.S. or Guatemalan citizens." The Advisory Board report did find that "credible allegations" of CIA assets committing human rights abuses required the CIA to reconsider its relationship with these individuals and to determine if the benefit of this relationship outweighed the potential costs.[61] Ignorant of HUMINT but wanting to send a message, Deutch alienated himself even more from the CIA workforce when on September 27, 1995, he fired two DO officers, demoted a third, and gave twenty-three others letters of reprimand for the handling of the Alpirez case.[62]

Deutch, who lacked intelligence experience, assumed leadership of the CIA between the SSCI Guatemala hearing and the release of the CIA inspector general's and Presidential Intelligence Advisory Board's reports. Deutch's ignorance of HUMINT operations became apparent shortly after his arrival when he started asking questions about safe houses and asset pay. These simple questions led to in-depth discussions regarding the character of CIA assets and what type of agents the CIA recruited.[63] Deutch eventually implemented the "Torricelli Rule," which restricted the CIA's recruitment of suspected human rights violators and criminals.[64] He also ordered a review of current CIA asset files and required justification for retaining any assets of questionable character. With Deutch already ordering the termination of one of the CIA's best assets based on human rights accusations, many believed that arguing to retain others was futile. The wisdom of Deutch's policy was later questioned, especially after the September 11, 2001, attacks highlighted a shortfall in CIA HUMINT assets within terrorist organizations.[65]

Controversy surrounding the CIA did not stop with the Ames spy case or the Guatemala allegations. On November 15, 1996, Deutch found himself being skewered during a town hall meeting in Los Angeles while responding to allegations that the CIA had ignored its Contra allies' involvement in introducing crack cocaine to Los Angeles. A *San Jose Mercury* article described how a South Los Angeles drug dealer had purchased cocaine from Nicaraguan drug dealers and the Nicaraguans had then used the proceeds to help fund the Contras. Although congressional and CIA inspector general investigations found the allegations false, many continued to believe that the CIA had played a role in fueling the crack cocaine epidemic. Fortunately for the CIA, Deutch's tenure was short-lived; a month after he spoke in Los Angeles, Deutch resigned as DCI.[66] As the CIA was being raked over the coals regarding its assets' human rights records, crack cocaine allegations, and spy cases, and as funding reductions were forcing it to close overseas stations, ongoing military operations were testing the DoD/CIA partnership.

Building a Partnership during Operations

During his Senate confirmation hearing in February 1993, DCI nominee James Woolsey quipped, "Our two surrounding oceans don't isolate us anymore. Yes, we have slain a large dragon, but we live now in a jungle filled with a bewildering variety of poisonous snakes. And in many ways, the dragon was easier to keep track of."[67] The CIA and the military were no longer chasing the Soviets or preparing to meet them on the plains of Europe; they were now trying to understand a confusing world while undergoing their own significant institutional downsizing and turmoil. Compounding this confusion were cuts in both personnel and budgets introduced during the George H. W. Bush administration and incorporated during President Clinton's tenure.[68] Despite declining budgets from 1990 to 1996 and mainly "flat budgets" from

1996 to 2000, the Intelligence Community still had to satiate the increasing intelligence appetite of multiplying consumers who were trying to come to terms with a post-Soviet environment and America's role in this world.[69]

Many pundits and experts thought the collapse of communism in eastern Europe signaled irrepressible progress toward a liberal democratic world, but the splintering of existing orders instead highlighted a tumultuous and unpredictable environment. In response to this splintering, the United States conducted various peacekeeping and humanitarian operations in the Balkans and Africa. Whereas the Desert Storm critiques centered on the Intelligence Community's analytical support to the combatant commander and BDA discrepancies, the post–Desert Storm expectations to provide Intelligence Community support down to the individual troops on the ground required more operational integration between CIA and DoD elements at the tactical level. It was one thing for the CIA to increase its analytical support to the military during infrequent major combat operations, but supporting numerous reoccurring MOOTW and establishing the necessary intelligence networks to generate the local knowledge that many peacekeeping and humanitarian conflicts required levied a significant tax on CIA resources during a period when they were already being reduced. It is one thing to provide a commander with an order of battle or intelligence on a country's infrastructure to inform major combat operations, but it is quite another to establish the asset networks necessary to provide atmospheric intelligence on the varied communities and competing interests that are often present within peacekeeping operations.

The number of MOOTW and reduced budgets forced the CIA to "surge" personnel to support military operations.[70] Although "surging" is often necessary, it becomes problematic for an organization dependent on engaging in long-term relationships to spot and develop individuals with access to information. Beyond the policy maker versus military support trade-off, the CIA required access and time to meet policy makers' increasing expectations to provide the intelligence needed to support the military at the operational and tactical levels, an extensive commitment many military commanders and policy makers' did not appreciate.[71] Despite these disadvantages, the CIA and DoD worked together during a period of austere budgets and personnel drawdowns to improve their relationship during operations.

In the late 1970s, Somalia became part of the Cold War surrogate conflict when the Soviet Union shifted support away from Somalian president Siad Barre and toward his Ethiopian enemy. In response, Barre sought assistance from the Carter administration, which was concerned about Soviet influence in North Africa and the Middle East.[72] The United States signed an agreement with Barre in 1980 to gain access to military installations in Somalia. The US-Somalia relationship deteriorated over time as the Cold War moved toward its conclusion and Barre became more despotic. In early 1991, the ten-year multitribal insurgency finally resulted in Barre's overthrow, and a civil war ensued.[73] By 1992, multiple clans were fighting for power, and a functioning government did not exist when the United Nations stepped in to ensure aid made it to Somalia's population. The United States initially did not have a large role in the mission, but this soon changed after President George H. W Bush, with pressure from Congress, decided that the United States was indispensable to the mission.[74]

On December 4, 1992, President Bush announced to the American people his decision to deploy roughly 25,000 US forces into Somalia in support of United Nations' operations. Within a week, the initial wave of US troops started arriving in Somalia as part of Operation Restore Hope. Commanding the American forces in Somalia was Lieutenant General Robert Johnston, commander of the First Marine Expeditionary Forces at Camp Pendleton, California. The Scots-born Johnston had come to the United States at eighteen and joined the marines after graduating from San Diego State University. An experienced officer, Johnston had been one of the first marines sent into Lebanon by General Bernard Rogers, supreme Allied commander Europe, to serve as part of a liaison team to Ambassador Philip Habib in August 1982. He subsequently commanded a battalion landing team as part of the American contingent to the MNF mission in Lebanon.[75] During Desert Storm, Johnston served as General Schwarzkopf's chief of staff at CENTCOM.[76]

From the beginning, CIA officers worked side by side with their DoD colleagues in support of military operations in Somalia. In addition to deploying as part of the National Intelligence Support Team that was providing Lieutenant General Johnston "national level, all-source intelligence support from throughout the Intelligence Community," the CIA DO deployed a group of officers to conduct intelligence preparation of the battlefield in support of follow-on forces.[77] On December 23, 1992, one of the CIA officers paid the ultimate sacrifice while conducting intelligence support to military operations.

Larry Freedman, a retired army special operations sergeant major, had served in Vietnam and been part of the mission to rescue hostages from the US embassy in Tehran in 1980. Freedman, who had enlisted in the army after a stint at Kansas State University, was part of a four-man team "conducting work for a humanitarian aid mission" around Bardera, Somalia, a town about 284 miles east of Mogadishu. During the mission, the vehicle Freedman and his three colleagues were riding in struck a land mine, which killed Freedman and injured the other officers.[78] The world was not initially told that the first US casualty in Somalia was a CIA officer, and Freedman's true affiliation was not known until Ted Gup wrote about it in *The Book of Honor: The Secret Lives and Deaths of CIA Officers* (2001). Although the world did not yet know about Freedman's sacrifice or his true affiliation, Lieutenant General Johnston knew and wrote Freedman's family a condolence letter that acknowledged the sacrifices Freedman had made in support of the Somalia mission.[79]

In March 1993, the United Nations decided to transition the mission in Somalia from a peacekeeping operation to a nation-building operation. To build Somalia's institutions, advisers in the Clinton administration believed it was necessary to remove impediments to development, such as clan leader Mohammed Aideed. Tasked with apprehending General Aideed was a special operations element known as Joint Task Force Ranger led by Major General William Garrison.[80] On October 3, 1993, Joint Task Force Ranger's attempt to capture Aideed resulted in some of the bloodiest one-day fighting American troops had experienced since Vietnam. That day, eighteen American troops died during the fighting, and the disturbing image of American troops being dragged through the streets of Mogadishu was seared into America's collective conscious.

The tragedy of Somalia is well known, but the collaboration between the DoD and the CIA in the Somalia mission is less known. Despite a lack of HUMINT sources, the CIA integrated its operations with Garrison's command as best it could. An SASC after-action review concluded, "Intelligence support to Joint Task Force Ranger was a major effort and demonstrated a high degree of cooperation and pooling of efforts by the several agencies involved. HUMINT was expected to be and proved the most difficult aspect of this effort. It did not succeed in locating Aideed but did locate his lieutenants."[81]

Colonel Jerry Boykin, the commander for Combat Applications Group (Airborne), was one of the military officers who voiced concern over HUMINT support in Somalia.[82] A career special forces officer, Boykin was in the Iranian Desert preparing to rescue the American hostages when the US aircraft collided, causing the mission to be aborted. Boykin, who had also served in Grenada and Panama, rose through the ranks before serving as the deputy USD for intelligence and then retiring as a lieutenant general.[83] During the Senate review of Joint Task Force Ranger, Boykin stated, "We don't have a good HUMINT program, certainly not for crisis or unanticipated situations,"[84] a telling comment for someone who as deputy USD for intelligence was involved in a controversial Pentagon program to build a separate DoD clandestine HUMINT capability under Secretary of Defense Rumsfeld. Although Boykin's opinion might have reflected reality somewhat, it ignored the long-term investment that is required to establish HUMINT assets and the significant resource constraints in developing networks that would be available if a crisis arose anywhere in the world. Boykin might not have enjoyed all the HUMINT resources he desired, but it was financially infeasible for the CIA or even the DoD to establish HUMINT networks throughout the world in anticipation that a mission *might* occur in some distant location that was not previously a priority.[85] In March 1994, five months after the tragic day recounted by author Mark Bowden in *Black Hawk Down* (1999), the American military mission in Somalia ended; at least temporarily.

During the same period that Somalia was spiraling out of control, Yugoslavia was fracturing into ethnic pieces. The multiple ethnic identities that Josip Tito had been able to hold together finally fell apart in 1991, a decade after his death. Against the wishes of the international community, which preferred stability in Yugoslavia, Slovenia, and Croatia, these nations declared their independence, and conflict quickly ensued. Slovenia was able to secure its independence after a relatively short war; Croatia was not as fortunate. Yugoslavia's Serbian president, Slobodan Milosevic, was not willing to part with Croatia so easily because it possessed a significant Serbian population.[86] Then in March 1992, Milosevic's and Serbia's attention shifted to Bosnia as the Bosnians declared independence from Yugoslavia.

Two months after Bosnia declared independence and before US troops hit the ground, DCI Gates and Deputy DCI Studeman established the Interagency Balkans Task Force to "centralize and coordinate collection and sanctions monitoring," while also "coordinating general military intelligence support to US policy and contingency planning and tactical intelligence support." The organization was led by a senior CIA analyst, with a senior DIA official as his deputy, and consisted of individuals from the CIA, the DIA, and the NSA. The Balkans Task Force eventually became the "longest-running" CIA task force at the time and evolved to include two deputies, one "a senior member of the JCS military intelligence" and the other a "CIA officer."[87]

In December 1995, the United Nations authorized NATO to conduct military operations to ensure enforcement of the Dayton Peace Accords, which had established a "cease-fire" between Bosnia, Croatia, and Yugoslavia (Serbia). As in Operation Enduring Hope in Somalia, Operation Joint Endeavor highlighted the evolving DoD/CIA relationship following Desert Storm.[88] The Intelligence Community once again committed to support military operations, a standard practice since Desert Storm. But in this case the DoD/CIA partnership went well beyond the standard practice and included a "unified integrated HUMINT Service" involving elements from the CIA

DO and the DIA DHS whose purpose was to synchronize HUMINT collection to meet the commanders' operational and force-protection needs. This unified CIA/DIA element operated out of an office in Tuzla, coordinating HUMINT collection efforts on force-protection requirements and atmospheric information such as identity and backgrounds on various leaders and the plans and intentions of the different groups. This type of unified organization was abnormal in the DoD/CIA partnership, but PDD-35 dictated that the CIA push its capability to the tactical level in support of military commanders. Twelve years earlier, following the marine barracks bombing in Beirut, the CIA had been blamed for failing to provide adequate force-protection intelligence. Only a month after Joint Endeavor began, a CIA officer was being credited with collecting information on minefield-emplacement procedures, likely saving lives of American and coalition forces.[89] Although the CIA's support of the operational commander appeared a tactical success, there is little doubt that increased tactical support resulted in reduced strategic intelligence collection.

The Clinton administration has been blamed for narrowly focusing on Bosnia in the Dayton Peace Accords while neglecting other issues in the region. Most notably, the accords neglected Kosovo, which some believed was Milosevic's biggest prize.[90] Richard Holbrooke, the lead negotiator for the Dayton Peace Accords, and Carl Bildt, the prime minister of Sweden and the European Union's top envoy at Dayton, argued that a peace accord was unachievable if Kosovo were part of the discussion. Believing that some degree of peace in the Balkans was a better option than chasing an unachievable yet preferable peace throughout the region, the negotiators temporarily set aside the Kosovo issue.[91]

Although American diplomats promised to deal with the Kosovo issue, some ethnic Albanians became impatient with the peaceful approach of the Democratic League of Kosovo, the leading voice for ethnic Albanians in Kosovo. In response to this frustration and determined to take action into their own hands, these ethnic Albanians in Kosovo started initiating attacks on Serbian targets in early 1996. Following up on these attacks, a little-known organization called the Kosovo Liberation Army declared a "guerrilla war" against "Serbian oppression." Hoping for a peaceful resolution to the conflict, the United States continued to encourage dialogue between Ibrahim Rugova, the Democratic League leader, and Slobodan Milosevic, but increased repressiveness by Milosevic made constructive dialogue difficult.[92] After numerous failed attempts to halt Serb actions in Kosovo, NATO undertook a seventy-eight-day bombing campaign, unleashing more than "14,000 strike missions" on "targets in Kosovo and Serbia."[93] This action, coupled with the threat of a ground invasion, resulted in the withdrawal of Serbian forces and the arrival of NATO's Kosovo Forces as part of Operation Joint Guardian.[94]

CIA support to military operations in Kosovo began with Operation Allied Force, the seventy-eight-day bombing campaign, and went well beyond its support for previous bombing campaigns. Its support for those earlier bombing campaigns had focused on the "strategic and planning level, such as analytical judgments on the kinds of targets that are the most important." During Operation Allied Force, however, its support went clear down to the tactical level, issuing targeting packages on "specific installations or buildings."[95] Instead of focusing at the national level, elements within the CIA were acting like an air intelligence unit, feeding information to drive the bombing operations. The CIA's support continued into Operation Joint Guardian, where it was part of the National Intelligence Support Team that deployed in support of military operations.

Although the CIA's involvement in the tactical target-nomination process was in line with PDD-35 guidance, this increased involvement did not come without incident. On May 7, 1999, NATO forces accidentally bombed the Chinese embassy in Belgrade when CIA misidentified the embassy building as the Yugoslav Federal Directorate for Supply and Procurement. Although Undersecretary of State Thomas Pickering proclaimed the incident "an error compounded by errors," some of these errors were directly related to the CIA becoming involved in a typically military target-nominating process without the requisite knowledge on how to accurately determine bombing locations and absent established targeting procedures and proper databases. Six weeks after the incident, DCI George Tenet explained to the HPSCI that although the CIA was taking measures to ensure a similar incident did not occur in the future, he pointed out that the "episode is unusual because the CIA does not normally assemble, on its own, target nomination packages containing the coordinates of specific installations or buildings." With both the executive and legislative branches pushing for increased CIA support to the military, the CIA's involvement in targeting and other tactical support to the military had inevitably increased.[96]

The use of unmanned aerial vehicles also started to gain more prominence during operations in Bosnia and Kosovo. Although both the CIA and the military had been testing drone technology for years, during Bosnia and Kosovo they worked together to train and deploy pilots to use drones to collect intelligence. The use of drones, especially by the CIA, was controversial, some fearing that this new technology would pull money away from traditional intelligence collection methods, in particular HUMINT.[97] Nevertheless, the Balkans marked the beginning of an operational use for drones that expanded exponentially after 9/11. It also brought the CIA further into tactical operations. Less than a decade later, a President's Foreign Intelligence Advisory Board member visiting the CIA for an organized tour stood in amazement as drones took center stage in the presentation. He left wondering if the CIA had been pushed too far to the tactical level at the cost of its national mission and support to policy makers.[98]

The integration of military operations with national intelligence at the tactical, operational, and strategic levels was even more remarkable when one considers that this integration occurred within multinational operations in the Balkans. Understanding that support to the military in multinational operations involved providing intelligence support to allies, the DCI had a task force develop procedures that ensured US and allied militaries received the necessary intelligence while at the same time protecting CIA sources and methods.[99] The interaction between the CIA and special operations also increased in the Balkans with SOF ground teams working closely with CIA officers.[100]

In 1991, the congressional committees reviewing intelligence support to military operations during Desert Storm probably had conventional war in mind; by 1995, the concept of "military operations" had significantly expanded to include MOOTW.[101] Although the term *phase zero: shaping* did not enter the military lexicon for another decade, the definition of MOOTW included military operations during peacetime to keep "tensions between nations below the threshold of armed conflict and maintain US influence in foreign lands."[102] The expanded definition of military operations, captured in the National Military Strategy of 1995, which articulated a "peacetime engagement," and the expectation of intelligence support to the military placed a considerable burden on the CIA.[103] The CIA could no longer temporarily surge officers from one area to focus on supporting military operations during war; the military was now conducting peacetime operations and depended on intelligence support. So despite reduced defense and intelligence budgets, the DoD and CIA continued to work together to develop new partnerships and procedures to meet these operational needs.

In 1998, President Clinton and Speaker of the House Newt Gingrich worked together to form another commission focused on how US national security institutions should transform in the post–Cold War world.[104] The US Commission on National Security in the 21st Century (Hart-Rudman Commission) began its work in October 1998. Cochaired by former senators Warren Rudman (R–NH) and Gary Hart (D–CO), the commission was composed of fourteen former government officials, business leaders, and media professionals, all with impressive national security credentials.

Whereas the Aspin-Brown Commission had focused on how the Intelligence Community had to transform to meet the post–Cold War requirements, the Hart-Rudman Commission sought to "redefine national security" in a post–Cold War environment.

The Hart-Rudman Commission pursued a bottom-up approach broken down into three phases: "understanding" the world, developing a strategy to respond to that world, and then adapting the national security structure to execute the strategy. During its two and a half years of existence, the commission produced three reports, each focused on one of the three phases. In its phase I report, it described a world that was becoming increasingly linked through rapid technology and whose economies were growing dependent on each other. The economic interconnectedness forced the United States and other "advanced countries" to become involved in the struggles of smaller, weaker states based on the fear that internal state failure would result in security threats to their interests. This involvement tested the notion of state sovereignty that had served as the foundation for the nation-state construct since the Treaty of Westphalia in 1648. This new world environment not only shaped the global role of the United States but also challenged the Intelligence Community with nontraditional threats. The commission further argued that many of these challenges, such as terrorism, would soon threaten the US homeland.[105]

Armed with a better appreciation of the world, the Hart-Rudman Commission transitioned to phase II. In April 2000, it published its phase II report, *Seeking a National Strategy: A Concert for Preserving Security and Promoting Freedom.* The report introduced six objectives the United States should pursue to protect and advanced its interests:

1. Defend the U.S. and ensure that it is safe from the dangers of a new era.
2. Maintain America's social cohesion, economic competitiveness, technological ingenuity, and military strength.
3. Assist the integration of key major powers, especially China, Russia, and India, into the mainstream of the emerging international system.
4. Promote, with others, the dynamism of the new global economy and improve the effectiveness of international institutions and international law.
5. Adapt U.S. alliances and other regional mechanisms to a new era in which America's partners seek greater autonomy and responsibility.
6. Help the international community tame the disintegrative forces spawned by an era of change.[106]

When the commission identified US strategic interests and objectives, it transitioned to phase III, which focused on building the "structure and processes" needed to pursue phase II objectives. Whereas phase I was descriptive and phase II spoke in broad strategic terms, phase III was critical of the US national security structure and prescribed specific changes necessary to prepare the United States for the dynamic world. The commission argued that the DoD was too large and inefficient and so recommended a 20–25 percent infrastructure reduction to streamline operations and make it more agile.

Unlike other post–Cold War commissions, the Hart-Rudman Commission did not mention a lack of intelligence support to military operations. In fact, it argued that a more dynamic world as well as reduced resources, concerns over terrorism, proliferation of nuclear weapons, "ethnic conflicts[,] and humanitarian emergencies" had "led to a focus on providing warning and crisis management, rather than on long-term analysis." The commission argued, "The results of these three developments is an intelligence community that is more demand-driven than it was two decades ago. That demand is also more driven by military consumers and therefore, what the Intelligence Community is doing is narrow and more short-term that it was two decades ago."[107] The commission further argued that long-term analysis of "important regions" had been ignored because of this short-term focus. This perspective is especially interesting because it was legislative and executive decisions over the previous decade that had deliberately pushed the Intelligence Community toward supporting the military consumer at the cost of neglecting the policy maker. To remedy this problem and to strengthen the link between strategy and intelligence, the commission recommended having the NSC set the national intelligence priorities.

The Hart-Rudman Commission also challenged the legacy of DCI Deutch and Senator Torricelli regarding HUMINT assets accused of human rights abuses. Arguing the importance of HUMINT collection for counterterrorism efforts and acknowledging that those with access to terrorist plans and intentions "are not liable to be model citizens of spotless virtue," it recommended reconsidering the restrictive guidelines emplaced by Deutch. The commission valued human rights but understood that Deutch and Torricelli's actions had significantly restricted the CIA's DO, potentially setting back US counterterrorism efforts.[108] Commission members were not the only ones voicing concern over Deutch and Torricelli's actions. Around the same period, the congressionally mandated National Commission on Terrorism argued that the human rights standards instituted in 1995 had "delayed vigorous efforts to recruit potentially useful informants" and recommended a

Director of Central Intelligence Directive stating that the "1995 guidelines will no longer apply to recruiting terrorist informants."[109] Unfortunately, the "Torricelli Rule" had already done damage to US counterterrorism efforts, and although it might be difficult to link the rule to counterterrorism intelligence shortfalls leading to 9/11, the rule certainly did not help.

The Hart-Rudman Commission's final report was released less than two weeks after President George W. Bush's inauguration, when the new administration was trying to find its footing. This timing, coupled with the absence of an event to compel policy maker actions, resulted in the Hart-Rudman Commission, like the Aspin-Brown before it, not leading to significant legislation.

As congressional committees were acknowledging improvements in intelligence support to military operations, the Aspin-Brown Commission and the Hart-Rudman Commission were raising concerns about military support consuming CIA resources and attention—a concern not limited to government commissions but also cited by influential former national security professionals, academics, and business leaders. A Council on Foreign Relations Task Force report in 1996 raised "concern about the influence over intelligence policy exerted by the Defense Department and defense-related concerns. There is a danger that spending on intelligence to support military operations will take priority over other important or even vital national security ends in which intelligence is needed."[110] Georgetown University's *Checklist for the Future of Intelligence,* a report intended to inform the Aspin-Brown Commission's work, argued that the commission should not "make recommendations that would excessively skew the focus of U.S. intelligence gathering toward purely military needs."[111] This discussion would have been useful over the previous five years, when congressional reviews and executive action were continually pushing national intelligence agencies, in particular the CIA, to focus their efforts on supporting the military.

While debates over the future of national security institutions were occurring on Capitol Hill, within commissions, and at policy and academic institutions, the CIA and the DoD were operating together in peacekeeping and nation-building operations. Although policy maker pronouncements highlighted the need for integrated DoD/CIA operations and structural changes displayed DoD/CIA willingness to adapt, operations were required to solidify the relationship. During the 1990s, peacekeeping and humanitarian operations provided a small-scale venue for the DoD/CIA relationship building. The decade looming on the horizon would bring a "global war" and two large-scale operations that would consume the focus of the national security establishment, while providing a shared mission focus that had been absent since the end of the Cold War. This experience would further solidify the DoD/CIA relationship but would also increase concern that the CIA and other elements within the Intelligence Community were becoming subordinated to the DoD.

6

A NEW ADMINISTRATION

Toward the end of Clinton's second term, concern started to build that the United States had cut too much bone from its defense and intelligence capabilities while at the same time deploying military forces more often than expected following victory in the Cold War. Uniformed military leadership argued that this increased operational tempo affected the military's ability to wage two midsize wars simultaneously, a standard introduced by Colin Powell and Dick Cheney in the last years of the George H. W. Bush administration.[1] With the budget balanced and the economy stronger than it had been in the past three decades, some argued it was time to reinvest the peace dividend in US national security organizations.

Although national security spending drastically increased after 9/11, the Clinton administration had already made modest increases in national security spending prior to leaving office, altering a reduction course that had begun in the late 1980s. Clinton's final budget included a roughly 3.8 percent increase in defense spending, the first "real" defense increase since Desert Storm but less than some in Congress desired.[2] Around this same period, the CIA started to enlarge a workforce that had not experienced growth in more than a decade. The number of CIA employment offers rose by more than 50 percent in 1998–1999, an important increase for an organization that had reduced the number of case officers worldwide in 1995 to the same number of officers cut by Stansfield Turner in the late 1970s.[3] Although this increased CIA capability was welcomed, it takes time to train and deploy case officers and years before their efforts at recruiting assets and developing networks bear fruit. This increased spending would continue, albeit at different levels and toward different programs, no matter who won the presidential election of 2000.

Campaign 2000

Al Gore entered the campaign in 2000 with high expectations that the Democratic Party could secure a third consecutive term. With President Clinton's second-term approval rating at greater than 60 percent and strong confidence in the economy, Gore entered the final days of the campaign slightly ahead of Texas governor George Bush, scion of the forty-first president.[4] On election night, the contest was closer than anyone expected, and so the selection of the forty-third president did not occur for more than a month after the election. On January 6, 2000, Congress certified George W. Bush the winner after one of the most contentious and drawn-out elections in American history.

During the campaign, both Bush's and Gore's platforms called for increased national security spending, but how each proposed allocating resources and employing the military was quite different. The Bush campaign argued for increased spending on missile defense, quality of life, military readiness, and research and development. Gore argued for increasing military pay while continuing to build a military that was flexible enough to execute his "forward-engagement" doctrine. Embracing elements of the Powell Doctrine, Bush argued that US forces should deploy only when "strategic" interests were at stake. These "strategic" interests did not include most of the humanitarian and peacekeeping missions that had occurred during the Clinton administration. Candidate Bush claimed he would not deploy US forces absent definable and achievable military objectives and an "exit plan" if things were to go awry.[5]

Gore criticized Bush for adopting a narrow perspective, focused largely on China and Russia, while ignoring America's responsibility to enforce peace and shepherd the world toward greater democracy, peace, and prosperity. Gore's campaign articulated a concept of "forward engagement," which included "trying to disrupt terrorist networks, even before they are ready to attack." Embracing a less-conventional approach with a limited missile-defense capability, Gore argued for developing a military force that could face unconventional threats "that do not respect national borders." His stance also called for "efforts to expand the rule of law, fight corruption, and improve democratic governance."[6]

In stark contrast to many of the arguments put forward for maintaining Iraq deployments circa 2006, Ari Fleischer, Bush's campaign spokesman and future White House press secretary, argued in 2000 that "the role of the United States military is not to be all things to all people. Governor Bush does not support an open-ended commitment to keep our troops as peacekeepers in the Balkans." Condoleezza Rice, the future national security adviser and secretary of state criticized Gore's "vision of an indefinite U.S. military deployment," arguing "that if he is elected, America's military will continue to be overdeployed, harming morale and re-enlistment rates, weakening our military's core mission."[7] The Bush administration fulfilled its promise to increase military pay and improve quality of life on installations, but it also surpassed the deployment rates of the Clinton years.

The 9/11 attacks and failures of conventional force to introduce democracy in Iraq, however, led President Bush to embrace a use of force consisting of elements more akin to Gore's platform than to his own. The president, who as a candidate had argued that the United States could not be the world's policeman, issued a National Strategy for Combating Terrorism in 2006 that called for "advancing effective democracies" and "eliminating physical safehavens."[8]

The Boys Are Back in Town . . . and Considering Intelligence Reform

Many of the top officials within the new Bush administration in the winter of 2001 had served with each other previously. Secretary of Defense Donald Rumsfeld had been a mentor to Vice President Richard Cheney, bringing him into the Office of Economic Opportunity during the Nixon administration when Cheney was a twenty-eight-year-old PhD student at the University of Wisconsin. A few years later Rumsfeld, then Gerald Ford's chief of staff, brought Cheney into the inner circle as his deputy chief of staff. Cheney subsequently became Ford's chief of staff when Rumsfeld replaced James Schlesinger as secretary of defense. These musical chairs made Rumsfeld the youngest secretary of defense and Cheney the youngest chief of staff in US history.

The Rumsfeld–Cheney connection was not the only relationship that extended back to previous administrations. Colin Powell, the new secretary of state, had served as the chairman of the JCS when Cheney was secretary of defense. Paul Wolfowitz, Rumsfeld's deputy in the DoD, had served with Secretary of State Powell and Powell's deputy, Richard Armitage, in the DoD during the Reagan administration. As James Mann points out in his book *The Rise of the Vulcans,* these relationships went beyond the top tier of the new administration and included many of their influential deputies and advisers.[9]

As secretary of defense in 1989, Cheney had plucked Rich Haver, a career navy intelligence professional, from a job as deputy of naval intelligence to serve as his intelligence adviser. After Desert Storm, Cheney made Haver the point man in reviewing intelligence performance during the war and the lead for intelligence reform efforts. A few days after the election in 2000, while the debate over the Florida ballots raged on, Vice President Dick Cheney once again turned to Rich Haver, this time asking him to lead the intelligence transition for the Bush team.

Haver had left government in 1999, when he departed the National Intelligence Council for a senior position within the defense industry. Soon after his conversation with the vice president elect in late 2000, Haver took a short trip from his northern Virginia home to Tysons Corner, a defense industry mecca at the junction of Route 123 and Leesburg Pike, less than fifteen miles from the White House. Over the years, Tysons Corner had transformed from a sleepy pastoral area into an important national security corridor into Washington, DC. On his first day working for his second Bush administration, Haver arrived at a nondescript three-story office building to meet with Dick Cheney and receive his marching orders.[10]

According to Haver, Cheney was interested in gaining an appreciation of how intelligence had evolved since he was secretary of defense in 1991 and told Haver to query the DCI and the congressional oversight committees' leadership about their interaction with Secretary of Defense William Cohen and President Clinton. He also asked Haver to find out what had happened to the intelligence budget for 1994–1999 that the previous Bush administration had left behind. In Haver's view, there was a limited relationship between many of the individuals responsible for guiding, directing, and overseeing intelligence during the Clinton administration. Haver said he confirmed that the intelligence budget left behind by the first Bush administration had been reduced significantly and told Cheney that the Clinton administration "had underfunded national intelligence by tens of billions of dollars."[11]

Vice President Cheney's experience in the executive and legislative branches had convinced him of the importance of intelligence. He had served as Ford's deputy chief of staff and then as chief of staff during the Church and Pike Committee hearings in the 1970s. Although he saw value in some of the hearings' findings, he also believed they were "sensational" and marked the unfortunate beginning of congressional usurpation of presidential power in foreign policy. As a congressman, Cheney had served on the HPSCI, personally observing CIA support to the Afghanistan mujahedeen during the Soviet occupation and gaining intimate knowledge of the Intelligence Community. When he became George H. W. Bush's secretary of defense, he "wanted to spend significant time on intelligence" and took a lead role in intelligence reform efforts following Desert Storm.[12] Now as vice president, Cheney once again prioritized intelligence, and his efforts were partially responsible for a second President Bush tackling intelligence reform early in his administration.

Shortly after Bush named Donald Rumsfeld his nominee for secretary of defense, Haver received an invite from Rumsfeld to dine at the Four Seasons in Georgetown, Rumsfeld's favorite haunt whenever he was in Washington, DC. Arriving late to dinner that evening, Rumsfeld apologized, explaining he had been meeting with Armitage, the administration's lead for the DoD transition. When asked if the meeting went well, Rumsfeld told Haver that he and Armitage had agreed the Pentagon was not big enough for both of them—Armitage ended up working for Powell at State.[13]

As Rumsfeld and Haver sat alone in a dim-lit room near the back of the restaurant ("a scene out of a movie," as Haver described it), Rumsfeld informed Haver that he was going to be his intelligence adviser. Away from government merely a year, Haver responded, "I already did that job for Cheney. Why do I want to do the same job again?" Rumsfeld retorted, "Look who you are talking to. Why do I want to do the same job again?" After a little more back-and-forth, Rumsfeld told Haver he was determined to reinvest in intelligence after years of neglect and highlighted three priorities: (1) "pump money back into the intelligence activity . . . but into the right places"; (2) fix the requirements process; and (3) establish an ASD for intelligence.[14] That evening, Rumsfeld made it clear to Haver that he had big plans for the Pentagon and wanted to give Haver the opportunity to finish the intelligence reform he had started ten years earlier. Haver's temporary job as the Cheney–Bush lead for intelligence had just evolved into a more permanent position within the administration.

Just as John Deutch's had arrived at the CIA in 1995, Rumsfeld stormed into the Pentagon criticizing its culture, alienating its leaders, and promising significant change. Rumsfeld argued that the DoD was a "bloated bureaucracy" and a "relic of the Cold War" that needed to transition to meet the demands of the changing world.[15] He looked to streamline the department's notoriously burdensome acquisition processes and to reduce what he viewed as bloated military staffs. Most importantly, he wanted to regain civilian control over the DoD, control he argued had been relinquished during the Clinton administration. Although Rumsfeld's pursuit of building a nimble organization capable of responding to unforeseen challenges was admirable, many of the reforms he pursued were not as novel as he portrayed.

His pursuit of streamlining the DoD's bureaucracy had been sought for years and had been part of Gore's NPR reinventing-government program. Rumsfeld's description of a stagnant DoD that had failed to evolve after the Cold War was not completely accurate, as Eric Shinseki's reform efforts under way in the army demonstrated.[16] Nor was Rumsfeld's capabilities-based approach as revolutionary as the Defense Planning Guidance of 2001 might lead one to believe, with the decade-long Revolution in Military Affairs already focusing in that direction. Despite the continuity between previous reform efforts and Rumsfeld's, his reform effort was contested as much for his approach as for its content. Instead of building a team, he created division.

Rumsfeld is truly a paradox. A man who gave his subordinates a copy of Thomas Schelling's foreword to Roberta Wohlstetter's book *Pearl Harbor: Warning and Decision*,[17] encouraging them to challenge their thinking, then created an environment that discouraged dissent. A man who circumvented the traditional military chain of command but would not tolerate being circumvented.[18] Many in the uniformed military did not appreciate these contradictions. Nor did these leaders, who had experienced significant turmoil in the 1990s, appreciate Rumsfeld's bluntness or arrogance. They agreed with the new secretary of defense that defense funding had to increase and that some reform was needed, but they did not appreciate him ignoring their views and depending largely on his civilian leadership for advice. Although traditionally loyal to the chain of command, the military leaders had given decades of their lives to the institution and expected reciprocity. Leaders such as the chairman of the JCS, General Hugh Shelton, had served in Vietnam and had survived the post-Vietnam military. Now Rumsfeld, returning to the Pentagon more than two decades after he had left an institution then suffering in the aftermath of Vietnam, was criticizing their leadership and neglecting their counsel.[19] Even though Rumsfeld's government background and business acumen brought some good ideas to the Pentagon, his confrontational approach sullied relationships he needed to realize transformative change.

During questioning in his confirmation hearings, Rumsfeld told the SASC that intelligence was his biggest concern, describing it as one issue that kept him up at night and identifying the improvement of intelligence as one of his top-five goals. He argued that the United States needed better intelligence to "know more about what people think and how they behave and how their behavior can be altered and what the capabilities are in this world." During his testimony, Rumsfeld not only focused on improving DoD intelligence capabilities but also declared his commitment to work with the DCI to establish "a strong spirit of cooperation between the DoD and the rest of the Intelligence Community."[20]

Once confirmed as secretary of defense, Rumsfeld did not waste any time tackling intelligence and initiated reform efforts only a month after assuming office, when on February 23, 2001, he sent Haver a paper titled "Visualizing the Intelligence System of 2025." The target of the document was wider than just DoD intelligence, focusing on developing "a new vision of intelligence, gathering, and utilization" for the United States. The document described characteristics of the post–Cold War environment, arguing that the current US intelligence system was "less than optimal in the face of new conditions and new requirements." The paper concluded by arguing for "a broad based working group or commission to review the collective needs of the National Command Authority and examine the potential and long-term requirements of both American security and American leadership and then propose a system that could meet those needs."[21] Rumsfeld's call to review US intelligence capabilities in a post–Cold War world was at least the fifth review in the past decade. Although his call appears innocuous, his actions to gain greater control of national intelligence capabilities following September 11, 2001, raises questions regarding whether his review was an initial attempt to expand DoD influence over national intelligence.

During the Ford administration, one of Rumsfeld's early intelligence initiatives had been to gain greater control of the DoD's intelligence bureaucracy. Despite responsibility for roughly 80 percent of US intelligence capabilities, the DoD did not have a point person dedicated to intelligence issues within the Pentagon. As Ford's secretary of defense from 1975 to 1977, Rumsfeld appointed an ASD for intelligence, a position established by Melvin Laird, Nixon's first secretary of defense, in 1971 upon the recommendation of a Blue Ribbon Defense Panel. In 1976, Rumsfeld also dual-hatted the ASD for intelligence as the DMI, giving the ASD for intelligence "line authority" over the majority of defense intelligence resources.[22] This change had essentially created an intelligence czar within the DoD that Rumsfeld could count on to lead DoD intelligence, to manage resources across entities, and to serve as a point of contact for intelligence issues.

Despite the importance Rumsfeld gave to this position, its existence was short-lived. Harold Brown, Carter's secretary of defense, had consolidated the ASD for intelligence position and the director of telecommunications and command-and-control systems into the new position of ASD for command, control, and communications.[23] By the time Rumsfeld returned to the Pentagon, intelligence shared an ASD's attention with two other important areas: command and communication. Rumsfeld's previous experience told him this had to change.

On May 9, 2001, President Bush issued *National Security Presidential Directive 5: Intelligence* to determine how the Intelligence Community had to evolve in the post–Cold War world, making him the third president to focus government efforts on reforming the Intelligence Community for the post–Cold War world. The directive ordered the DCI to establish "two separate panels," one comprising Intelligence Community professionals and the other comprising outside government leaders. These two panels would assess the intelligence needs of the United States and then recommend the structure and resources necessary to meet those needs.[24] The responsibility for chairing the internal committee was given to Joan Dempsey, a career intelligence professional who served as the deputy DCI for community management under George Tenet. DCI Tenet selected Brent Scowcroft, the retired lieutenant general and George H. W. Bush's national security adviser, to chair the external committee.[25] Unfortunately, tragedy struck, delaying the external committee's report and ending the internal committee's review.

7

9/11 AND THE GLOBAL
WAR ON TERRORISM

By September 2001, Donald Rumsfeld's popularity with the military was rapidly diminishing. A conservative institution whose officer corps self-identifies as Republican at a rate higher than the rest of the population, military officers overwhelmingly supported Bush during the election in 2000 and had high expectations for his administration.[1] Following a strained relationship with President Clinton, the military was looking forward to a change in the White House, particularly with candidate Bush promising pay increases and quality-of-life improvements for military personnel—campaign promises he initiated action on with *National Security Presidential Directive 2: Improving Military Quality of Life*, on February 15, 2001.[2] The military's honeymoon with the new administration ended a few months later, however, when Rumsfeld's alienation of the uniformed military leadership had some officers almost reminiscing about the good ol' days of the Clinton administration.[3]

Rumsfeld's approach not only frustrated his underlings but upset many within Congress. When some of his civilian deputies were circulating a proposal to cut the army by two divisions, bringing it down from ten to eight divisions, a bipartisan group of ninety-two members of Congress sent him a letter warning against this action.[4] Rumsfeld's actions and disregard for military leadership also caught the ire of retired flag officers, a powerful force in the defense community. Retired army general Gordon Sullivan, who had served as secretary of the army during the George H. W. Bush and Clinton administrations, publicly excoriated Rumsfeld for coming to "the easy, but erroneous conclusion that by spending hundreds of billions of dollars weaponizing space, developing a national missile defense, and buying long-range precision weapons, we can avoid the ugly realities of conflict,"[5] a statement that became all too relevant in the coming years.

The frustration with Rumsfeld culminated on September 10, 2001, when he castigated the Pentagon's bureaucracy and articulated his mission to liberate it from itself. Although he tried to distance the Pentagon's bureaucratic culture from the employees who labored within it, his messianic tone only reinforced his image as a patronizing curmudgeon. The next day tragedy struck, providing the secretary of defense an opportunity to transform from a cankerous influence in a peacetime Pentagon to a brave leader of a military at war. As Dale Herspring discusses in his book *Rumsfeld's Wars,* Donald Rumsfeld's unpopularity and the likelihood of his becoming the first cabinet member fired ended with the September 11, 2001, attacks.[6] The photo of Rumsfeld carrying the wounded out of the burning Pentagon and stories of him ignoring personal risk to assist with immediate response efforts seared within America's collective mind the image of a fearless leader unwilling to back down. In the coming days, weeks, and months, his mannerisms during press conferences, which had been considered bombastic and irreverent before 9/11, were now considered decisive and assertive—qualities many sought after the terrorist attacks. The image of a man in charge was in stark contrast to what Rumsfeld perceived happening with regard to the DoD's initial role in Afghanistan.

On September 20, 2001, with fires smoldering at the Pentagon and the Twin Towers, President George W. Bush annunciated his vision for a "war on terror" that would "not end until every terrorist group of global reach has been found, stopped and defeated."[7] Days before Bush's speech, CIA, SOCOM, and CENTCOM personnel were conducting the initial planning for a US response. On September 13, 2001, CIA officers briefed the NSC on a plan to insert CIA teams with the Northern Alliance to pave the way for follow-on forces.[8] A week after Bush's speech, the first CIA teams entered Afghanistan.[9]

Rumsfeld was not happy that CIA officers were the first boots on the ground in Afghanistan and did not hide this frustration from his subordinates. On September 19, he called all the service intelligence chiefs and the directors of the DIA, the NSA, and the National Imagery and Mapping Agency to badger them for what he perceived as an intelligence failure—not that of 9/11, but that of the CIA beating DoD into Afghanistan. That day he charged the leaders of defense intelligence with finding new ways to advance DoD operations.[10]

Rumsfeld viewed the DoD and himself as the first among unequals and did not want to depend on another organization to enable his department's operations. Although the CIA had connections in Afghanistan and it was a logical plan to have the agency use these relationships to open the door for follow-on forces, Rumsfeld instead wanted the DoD to be in control of operations and self-sufficient. He constantly lectured his subordinates about ridding the DoD of its dependence on the CIA, comparing the DoD's relationship to the CIA to a baby bird hungrily resting in a nest waiting to be fed by its mother.[11] To make DoD independent, he had to go back to what gave him insomnia: intelligence.

In Senate hearings on his nomination as secretary of defense, Rumsfeld's description of his initial intelligence reform efforts embraced a community approach, focused not just on providing the military the necessary intelligence to develop plans and inform operations but also on creating an intelligence system that provided the United States a better understanding of adversaries' "attitudes and behaviors and motivations."[12] His stated goal of ensuring that the Intelligence Community would be designed to respond to the nation's needs was admirable, but it is unclear whether he was being nonparochial or if he was motivated by a desire to expand DoD influence. If his motivations were initially nonparochial, they shifted after he became frustrated with DoD's dependence on the CIA. At that point, his determination to build the Intelligence Community shifted toward building the DoD's own intelligence capability and achieving self-sufficiency. Rumsfeld was no longer as concerned with the broader Intelligence Community; he was now concerned that the DoD had the intelligence capability necessary to wage war and lead America's efforts in the GWOT.

DoD Counterterrorism Reform and Finalizing the Position of Undersecretary of Defense for Intelligence

On September 26, 2001, the same day CIA teams arrived in Afghanistan, Rumsfeld sent DCI George Tenet a new organizational concept that, if implemented, could help DoD reduce reliance on CIA. The Joint Intelligence Task Force–Counterterrorism (JITF-CT) was proposed by Vice Admiral Thomas Wilson, the DIA director who had previously served as the associate DCI for military support and before that as the J2 director for the JCS. The organization described in Wilson's proposal as "supporting a unified national campaign" would have given the DoD a lead role in counterterrorism efforts. The envisioned DoD organization would be the centerpiece of US counterterrorism efforts, with access to "all information" and the capability to "generate actionable intelligence to drive planning and operations," while also providing threat warning and assisting in diplomacy and policy development. Although led by the DoD, the proposed organization would have elements from the CIA, the FBI, the Department of State, the Treasury, the

Federal Aviation Administration, law enforcement agencies, allies (Canada, Great Britain, Israel), and other members of the undefined "coalition," which would operate out of DIA Headquarters at Bolling Air Force Base in Washington, DC, and other deployed locations.[13] The envisioned JITF-CT would place the DoD at the center of US counterterrorism efforts, possibly usurping authority and responsibility from the CIA and the FBI. Although a new concept that would have significantly expanded the DoD's role, the proposed JITF-CT in fact built upon an already established organization.

After the bombing of the USS *Cole* in October 2000, CENTCOM commander General Tommy Franks and his J2, Major General Keith Alexander, met with the chairman of the JCS, General Hugh Shelton and his J2, Rear Admiral Lowell Jacoby, at the army's Intelligence and Security Command Headquarters near Washington, DC. Franks and Alexander proposed placing CENTCOM in charge of the global counterterrorism mission for the DoD. Concerned with a regional combatant commander trying to gain a worldwide mission but aware that the DoD had to improve its counterterrorism efforts, Shelton asked Jacoby to devise a "counterproposal." Jacoby's counterproposal recommended keeping regional commanders responsible for counterterrorism within their areas of responsibility but establishing a "central repository" of terrorist threats and warnings to support these commanders.[14] Jacoby's argument was that the DoD required a "tailored warning down to the unit level" to identify potential attacks on US forces, and this requirement exceeded what the CIA's CTC could provide. A central repository would also ensure the dissemination of intelligence regarding potential attacks, where the planning occurred in one combatant command area of responsibility but targeted another combatant command's area of responsibility.

Supporting the proposal but not wanting to conflict with CIA operations, Shelton ran the recommendation past DCI Tenet and Cofer Black, the chief of the CIA's CTC. Tenet and Black confirmed that the CIA was unable to provide force-protection intelligence but was willing to support DoD efforts. The CIA sent the DoD "additional resources," and the DoD sent officers to work with the CIA. Prior to 9/11, this organization was not called JITF-CT and was structured to provide terrorist warning, not finished analysis. In 2002, the DoD established the JITF-CT, using Jacoby's earlier organization as a foundation, but the task force did not possess the responsibilities laid out in the proposal Rumsfeld sent Tenet. As of 2016, JITF-CT conducted analysis and assessments on threats to "DoD personnel, facilities, and interests" while also providing some analytical support to operations— important functions but not the center of the US counterterrorism effort.[15]

In the early days of the administration, prior to 9/11 and the JITF-CT proposal, Rumsfeld was looking to resurrect the ASD for intelligence position that had existed during his time in the Ford administration. To confirm the need for this position, Rumsfeld told Haver to "birddog" John Stenbit, the ASD for command, control, communications, and intelligence, to assess how much attention he focused on intelligence in relation to his other responsibilities (i.e., command, control, and communication). Rumsfeld personally liked Stenbit but did not see how, with such a demanding portfolio, Stenbit could dedicate enough time to intelligence. Rumsfeld wanted a senior leader dedicated to intelligence who could ensure that the defense intelligence needs of the president, the military services, the CIA, and other departments were met. With Haver confirming Rumsfeld's concerns that Stenbit was spending most of his time on command and control, the secretary of defense moved forward with the ASD for intelligence proposal.[16]

Secretary of Defense Rumsfeld was not the best at motivating subordinates or building organizational cohesion, but he was intelligent and politically astute, and he understood that DoD budget constraints were not an issue immediately after 9/11. In mid-September 2001, Rich Haver received a phone call from Larry De Rita, Rumsfeld's special assistant. De Rita told Haver that Rumsfeld wanted him to "bring down all that stuff on the ASD [for intelligence]; we are going to send it to the Hill as part of legislative initiatives." When Haver warned De Rita that "prep work" to inform Congress had not been done, De Rita responded that Rumsfeld "did not care"; he just wanted to get the concept before Congress for discussion. Over the next week, Haver and De Rita used the documents Haver compiled to "develop a legislative proposal." Congress discussed the ASD for intelligence proposal during the hectic days immediately following 9/11, but more pressing concerns captured their attention, and the proposal was set aside. That December, as Congress was preparing for the holiday season, Rumsfeld told Haver to prepare the ASD for intelligence packet for the next session. It was finally time to initiate reform.

Haver and Rumsfeld had just returned to the Pentagon from an ASD for intelligence discussion with the Intelligence and Security Command commander, Lieutenant General Keith Alexander, when Rumsfeld sensed Haver's reservations about the proposal. On the escalator back to the secretary of defense's office, Haver explained to Rumsfeld that he did not believe an assistant secretary possessed the authority or influence to oversee the vast defense intelligence structure. In the Office of Secretary of Defense, there are seventeen assistant secretaries and only five undersecretaries. Haver explained to

Rumsfeld that he "may or may not answer" a phone call from an assistant secretary, but he would return a phone call from an undersecretary "right away." Without hesitating, Rumsfeld told Haver to make the position being proposed an undersecretary.[17] On December 2, 2002, the National Defense Authorization Act of 2003 established the position of undersecretary of defense for intelligence.[18] In 2005, President Bush made the USD for intelligence the number three official within the DoD directly below the secretary of defense and the deputy secretary of defense, highlighting how much the administration valued intelligence support to operations. Based on his position, experience, and knowledge of the Intelligence Community, Rich Haver was the logical choice to become the first USD for intelligence, but this did not happen. Prior to his return to the Pentagon in 2001, Haver had told Cheney and Rumsfeld that he would serve in the administration for only two years, and he followed through on that assertion, leaving the administration in the summer of 2003 when he accepted an executive position with Northrup Gruman.

Instead of finding another intelligence professional to serve as the first USD for intelligence, Rumsfeld reached out to one of his closest aides, Stephen Cambone. Tenacious and stubborn, Cambone is a determined ideologue who in 2012 argued that the future will prove that the US invasion of Iraq was the "greatest decision of the century."[19] Cambone spent his early career moving between academia and government, and in 1998 Rumsfeld selected him to be his staff director for the Commission to Assess the Ballistic Missile Threat to the United States. Early in the Bush administration, Cambone gained a reputation as the secretary of defense's "henchman" for aggressively pursuing Rumsfeld's reform vision. Although no doubt intelligent, Cambone was probably selected for his loyalty and indefatigability, not for his expertise in intelligence.[20] Some perceived his appointment as USD for intelligence as an element of Rumsfeld's strategy to assert more authority over the Intelligence Community. It was more likely that Rumsfeld chose Cambone because he trusted him to implement his (Rumsfeld's) vision for building a self-sufficient DoD. Rumsfeld did not want to run the Intelligence Community, but he did want to increase the DoD's influence, independence, and role in the intelligence domain.[21] To assist Cambone, Rumsfeld selected an experienced special operator who proved to be as controversial and ideologically driven as both Cambone and Rumsfeld.

Lieutenant General Jerry Boykin, the career special operations officer who criticized HUMINT support for Joint Task Force Ranger in Somalia, where he served as the commander for Combat Applications Group (Airborne), was selected as the deputy USD for intelligence. Boykin's special operations experience and his time detailed to the CIA must have made him an attractive candidate to help achieve Rumsfeld's vision for increasing DoD's HUMINT capability. According to Boykin, it was Rumsfeld's annoyance at the DoD's dependence on the CIA that led to the establishment of the USD for intelligence position.[22] Boykin and Cambone soon initiated a plan to sever that dependence, even if it meant a duplication of intelligence collection efforts, which Congress and the executive branch had been trying to eliminate for the past decade.

HUMINT Independence

In late 2004 and early 2005, controversy struck Rumsfeld's intelligence reform efforts when articles about the DoD's HUMINT activities started appearing in newspapers. According to the articles, Rumsfeld and his advisers had concluded that the secretary of defense possessed greater HUMINT authority than had previously been understood and wanted to build a capability to exploit this authority. The articles described a new HUMINT collection organization called the Strategic Support Branch (SSB) that was responsible for conducting clandestine operations throughout the world. According to the articles, the SSB was established because Rumsfeld was frustrated with CIA support to the DoD's operations and disagreed with Tenet on priorities.[23] The articles were not completely accurate, but they were accurate enough to raise concern within the legislative intelligence oversight committees.

In early 2002, Rumsfeld had his lawyers review the DoD's HUMINT collection authorities and subsequently pressured USD Cambone and his deputy, Boykin, to develop a better HUMINT capability.[24] Major General (ret.) Michael Ennis, then director of DoD HUMINT, said later that Rumsfeld "did not have any confidence in the DIA or DHS" because they "lacked money and were cautious not to trample on CIA's turf." So Cambone and Boykin instead worked through SOCOM to conduct the type of operations described in the newspaper articles. The always coy Rumsfeld was careful not to call the activities intelligence and instead referred to them as the work of the SSB.[25] Although the articles accurately described Rumsfeld's SSB, they mistakenly placed it under the direction and authority of Vice Admiral Jacoby and the DIA. The DIA was working on its own program to build DoD HUMINT capacity, but this program was focused on providing tactical intelligence support to the troops on the ground in Iraq and Afghanistan, something that was clearly the DoD's responsibility.[26]

The Defense HUMINT Management Office (DHMO), the DIA office

responsible for "deconflicting and enabling DoD HUMINT activities," was established in December 2004.[27] Ennis, a Marine Corps major general, was the first director of the DHMO, overseeing the rejuvenation of the military's tactical HUMINT capability. As a young infantry lieutenant, Ennis had been close friends with Lieutenant Jim Mattis, a fellow infantry officer. One day Ennis and Mattis were discussing whether Ennis should remain an infantry officer or become a foreign-area officer. After some discussion, Mattis said, "Mike, you do that [foreign-area officer] shit, and I will stay with infantry, and we will see where we are in twenty years." Thirty some years later, both were general officers at the top of their chosen career fields. Mattis rose to four stars and retired as the CENTCOM commander. Ennis spent his career as a foreign-area officer in Russia, as an intelligence officer serving at the USMLM in Potsdam, as the director of Marine Corps Intelligence, and as the first CIA deputy director for community HUMINT.

DoD's tactical HUMINT capability had been a casualty of the "peace dividend"; with the Cold War over and budgets being slashed, the military services had reduced their number of counterintelligence HUMINT collectors and interrogators to create space for other requirements. This proved to be a poor decision when battalions, brigades, and divisions found themselves in dire need of tactical HUMINT support in Afghanistan and Iraq. The tactical HUMINT these troops required was not the clandestine HUMINT collection Rumsfeld was trying to build with the SSB but more in line with the tactical counterintelligence and interrogator capability that had been "decimated" in the 1990s.[28] Commanders on the ground required HUMINT capabilities that could collect information on tactical threats to coalition forces and local atmospherics in their areas of operation, information that could often be attained without depleting the finite DHS clandestine-officer pool.

The tactical HUMINT shortfalls forced the army to pull HUMINT-trained officers from the DIA's DHS to support tactical units in Iraq and Afghanistan, even if these HUMINT officers possessed different skill sets, such as more advanced fieldcraft training, than what was required by commanders. This decision negatively affected the DIA's ability to conduct HUMINT operations, creating an additional problem for the military. To remedy this problem, Major General Ennis and his DHMO team looked for ways to expand the military's HUMINT-training capacity. The DHMO team started from scratch, without a training plan, course syllabus, or even a training location. Lieutenant Colonel Bridget Kimura, a reserve officer who worked for Ennis, was able to secure training facilities in South Central Texas. To quickly develop a training program, they adapted a CIA syllabus to fit their tactical needs, reducing the program of instruction from six months to three months. The tactical HUMINT teams operated on the battlefield and did not require the same level of training as CIA officers. The graduates of this course were part of the Strategic Support Teams (originally called Human Augmentation Teams) that deployed in support of tactical units in Iraq and Afghanistan.

The CIA and congressional committees were not concerned with the DIA's Strategic Support Teams because the latter were created to fill a tactical HUMINT gap within military units, something clearly a DoD responsibility. The DIA was also careful to discuss the concept with the legislative oversight committees and requested additional funding through Congress.[29] However, Cambone and Boykin did not discuss the SSB with Congress, and the SSB used "reprogrammed funds without explicit congressional authority or appropriation."[30] Congress was also concerned that the SSB could cause confusion in the field or risk an intelligence blowback if proper coordination did not occur. Tensions surfaced between the CIA and the DoD when such confusion was caused in the field, potentially putting operations at risk.

Congressional and newspaper inquiries discovered that the SSB was originally established in April 2002.[31] Two months later, in July 2002, Secretary of Defense Rumsfeld identified SOCOM as the lead in the global counterterrorism fight and gave it the authority to coordinate and wage the DoD's counterterrorism operations across the different Geographic Combatant Command territories.[32] This decision and the concept of "preemptive" action articulated in President Bush's West Point speech in June 2002 and codified in the National Security Strategy of 2002 not only were significant steps in expanding the DoD's role in foreign policy but also created conditions for the military to justify trespassing on CIA turf.[33] If the GWOT was truly global, then the DoD could argue that what appeared to be clandestine operations were merely preparation for future combat operations, or what the military calls "intelligence preparation of the battlefield," thus giving the US military the ability to operate globally without limitations.[34]

The CIA's chiefs of station are overall responsible for clandestine operations within nonwarzone countries and were angry about their lack of notification about DoD operations. During testimony before one of the Homeland Security and Government Affairs Committees, the director of the NCS, Jose 𝒱 Rodriguez contradicted earlier testimony from Cambone and SOCOM commander General Bryan Brown. Cambone and Brown told the committee there were no issues between the CIA and the DoD, but Rodriguez disagreed, telling the committee there was still inadequate coordination between the DoD and the CIA.[35] The failure to coordinate was a serious transgression that not only duplicated CIA efforts and ignored the CIA's role in coordinating overseas intelligence operations but also risked blowback in the countries where the DoD was conducting intelligence preparation of the battlefield. Neither Cambone nor Brown deserve blame for this failure because the guidance not to coordinate with the CIA came directly from Rumsfeld, who argued that the capability was the DoD's and thus there was no need to coordinate. Rumsfeld was determined to make the DoD self-sufficient, not the CIA's "baby bird" any longer.[36]

The two organizations eventually worked through their coordination issues, but congressional concern lingered. In the IAA of 2010, the HPSCI stated that the military often hid intelligence activities under the guise of operational preparation of the environment to avoid HPSCI and SSCI oversight.[37] HPSCI members argued that the potential damage these activities could cause was as great as the potential damage other clandestine intelligence activities under HPSCI's purview could cause, and so HPSCI should be briefed on these activities.[38]

The creation of the SSB was not Cambone and Rumsfeld's only attempt at usurping power and authority from the CIA. In a memo sent in September 2004, Cambone raised the question whether the DoD should take over the CIA's unconventional-warfare activities, offering an earlier CIA mission in Iraq as an example. That mission involved the CIA setting up a base in the mid-1990s to work with Saddam Hussein's opposition and to maintain a presence in the region. The mission was temporarily halted in 1996 after a controversy involving Ahmad Chalabi, founder of the Iraqi National Congress, and then was reestablished in the run-up to the Iraq War.[39] Cambone's memo went beyond this one mission and suggested stripping covert action from the CIA and "distribut[ing] the missions among various departments and agencies."[40] Cambone was not the first to raise concern about CIA covert action, but his criticism was not due to the effectiveness of covert action as a foreign-policy tool or the ease with which policy makers resorted to its use; his motivation was parochial.

Cambone's memo highlighted an ongoing debate in the national security community that became more relevant with the GWOT. The US government has conducted covert actions throughout its history, but that use has been a particularly controversial topic since the early 1970s.[41] In response to the CIA's alleged involvement in the overthrow of Chilean president Salvador Allende, Congress passed the Hughes-Ryan Amendment, limiting the executive branch's ability to conduct covert action by requiring a presidential finding for all such actions.[42] Subsequent controversies over covert action in

South America and the Middle East led to additional executive orders and legislation, further limiting its use without proper notification and oversight.

The coexistence of a covert-action arm within a clandestine foreign-intelligence collection agency has caused some friction since the CIA's founding. Both covert action and paramilitary operations are offensive in nature, looking to shape reality, whereas foreign-intelligence collection looks to understand the world as it is. DCI Richard Helms, who served in the OSS before embarking on a long career in the CIA, voiced concern with covert action being employed too often as the president's favored foreign-policy tool instead of lengthy diplomatic efforts. Despite these concerns, Helms understood that covert action was a necessary tool to have in the US arsenal and that retaining it within the CIA provided the compartmentalization and ease of deniability that covert actions require.[43] Although not always ideal, maintaining the covert-action mission within the organization responsible for foreign-intelligence collection was the best possible approach.

The United States Code Title 50 definition of "covert action" states that "traditional diplomatic or military activities or routine support to such activities" are not considered covert activities and do not require a presidential finding.[44] Although this distinction between traditional military activities and covert actions is understandable in print, it is more problematic in practice. In 1991, Congress clarified the definition of "traditional military activities" stating that they "include activities by military personnel under the direction and control of a United States military commander (whether or not the U.S. sponsorship of such activities is apparent or later to be acknowledged) preceding and related to hostilities which are either anticipated to involve U.S. military forces, or where such hostilities involving United States military forces are ongoing, and, where the fact of the U.S. role in the overall operation is apparent or to be acknowledged publicly."[45] Since 2001, even this expanded definition of what constitutes and does not constitute covert action has become problematic. The legal definition of covert action does not specify time horizons but merely states that the "role of the United States Government will not be apparent or acknowledged publicly."[46] Arguably, if the US military plans to acknowledge an activity publicly in the undefined future, that activity by definition is not a covert action.

The definition of covert action developed in 1991 was premised on a traditional nation-state military conflict within a limited and defined theater of war. Since 2001, however, the United States has been waging "war" against a global nonstate actor. Therefore, the military can posit that its "operational preparation of the environment" in the numerous countries where the identified terrorist organizations reside constitutes traditional military activity. In an interview in 2012, former SSCI chair Senator Pat Roberts (R–KA) stated that one of the specific tests of whether an activity is covert or not is if the activity will be acknowledged if it is revealed publicly. According to Senator Roberts, an activity is not covert if there is a willingness to acknowledge it if it is revealed publicly.[47] Although this definition of covert action appears to meet the letter of the law, it is debatable whether it completely meets the post–Church Committee spirit of the law. The discussion over the CIA retaining covert-action authority quieted down after Rumsfeld and Cambone left office.[48]

In 2012, USD for intelligence Michael Vickers, a former CIA case officer who had gained notoriety for the depiction of him in the film *Charlie Wilson's War* (Mike Nichols, 2007), and DIA director Michael Flynn, an army lieutenant general who had served as General Stanley McChrystal's J2 and helped develop the fusion concept that brought together intelligence capabilities in Iraq and Afghanistan, proposed establishing a Defense Clandestine Service (DCS) to correct shortfalls in DoD HUMINT.[49] The DCS idea garnered support from both the DoD and the CIA's NCS. The DoD looked at the DCS as increasing its ability to collect much-needed intelligence on global issues, and the NCS embraced the idea of more DoD HUMINT collectors available to collect intelligence to meet military commanders' requirements, thus freeing up the CIA to collect on strategic issues.[50] Military HUMINT collection requirements were taxing CIA capability, with one chief of station estimating that more than 75 percent of what was required of him was military driven and wondering when the military was going to collect against its own needs.[51] The DCS would also serve as an opportunity to break down the parochialism by introducing a greater number of DoD case officers who were "Farm" trained, thus furthering the interaction between the DoD and the CIA. The new DoD case officers would work closely with CIA stations abroad, thus ensuring deconfliction of clandestine collection activities, something that had not always occurred in the past, as exemplified by Rumsfeld's SSB initiative.[52]

Despite support from both the CIA and the DoD, the DCS concept met congressional resistance when the Defense Authorization Bill of 2013 halted its establishment, citing past career-management issues with DoD clandestine operatives.[53] According to former senior intelligence officials, Congress was not properly briefed on the DCS concept before the concept was publicly released, annoying Congress and resulting in its nonsupport.[54] Although the DCS was eventually established, it has not achieved the status or strength envisioned by Vickers and Flynn.[55]

Intelligence Community Reforms

Between November 2002 and March 2005, the US government conducted two significant commissions. The first, the National Commission on Terrorist Attacks upon the United States (9/11 Commission), was established to "investigate facts and circumstances relating to the terrorist attacks of September 11, 2001."[56] The 9/11 Commission conducted an exhaustive review, focused not only on the 9/11 attacks but also on the rise of bin Laden, the associated terrorism threat, and US actions against the threat. It concluded by recommending a "global strategy" and changes to the national security structure to ensure that the US government was organized to implement this strategy. Many of the recommendations were embraced by Congress and implemented in the Intelligence Reform and Terrorism Prevention Act (IRTPA) of 2004. The DNI position, which had been recommended by the Boren and McCurdy proposals in the 1990s, was established, as was the National Counterterrorism Center, to create a unity of effort against terrorism. Within the National Counterterrorism Center, the Directorate of Strategic Operational Planning was set up to "conduct strategic operational planning for counterterrorism activities, integrating all instruments of national power, including diplomatic, financial, military, intelligence, homeland security, and law enforcement activities within and among agencies."[57] This directorate was a much-needed organization to coordinate government planning, but planning was also an activity the DoD was more capable of conducting than other government agencies, thus necessitating an influential role for DoD in it.[58]

The IRTPA also mandated that the CIA and the DoD "develop joint procedures to be used by the DoD and the CIA to improve coordination and deconfliction of operations that involve elements of both the Armed Forces and the CIA consistent with national security and the protection of human intelligence sources and methods."[59] These coordination procedures were much needed during a period when Rumsfeld was trying to assert what he viewed was his expanded authority under US law to conduct intelligence operations in support of possible future military operations. As mentioned earlier, Rumsfeld directed operations that created significant tension between the DoD and the CIA.

The 9/11 Commission Report described the growing influence the military had over technical collection capabilities within the Intelligence Community following Desert Storm. Although it understood the military's grab for greater control and believed greater DoD control appropriate to support operations, the committee was concerned about the unintended consequence of the DCI losing control of these organizations.[60] The commission appreciated the military's need for intelligence but wanted a DNI who actually ran the Intelligence Community and possessed the ability to shift resources between all community members.

Although Rumsfeld's push for Intelligence Community reform prior to 9/11 appeared on its surface to be nonparochial, his stance after 9/11 was centered on what was in DoD's best interest. When congressional discussion started to arise about establishing a DNI position, Rumsfeld rallied his staff to prepare arguments about why this was a "bum idea." As the recommendation to establish a DNI gained traction and its establishment was certain, Rumsfeld switched his focus to weakening the position. He tried to distance himself from the broader Intelligence Community and discussions regarding intelligence failures, arguing that DoD capabilities should not be taken away just because the FBI and the CIA could not coordinate.[61] When Lieutenant General (ret.) James Clapper, the NGA director at the time, and General Mike Hayden, the NSA director, told Rumsfeld they supported their two agencies becoming independent from the DoD and placed under the DNI, he became visibly angry, telling them, "It is a terrible idea; I can't support it."[62] Rumsfeld wanted intelligence to support DoD efforts, but he also wanted to build DoD's intelligence capabilities separate from the Intelligence Community, as the establishment of the SSB highlighted. A line from James Joyce's novel *Ulysses* encapsulates Rumsfeld's opinion on intelligence capability: "What's yours is mine and what's mine is my own."[63] So much for a community.

The most significant change the 9/11 Commission recommended regarding the DoD/CIA relationship was removing the CIA's paramilitary capability and placing it under SOCOM to centralize the capability for operations and training.[64] The commission argued that it was not efficient for the United States to have two separate paramilitary organizations, one residing in the CIA and the other in DoD's SOCOM. Each of these government entities, the CIA and the DoD, should instead "concentrate on its comparative advantages in building capabilities for joint missions." The commission clearly placed the military in the lead for operations, arguing, "CIA experts should be integrated into the military's training, exercises, and planning. To quote a CIA official now serving in the field: 'one fight, one team.'"[65]

According to Senator Roberts, who was the SSCI chairman when the IRTPA was passed, the 9/11 Commission recommended placing all paramilitary in the DoD because commission members believed, despite the CIA's successful early Afghanistan operations, that "the CIA did not invest sufficiently in a robust paramilitary capability prior to 9/11, but instead relied on foreign proxies." Senator Roberts said later, in 2013, that the CIA had developed its paramilitary capabilities and had "made progress" in its coordination efforts with DoD during the period between the commission's investigation and the report's release. He "was comfortable" with the changes made and believed the new "procedures worked well to prevent conflict and duplication," which was Congress's main concern.[66] The paramilitary recommendation did not make it into the IRTPA, but the legislation mandated further operational "coordination and deconfliction" measures between DoD and CIA entities and agreement on the strategic objectives being pursued when the two were conducting joint operations. In 2005, President Bush ordered the CIA and the DoD to provide recommendations on whether paramilitary operations should be shifted to the DoD. In response, both the CIA and the DoD recommended that the CIA retain its paramilitary capabilities. Since receiving the CIA and DoD responses, Congress has shown little interest in revisiting this debate.[67]

The second commission, the Commission on the Intelligence Capabilities of the United States regarding Weapons of Mass Destruction (Silberman-Robb Commission), was meeting when the 9/11 Commission issued its report and when the IRTPA passed Congress. President Bush's Executive Order 13328 established the Silberman-Robb Commission on February 6, 2004, to "assess whether the Intelligence Community is sufficiently authorized, organized, equipped, trained, and resourced to identify and warn in a timely manner" against the WMD threat and "other related threats of the 21st Century."[68] On March 31, 2005, the Silberman-Robb Commission published a report that identified seventy-four recommendations for "improving the Intelligence Community."[69] After review of these recommendations by multiple "interagency expert panels," the president decided to pursue seventy of the recommended changes and have the Intelligence Community consider three of the remaining four before taking action. The final recommendation dealt with an expanded role for the military in covert action, which Bush decided not to pursue.[70]

The recommendations focused on strengthening the community foundation, a process that was first initiated with the IRTPA legislation that created the DNI. Regarding the DoD/CIA relationship, the most notable change was the creation of the National Clandestine Service within the CIA, which would be responsible "for coordination, deconfliction, and evaluation of clandestine HUMINT operations across the Intelligence Community." On its surface, the creation of the NCS appeared merely to be a name change for the CIA's DO. With the NCS, a CIA DO officer would see little change in his or her job responsibilities or how the CIA HUMINT arm operated. Change did occur, however, in the authority given to the DCIA to integrate and synchronize HUMINT operations across the Intelligence Community to reduce redundancy and better allocate community resources—all in an effort to improve HUMINT operations.[71]

Reforming Defense Initiative

A month after the Silberman-Robb Commission released its report, Stephen Cambone and DIA director Vice Admiral Jacoby testified before the SSCI on the DoD's Remodeling Defense Initiative (RDI). The RDI grew out of two earlier studies undertaken shortly after Cambone became the USD for intelligence. Similar to numerous post–Desert Storm reviews, the first study was initiated in 2004 to review what intelligence support the combatant commanders and others required on future battlefields. The second study focused on how to rebuild defense HUMINT after years of neglect and during two wars, when the military was in dire need of HUMINT support. These two studies provided the first two objectives for the RDI: to meet the needs of the combatant commanders and to build defense HUMINT. The final RDI objective focused on increasing jointness among the service intelligence organizations to ensure that combatant commanders' intelligence needs were met while also reducing unnecessary duplication.

The RDI initiative was fundamentally about making DoD intelligence a community and ensuring that this community was structured to best support the needs of the commanders in the field rather than focused solely on the requirements of individual military services. The RDI also sought increased operationalization of intelligence through the transformation of JICs into Joint Intelligence Operations Centers (JIOCs) and the introduction of intelligence campaign plans.

JICs were first established during Desert Storm to reduce the cost of intelligence support to combatant commanders.[72] The motivation to create JICs was driven by the fiscal environment, but increased jointness and the improved linking of intelligence to operations were results of their creation. The JIOC concept was Cambone's attempt to operationalize intelligence by theoretically increasing the linkages between operations and intelligence. Although the creation of the JIOCs sounded good to individuals unfamiliar with the workings of military operations, in reality the only thing that changed was the acronym. In a combatant command, the J3 director is responsible for short-term planning and execution of operations, whereas the J5 director is responsible for long-term planning. Intelligence (J2) personnel were already involved in planning efforts and were present within the J3's operation center. Operations are driven by the J3, but the JIOC was purely J2, so there was no increased operationalization of intelligence.[73]

Unlike the JIOC concept, the idea for intelligence campaign plans brought value to operationalization of intelligence because it encouraged a discussion with the commander on priorities for allocating finite intelligence capabilities. Understanding the priorities of all the combatant commanders allowed the DoD intelligence community, under the USD for intelligence, to shift intelligence resources as necessary and to inform the DNI on defense intelligence requirements for future budget requests and capability development.

The RDI also sought to identify the available intelligence collection capabilities and to ensure that the collection requirements went to the best-positioned capability. It established the DIA director as Strategic Command's "functional component commander" for intelligence, surveillance, and reconnaissance. The DIA director was responsible for parsing out the collection requirements to the asset (DoD or national intelligence) that was best positioned to collect on the requirement. Regarding HUMINT, the RDI looked to build upon the changes instituted with the establishment of DHMO in 2004. This meant increasing the military's HUMINT strength while also providing a centralized point for identifying intelligence collection requirements and "deconflicting and enabling DoD HUMINT activities." Similar to the intelligence, surveillance, and reconnaissance initiative, the RDI looked to bring together "DNI-directed HUMINT and [combatant commander]–requested or authorized activities in a seamless and mutually supporting manner."[74] In other words, the DoD wanted to ensure that DoD HUMINT and CIA HUMINT worked together to support commanders' collection requirements with the best-positioned asset. During his RDI briefing to the SASC on April 28, 2005, Cambone reiterated that the DoD was "ready and eager to help the DNI," but the briefing made it clear that the DoD's focus was building DoD capability.[75]

DoD/CIA during Operations

As intelligence reform was ongoing in this period, the CIA and the DoD were working together in Iraq and Afghanistan. The policy pronouncements and organizational changes made in the 1990s conditioned the environment for greater DoD/CIA interoperability.[76] Since Desert Storm, the CIA had increased its focus on support to military operations, and the evolving DoD/CIA relationship had been tested in small-scale operations. The military and the CIA became more familiar with each other during these operations, but the lack of a significant unifying threat to the United States kept the collaboration at low levels. Out of tragedy often grows common purpose: the terrorist attacks on the World Trade Center and the Pentagon gave the US national security apparatus a new focus and helped establish a common purpose for the CIA and the DoD.

The CIA/SOF partnership took off shortly after 9/11 when combined cross-functional teams supported the Northern Alliance's efforts to overthrow the Taliban.[77] Although these composite teams did not always agree and friction did occur, the DoD/CIA partnership strengthened out of a need to benefit from each other's capabilities.[78] The melding together of the DoD's military capabilities and the CIA's intelligence and paramilitary capabilities provided a good template for counterterrorism operations, which were increasing in importance for both organizations. Since 1986, the CIA's CTC had served as the leading intelligence organization focused on international terrorism.[79] Although SOCOM was created partially in response to terrorist attacks in the 1980s, its primary focus was low-intensity conflicts.[80] This focus changed after Rumsfeld identified SOCOM as the DoD's lead in the GWOT and gave it authority to coordinate and wage the DoD's counterterrorism fight across the different geographic combatant command territories. The elevation of SOCOM as the DoD counterterrorism lead helped formalize a relationship that had already grown out of necessity.

This relationship expanded further in Afghanistan under the leadership of General John Abizaid, the CENTCOM commander, and DCI George Tenet when they worked together to set up the Joint Interagency Task Force to drive counterterrorism operations in Afghanistan and Pakistan. As described in General Stanley McChrystal's autobiography, *My Share of the Task,* the Joint Interagency Task Force "would be a way to fuse the various intelligence agencies' specialties in order to better understand the enemy." It brought together the talent, expertise access, and capabilities of the CIA, the NSA, the FBI, the DIA, the NGA, and other agencies to execute counterterrorism operations in Pakistan and Afghanistan.[81] It also served as a good template for future interagency operations, demonstrating how multiple elements of national power could come together to wage war.

During the run-up to the Iraq War, the CIA/SOF partnership continued to grow. In the summer of 2002, CIA teams operating in Kurdistan and adjacent countries began introducing soldiers to Iraqis who could help convince Iraqi soldiers to surrender prior to conflict initiation. These CIA teams assisted with the preparation of the battlefield and military planning by developing relationships that enabled future operations and by providing intelligence to CENTCOM in support of planning efforts. At CENTCOM, the designated CIA lead in Iraq worked with General Tommy Franks and his staff during the preparation for war. In Iraq, the integration of DoD/CIA operations manifested both formally and informally. Formally, CIA officers were "feeding real-time information to the warfighters," and these fighters' locations were coordinated with military elements to protect against accidental fratricide.[82] Informally, military and CIA personnel on the ground were reaching out to each other and developing partnerships.

On April 5 and 7, 2003, Colonel David Perkins, commander of Second Brigade, Third Infantry Division, led "Thunder Runs" into Baghdad to disrupt the Iraqi defense and to "create as much chaos" as possible in the Iraqi capital.[83] In October 2012, Perkins recalled how a CIA officer arrived at his tactical operations center on the evening prior to his unit's assault into Baghdad. The CIA officer, who turned out to be the future Baghdad chief of station, asked if he could accompany Perkins into the capital city. Not only did Perkins agree, but upon arrival in Baghdad he and the CIA station chief also cooperated and supported each other's operations. Although unplanned, this encounter set a positive tone for future DoD/CIA interactions.[84]

The fortuitous interaction between Colonel Perkins and the CIA in the early days of Iraq mark the initial stages of a relationship between the CIA and conventional forces that was unparalleled in history. The CIA deployed numerous Crisis Operations Liaison Teams to the region in support of military forces. These teams worked closely with military partners, providing intelligence and linking military commanders with HUMINT and other CIA capabilities. In support of these operations, the CIA established the two largest stations since the Vietnam-era Saigon Station in Baghdad and Kabul.[85] Although not all the CIA's work in Afghanistan and Iraq focused on supporting military operations, a significant portion of it did. However, whereas the DoD/CIA partnership in Iraq and Afghanistan strengthened as the wars progressed, the one back in Washington, DC, was more tumultuous.

Rumsfeld's frustration with the DoD's inability to be operationally self-sufficient caused friction during the early days of the Afghanistan War, not only within the DoD but also between the DoD and the CIA. Rumsfeld had a good relationship with DCI Tenet, lunching with him weekly to discuss issues of common concern, but despite Rumsfeld's good professional relationship with the DCI, other CIA leaders viewed the secretary of defense the same way many of his subordinates did: as a stubborn leader with control issues.[86] Rumsfeld valued intelligence and had been one of the officials who had pushed for intelligence reform early on in the George W. Bush administration. Yet although he valued intelligence and was supportive of strengthening the CIA, he also wanted the DoD to have the central role in the GWOT: a strong CIA was good only as long as it did not appear to weaken or impede DoD operations and, more importantly, Rumsfeld's power.

Tension between the CIA and elements within Rumsfeld's Pentagon preceded the establishment of the USD for intelligence position and the Strategic Support Teams. Dissatisfied with the CIA's Iraq analysis, Douglas Feith, Rumsfeld's USD for policy, put together his own intelligence team to build a case against Saddam Hussein. Feith, an experienced lawyer, approached his newfound job as an intelligence analyst with the vigor of an attorney serving his client, not as a professional analyst searching for understanding. Ideologues such as Feith and his subordinates had advocated for Saddam's overthrow prior to 9/11 and so seized the tragedy on 9/11 as an opportunity to push their agenda.[87] Feith's policy-planning shop was using raw intelligence to build a case linking Saddam's regime to the 9/11 terrorists and then presenting their argument to Paul Wolfowitz, the deputy secretary of defense. Wolfowitz took this information and sent Vice Admiral Jacoby "snowflakes" (short memos) asking him to look into supposed connections between Saddam Hussein and the 9/11 terrorists. Jacoby and the rest of the Intelligence Community found no link between Saddam and 9/11, but this did not discourage Feith and his subordinates from prosecuting the case anyway.

In the summer of 2002, as the drumbeat for war with Iraq was intensifying, Jacoby, then acting DIA director, received a phone call from DCI Tenet telling him to "get your ass" to CIA Headquarters for a meeting the next day at 3:00 p.m. Tenet wanted Jacoby, the senior uniform intelligence officer, present for a briefing from members of Feith's policy-planning shop. Jacoby, still uncertain what the meeting was about, did what he was told and took his seat alongside a group of CIA officers that included deputy DCI John McLaughlin and CIA deputy director for intelligence Jamie Miscik. A short time later, two of Feith's subordinates, a navy lieutenant and a civilian, arrived announcing they were there to brief the CIA on a connection between Al Qaeda and Iraq. Not completely surprised because Wolfowitz and Feith had been pushing for the overthrow of Iraq even before 9/11, Jacoby considered the meeting "really goofy," and DCI Tenet must have considered it annoying. Tenet halted the meeting before the self-confidant lieutenant could show his slides and then promised to have people in the DCI's office review the documents and get back with Feith. Tenet escorted the visibly disappointed lieutenant and civilian to the door before telling his subordinates not to waste time chasing the policy-planning shop's ideologically driven fantasies.[88]

An Intelligence House Cleaning

Porter Goss, an eight-term Republican congressman from Florida who served as HPSCI chairman from 1997 to 2004, replaced George Tenet as DCI in 2004. Goss served as the last DCI and, following the establishment of the DNI in 2005, as the first DCIA. For Goss, who had served as a CIA case officer for about a decade in the 1960s, his return to Langley was somewhat of a homecoming. His experience as an intelligence officer, a member of the Aspin-Brown Commission, and head of the HPSCI gave him a diverse knowledge of intelligence, making him, at least on paper, an ideal candidate to lead the Intelligence Community. Two months after Goss became the DCI, President Bush told him to grow the clandestine service by 50 percent. With the president's support, Goss began to increase the number of operation officers and analysts to help wage the GWOT, a welcome development considering the increasing demand for CIA capability.[89] Yet, despite Goss's background and efforts to grow the agency, he quickly ran afoul of the CIA workforce.

Accompanying Goss to the CIA were a group of his HPSCI staffers pejoratively referred to as the "Gosslings." This imperious group of advisers wreaked havoc throughout the CIA and caused friction with some senior CIA officers. In November 2004, two months after Porter Goss became DCI, Stephen Kappes, the DDO, resigned after a confrontation with Goss's chief of staff, Patrick Murray. According to reports, Murray had castigated Mary Graham, the CIA's counterintelligence chief, for not stopping purported leaks about Goss's nominees for senior CIA positions. Angered by the treatment of one of his subordinates, Michael Sulick, the number two official in the CIA DO, confronted Murray about his behavior. Murray responded by telling Kappes to fire Sulick, but Sulick and Kappes resigned from the agency instead.

Murray's anger stemmed from the failed nomination of Michael Kostiw to serve as the CIA's executive director when it came to light that Kostiw had resigned from the CIA years earlier following an alleged shoplifting incident. Piling poor executive decision upon poor executive decision, and despite warnings from senior CIA officers, Goss then nominated Dusty Foggo, an officer within the CIA's Directorate of Support, to be the executive director. In 2006, Foggo was sentenced to thirty-seven months in prison on corruption and fraud charges for directing government contracts to a boyhood friend in return for gifts and financial rewards. Failing to make a lasting imprint on the CIA, Goss and the Gosslings departed Langley after a rocky nineteen months. Goss's successor not only brought Kappes and Sulick back to Langley but also promoted Kappes to the position of deputy director and Sulick to the position of NCS director.[90]

Air force general Michael Hayden, an experienced intelligence officer who had served as the director of the NSA and first deputy DNI, replaced Goss at the CIA. Hayden, a native of Pittsburg and graduate of Duquesne University, is a cerebral intelligence professional who is well liked by those he leads. His early actions, such as bringing back Stephen Kappes and Michael Sulick, were popular with the CIA workforce and helped rectify some of the mistakes his predecessor made. Although Hayden's status as an active-duty air force general caused some apprehension early on among those who feared a military takeover of national intelligence, his nonparochial style eased those concerns.

Goss's resignation in May 2006 was followed by the resignations of Donald Rumsfeld and Stephen Cambone in December 2006 and of DNI John Negroponte a month later. Negroponte was replaced by Michael McConnell, the former NSA director who was Powell's J2 during Desert Storm. Replacing Cambone was James Clapper, the retired air force lieutenant general who had served as the air force G2 during Desert Storm and then as the DIA director before retiring from the military in 1995. A few years into his retirement, Clapper returned to the Intelligence Community as the NGA director. To replace Rumsfeld, Bush asked former DCI and then president of Texas A&M University Robert Gates to be secretary of defense. Having served with Bush's father and unwilling to look the other way when his nation needed him, Gates reluctantly departed a position he loved to return to government service.[91] These four gentlemen knew each other well, and, unlike their predecessors except Goss, all brought an intelligence background to their new positions.

Gates arrived at the Pentagon preaching the importance of finding balance in US foreign policy between the DoD, the Intelligence Community, and the State Department. Encouraging greater State Department funding, Gates requested that funds transferred from the DoD to the State Department for certain activities, as stipulated in Section 1207 of the National Defense Authorization Act of 2006, be increased. Originally devised through collaboration between Secretary of Defense Rumsfeld and Secretary of State Condoleezza Rice to establish the State Department's Office of Reconstruction and Stabilization, Gates requested doubling Section 1207 funding to $200 million per year. Although the leader of the DoD, Gates was concerned with his department's influence over the Intelligence Community and with the militarization of foreign policy. In a speech given in July 2008, Gates stated, "As a career CIA officer I watched with some dismay the increasing dominance of the defense 800-pound gorilla in the intelligence arena over the years." He argued that "the lines separating war, peace, diplomacy, and development have become blurred" and that the US national security organizations had to appreciate the role each played individually and collectively.[92]

Early on in their new assignments, Gates, McConnell, and Clapper showed that they were going to bring a new collaborative approach to how the Intelligence Community operated. In his autobiography, *Duty*, Gates describes how he worked with McConnell, Clapper, and Hayden "to remedy the deficiencies of the 2004 Intelligence Reform Act and bring the Intelligence Community closer together."[93] One of their first actions made the USD for intelligence a leader in the Intelligence Community, not just in the DoD. This was a significant change that made the USD for intelligence subordinate not only to the secretary of defense but also to the DNI, thus giving the DNI a degree of authority and control that Rumsfeld sought to avoid. Rumsfeld had created the USD for intelligence position to organize and shield DoD intelligence efforts and wanted the position to remain independent of the Intelligence Community. In May 2007, Gates and McConnell went against Rumsfeld's vision when they agreed to dual-hat the USD for intelligence as the DNI's DMI. This new role strengthened the DNI's influence over the Intelligence Community and alleviated some of the concerns that the USD for intelligence would usurp control from the DNI.[94] As Gates points out, the personalities of these four gentlemen—McConnell, Clapper, Hayden, and Gates—allowed them to "mitigate otherwise intractable hostility" between the CIA, the DoD, and the Intelligence Community.[95] Much of this hostility was caused by the parochial approach taken by Rumsfeld and Cambone as well as by their and Goss's alienation of their own organizations. Gates, McConnell, Hayden, and Clapper initiated the long process of healing those wounds. The improvement of the DoD/CIA relationship in Washington was reinforced with an increasing partnership in the field, in which military leaders such as Generals David Petraeus and Stanley McChrystal worked closely with their CIA counterparts in Iraq and Afghanistan. Although mission requirements drove the DoD/CIA partnership, nonparochial officials from both organizations deserve credit for their actions. Personalities matter, and the tone of cooperation set by leaders in both Washington and in the warzones encouraged cooperation at lower levels.[96]

The increasingly operational DoD/CIA relationship was understandable because the US foreign-policy focus was being consumed by Iraq, Afghanistan, and the GWOT. The military lacked HUMINT collectors and depended on the CIA's significantly larger and better-trained HUMINT capability in Iraq and Afghanistan. Yet although the collaboration efforts between DoD and CIA leaders was commendable, the evolving DoD/CIA relationship did not come without cost. The CIA's increased focus on paramilitary actions and support to military operations hastened the agency's shift away from its traditional focus of support to policy makers—a shift that had been occurring since the early 1990s. This focus not only risked subordinating the CIA to military operations but also could result in the CIA becoming a twenty-first-century OSS, something Hayden warned incoming DCIA Petraeus about in 2011.[97]

During the election of 2008, candidate Barack Obama promised to "renew the American dream" by improving the economy, tackling poverty, and increasing access to health care. Similar to Bill Clinton's platform, Obama's platform was focused on domestic issues, but, unlike in 1992, the ongoing wars in Iraq and Afghanistan and the GWOT did not allow Obama to ignore national security issues. He promised to continue the intelligence reform initiated with the IRTPA and to better prepare the military for the type of conflicts it was conducting in the post-9/11 world. With a majority of Americans believing the invasion of Iraq a mistake and the Republican candidate for president John McCain arguing that "maybe 100 years" was the length of time the US military would be in Iraq, Obama won the election with nearly 53 percent of the popular vote.[98] Barack Obama was inaugurated as the forty-fourth president of the United States on January 20, 2009, and two months later he ended the GWOT and the long war. Although official documents no longer referred to a "global war on terrorism" or the "long war," the wars in Iraq and Afghanistan and America's counterterrorism operations nevertheless raged on.

8

EVERYTHING COMES WITH A COST

Improved Operations, Organizational Subordination, and Strategic Shortfalls

While the military has a role in the Intelligence Community, it would be a mistake to place our entire Intelligence Community or operation in the Department of Defense at a time when competition for world leadership is being increasingly defined in economic and social terms. Nor can the State Department be expected to totally meet the intelligence needs of our government. It is not equipped to provide the kinds of intelligence needed by our military services. Furthermore, the collection of raw intelligence is not always consistent with the process of diplomacy. For intelligence to be as objective as possible, the producers of intelligence should not be subordinate to any consumer agency, whether the State Department or Defense Department.
—Senator David Boren, interview, November 20, 2012

A lot of things are going to be neglected while you're providing military intelligence. Military Intelligence is important, but it is not the whole world.
—Lee Hamilton, former congressman and 9/11 Commission cochair, quoted in Loch K. Johnson, *Threat on the Horizon*

The relationship between central intelligence and the military was an issue even before the founding of the CIA and DoD through the National Security Act of 1947. The report produced by the Army Pearl Harbor Board specifically noted the requirement for an intelligence capability to "know as much about other major world powers as they know about us," while pointing out that this responsibility was not just the military's but "a national

151

problem."[1] To ensure the independence of the CIA, the National Security Act of 1947 required the DCI, even if a military officer, to sever chain-of-command and reporting connections to the DoD and the military services.[2] In 1949, the Eberstadt Report and the Dulles-Jackson-Correa Report recommended improving coordination within the Intelligence Community and the empowerment of the DCI but still supported the DCI's independence. These two reports also recommended the CIA remain the lead for both clandestine operations and covert action, a decision that was upheld in future reviews, although the Eberstadt Report argued that the JCS should assume responsibility for clandestine operations during war. The Dulles Report was so concerned with the militarization of the CIA that it questioned the "number of military personnel assigned" and argued that the "DCI should be a civilian."[3]

Despite six of the DCIs/DCIAs being active-duty flag officers, the CIA and the DoD have maintained separate and distinct cultures. The two organizations have operated together over the years, particularly during the Vietnam War, when they conducted pacification programs and paramilitary operations together, but at that time their cooperation never reached the degree it has since 9/11. In the Vietnam era, the CIA, the DoD, and other US agencies integrated activities as part of the Military Assistance Command Vietnam's Civil Operations and Rural Development Support program. Ostensibly subordinate to the former, the latter was built to support mutual pacification efforts, and the CIA played a significant role in developing, leading, and executing these programs.[4] Beginning in the 1990s and proliferating after 9/11, the CIA began not only to work with the DoD but also, pushed by policy makers, to adopt a supporting role during military operations. Although this role was never technically a subordinate relationship, PDD-35 and the numerous criticisms directed toward the CIA raised expectations that the CIA was available and responsive to commanders' needs.

Beginning in the 1980s, policy makers started pushing for increased intelligence support to military operations as well for improvement of how the military planned and conducted joint operations. The call for increased intelligence support to military operations was an important development because it reflected a subordination of national intelligence capabilities to military commanders during conflicts, something that had been recommended in the Eberstadt Report during periods of war but had never been implemented. Congress was now asking the CIA to conduct operations in support of force protection, military planning, and military operations, and not just during declared wars or as part of a collective interagency effort. It appeared that Congress expected the CIA to put its resources at the military commander's disposal rather than just mutually work toward national policy objectives. Although this change was significant, it was still manageable if military operations were viewed as temporary in nature, allowing the CIA and others to surge in support without shifting too much focus away from long-term analysis and support to policy makers. This level of support was problematic following September 11, 2001, when the United States entered a perpetual state of war.

In 1986, Congress passed the Goldwater-Nichols Department of Defense Reorganization Act, a law that weakened the military services' authority but improved how they conducted joint operations. In addition to softening the service parochialism, the legislation centralized authority within the DoD and established a planning structure that linked defense strategy and contingency planning with national security strategy. Centralizing DoD power under the concept of jointness also increased the influence of the joint regional combatant commanders, giving them a more significant role in US foreign policy. Although intelligence support to military operations and service interoperability had been mentioned as issues in previous after-action reviews, Goldwater-Nichols focused on service interoperability and did not resolve the intelligence support to operations deficiency. The invasion of Panama in 1989 confirmed that Goldwater-Nichols improved joint interoperability, but it also highlighted the fact that intelligence support remained an issue.

The congressional supporters of defense reform viewed increased intelligence support to military operations as part and parcel of the changes brought about by Goldwater-Nichols. With the military on the path to improved service interoperability, Congress now wanted to turn to "the civilian side of the coin" to improve interagency operations.[5] The Goldwater-Nichols legislation might have weakened service barriers that limited interoperability, but the military still required greater intelligence resources to support the planning and operations of the joint force. With the Cold War over and the White House and Congress pursuing reductions in spending and slashing redundancy, the expectation was that national intelligence capabilities had to increase the role of the Intelligence Community in military operations.

Embracing the call for improved national intelligence support to military operations, the CIA came together with its military intelligence brethren to serve the troops on the ground during Desert Storm in 1991. Despite this novel effort, criticism over intelligence support during the war subsequently surfaced in congressional testimony and on the front pages of the leading US newspapers. Wanting to improve support to the military and at the same time to get General Schwarzkopf and the pressure he brought to bear "off their back," CIA officials embraced changes.[6] These changes included the addition of a military flag officer and the establishment of an office that focused on improving the CIA's support to military operations. Even before these changes were fully implemented, however, the CIA was already sending officers and resources in support of military operations. Unlike its support in Vietnam, these CIA actions were focused largely on supporting the military commander and his operations, not on conducting unified, separate, or parallel operations.

In Somalia, the CIA deployed capability as part of the National Intelligence Support Team to the operational commander and a separate HUMINT team to conduct intelligence preparation of the battlefield, assuming a supporting role to the military in both cases. In Bosnia, the CIA once again deployed as part of the National Intelligence Support Team and became part of a HUMINT effort to ensure the commander's operational and force-protection needs were met. Back in Washington, the DCI established the Balkan Task Force, whose responsibility included tactical intelligence support to the military. In Kosovo, the CIA expanded its support to the military operations by becoming part of the air campaign's targeting effort, a role atypical of how CIA had operated in the past, subordinating the CIA to the military's needs.

The rise in importance of national intelligence support to military operations, which reached its pinnacle when President Clinton made it the top priority through PDD-35, paralleled the rise of the DoD's influence in foreign policy and its increasing role as America's favorite foreign-policy tool.[7] As the Cold War was ending, the DoD gradually shifted away from preparing for large-scale operations and toward low-intensity conflicts and peacekeeping operations. Believing that US military power was indispensable within the post–Cold War "New World Order," elected officials regularly turned to the DoD.

In 1994, the Clinton administration published its first National Security Strategy, which focused on the United States engaging globally in order to enlarge the number of its democratic allies throughout the world.[8] This engagement strategy became more assertive when the National Security Strategy of 1997 declared that the military and other elements of national power should be used to "shape the international environment."[9] Over time, this new policy of "shaping the environment" moved beyond broad strategy documents and became part of military doctrine and lexicon. In 2006, the DoD's *Joint Publication 3-0: Joint Operations* expanded its "phasing model" from four phases to six, incorporating "phase zero: shaping," which involved ongoing military operations "to enhance international legitimacy and gain multinational cooperation in support of defined military and national strategic objective(s)."[10] Although this phase was not yet formally written into doctrine in 1997, empowered combatant commanders were now engaged in ongoing shaping operations and planning efforts that required significant intelligence support to enable. This increased intelligence requirement was problematic for an Intelligence Community that was already dealing with significant capability cuts.

In the late 1990s, some policy makers and national security professionals became concerned that intelligence support to military operations had gone too far, weakening the long-term analysis required for strategy development and to support policy makers. Despite these concerns, no major changes to either the national intelligence organizations or its priorities were implemented. These concerns were forgotten after 9/11, as the United States shifted to global counterterrorism efforts and policy makers increasingly focused on tactical and operational actions. Instead of being as concerned with the position of the United States in relation to Russia, China, and other world powers, American policy makers became obsessed with defeating a nonstate actor and the tactics that actor employed. In pursuit of this objective, the CIA focused a significant amount of its resources on global counterterrorism efforts and in support of military operations in Iraq and Afghanistan.

As the CIA and the DoD were waging two wars, the US Intelligence Community was undergoing reform. The Intelligence Reform Terrorism Prevention Act of 2004 implemented recommendations that had preceded the 9/11 attacks, but a significant portion of the reform measures were focused on making the Intelligence Community better postured to identify terrorist threats and conduct operations to defeat them. The citizens of the United States do not yet know whether the IRTPA and other post-9/11 reforms are responsible for preventing domestic terrorist attacks, but it is safe to say that measures have improved interoperability among many agencies and departments, including the CIA and the DoD—but at what cost?

The evolution of the DoD/CIA relationship over the past twenty-five years is both encouraging and astounding, while at the same time reinforcing US foreign-policy trends that are disconcerting. Although there might be nuanced disagreement over why the relationship has improved, with some individuals pointing to Desert Storm and others to 9/11, there seems to be universal agreement among current and former senior leaders within both the DoD and the CIA that the relationship has never been better. Garry Reid, a former principal deputy ASD for special operations and low-intensity conflict and a former special operations soldier with more than twenty-eight years of service, stated in 2012 that "overall the relationship has never been stronger across the board."[11] The CIA sends representatives to dozens of military commands and professional military schools, and in 2012 DoD students made up 25 percent of the student population at the Farm.

Historians in the CIA's Center for the Study of Intelligence stated that interviews with CIA personnel highlight significant improvement in the CIA's relationship with other government organizations since 9/11. These improved partnerships have resulted in less parochialism and increased collaboration. Most important, the officers recognize the value of these partnerships and are now more receptive to engaging their interagency colleagues instead of operating alone. Even during periods when the structure has not completely evolved to enhance partnerships, officers find new and innovative ways to work around constraints.[12] Although these officers still understand and appreciate the difference in their two organizations' missions and cultures, they now view each other as indispensable members of the larger US national security profession.

Doug Wise, an experienced and respected intelligence leader and retired military officer who has been involved in some of America's most significant operations in the post–Cold War and post-9/11 period, compared today's DoD/CIA partnership to their relationship when he was a military liaison in the late 1980s and early 1990s. When he first arrived at the CIA, there were only a handful of liaison officers located at CIA Headquarters in Langley, Virginia. Today, hundreds of uniformed personnel (active, guard, and reserve) serve at these headquarters, and nearly half of those individuals are active-duty service members. Yet although Wise said the relationship has never been better, he also pointed out that over the past decade the CIA has served largely in a "supporting" role to the military's "supported" status, and the question remains whether the DoD can handle a role reversal.[13]

Although organizational leaders highlighted improvements in the DoD/CIA relationship and understood the necessity of interoperability after the 9/11 attacks, many also appreciated the trade-offs. In 2012, former deputy DCIA John McLaughlin said intelligence support for force protection is a top intelligence priority but warned that support to military operations necessarily takes resources away from other global missions.[14] That same year, former SSCI chair David Boren voiced concern with the CIA mission becoming subordinate to military operations: "I think there is great danger if the CIA becomes primarily an agency dedicated to the support of military operations; it will neglect its primary role of providing objective intelligence to the policy makers." Boren believed CIA's "military support roles in Iraq and Afghanistan had resulted in reduced intelligence collection and analysis in parts of the world which are more vital to America's long term interests."[15]

Boren also worried that a greater "emphasis on a military support role runs the risk of compromising the objectivity in intelligence analysis," a concern shared by Richard Russell, a university professor and former CIA analyst who argued that CIA analytical support to certain programs are intensive and drain analytical resources from other areas. Boren went even further, expressing concerns regarding the influence of the DoD on CIA: "I do not think it is healthy when a person whose principal experience has been in the military is asked to serve as director of the CIA; it tends to bias policy in a way that places too much emphasis on military intervention instead of carefully evaluating the use of diplomacy and other policy tools."[16] Robert Gates agreed with this sentiment as a "general rule" but also stated that he did not believe the DNI can contain the military commanders' growing appetite for intelligence.[17]

Former military leaders have also voiced concern with the future implications of the DoD/CIA relationship. Former DCI Admiral William Studeman acknowledged to Loch Johnson that support to military operations "presented an endless demand on America's finite intelligence resources."[18] Studeman later pointed out that the United States had dropped fundamental intelligence coverage because it focused on "Lucy and the football" (i.e., terrorism),[19] a sentiment shared by former deputy DCIA for HUMINT Major General (ret.) Michael Ennis, who believes the CIA's focus on tactical collection had distracted it from strategic collection. Although Ennis commented that the military does not fundamentally understand HUMINT and often alienates HUMINT officers, he argued for an enhanced clandestine service that has the resources to support both national and military collection requirements, with military officers that understand the type of HUMINT intelligence commanders require working alongside civilian counterparts who are focused on strategic issues.[20] This would enable the military to benefit from the civilian expertise in HUMINT operations and training while also maintaining officers focused on military intelligence collection requirements who understand military operations.

Former DCIA General (ret.) Michael Hayden and former deputy DCI Admiral (ret.) Bobby Ray Inman highlighted that focusing CIA HUMINT capability on supporting military operations has greater potential repercussions for strategic analysis than focusing technical intelligence collection toward military operations would have. Signals intelligence and other passive technical collection systems are able to compile large amounts of data that can be exploited for either tactical or strategic analysis, unlike HUMINT collection, in which the individual asset normally has access to limited detailed information. Focusing on individuals with access to information that supports military operations necessarily distracts from spotting, assessing, and developing individuals with access to strategic information—a time-consuming endeavor that cannot easily be surged. Robert Gates, the former DCI and secretary of defense, made a similar argument when he posited that technical collection should be distributed between military and national intelligence requirements but that the tactical HUMINT support to military operations should come from the DIA and the services.[21]

Admiral Inman also raised concern regarding what he saw as the CIA's increasing focus on tactical operations, which he believed was first attempted by Admiral Stansfield Turner and then realized after 9/11. Inman argued that the CIA pursued a tactical focus to maintain relevance, but he believed this was often driven by presidents who were enamored of tactical operations and tales of derring-do.[22] Hayden voiced a similar concern when in 2011 he warned the new DCIA, David Petraeus, that the CIA risked becoming a twenty-first-century OSS, an organization conducting paramilitary operations to win conflicts instead of conducting intelligence collection operations to inform strategic analysis.[23] Salivating for immediate results and seemingly as concerned with drone strikes and the targeting of individual terrorists as they are with the relative position of the United States in the world, policy makers have driven the CIA to this tactical focus. This increasing CIA focus on tactical operations is a symptom of a broader issue: the militarization of foreign policy.[24]

In 2008, Gates warned of the "creeping militarization" of US foreign policy. Arguing that the United States "cannot kill or capture our way to victory," Gates stated the military should take a "supporting role" to diplomats in "America's engagement with the rest of the world."[25] Loch Johnson, a former staffer on both the Church Committee and the Aspin-Brown Commission and a well-known intelligence studies academic, raises a similar question: "I continued to wonder if at least a few more resources directed toward national (civilian) intelligence targets wouldn't make the United States more effective at diplomacy and less drawn toward war fighting."[26] This concern is not limited to civilians but is also held by some former military professionals. Karl Eikenberry, a retired lieutenant general and former ambassador to Afghanistan, argued in 2012 that the militarization of US foreign policy and an unequal investment in DoD over other departments have resulted in the military becoming the "starting and relief pitcher for a number of foreign policy problems."[27]

In a speech given at Kansas State University in 2010, Michael Mullen, former chairman of the JCS, articulated his concern with the DoD's increasing role in foreign policy: "My fear, quite frankly, is that we aren't moving fast enough in this regard. U.S. foreign policy is still too dominated by the military, too dependent upon the generals and admirals who lead our major overseas commands. It's one thing to be able and willing to serve as emergency responders; quite another to always have to be the fire chief."[28] In an earlier interview, Mullen described a vicious cycle of policy makers turning to the military and increasing funding to the DoD because they have greater trust in military capability than in other agencies, and this greater funding in turn makes the military even more capable in relation to its national security brethren.[29] Instead of correcting a significant imbalance in resourcing national security capabilities, policy makers just turn to the military to handle an increasing array of missions. The military then becomes the lead while other organizations find themselves in supporting roles.

This tension and the unequal influence of DoD's priorities have been noted in the field. For example, in 2010, as US troops were preparing to depart from Iraq, the military was focused on short-term conditions to ensure the smooth transition to Iraqi forces, whereas the State Department and other agencies were focused on longer-term objectives. Although all were in pursuit of national policy, the short-term military focus was sometimes at odds with the longer-term perspective. This friction was articulated best by an interagency leader, who stated that although the CIA wanted to assist the military as much as possible, it had to consider the long-term effects of its actions. According to him, "the military is on a sprint to 2011 and we are running a marathon."[30]

Although the evolution of the DoD/CIA relationship has brought greater cooperation and resolved many of the issues identified in the late 1980s and 1990s regarding intelligence support to military operations, it has not come without cost. The DoD already controls an estimated 80–90 percent of Intelligence Community funding, and even national intelligence organizations such as the NRO, the NSA, and the NGA have a significant military contingent or serve as a combat-support agency or both. This leaves the CIA as the only truly independent intelligence organization within the Intelligence Community. It is thus important that the CIA, as the only independent agency not focused on serving the needs of a single department, retains a focus on supporting policy makers with the strategic analysis and warning it was created to provide.

Since the Gulf War and particularly after 9/11, this focus has been significantly distracted by the CIA's support to military operations and its involvement in offensive counterterrorism operations, resulting in less long-term analysis focused on the broader world.[31] The CIA rightly has a role in the counterterrorism fight, and the DoD and the CIA should maintain a strong relationship, but the CIA's focus on these two missions has consumed an inordinate amount of its attention and resources. As Senator Boren pointed out in 2013 when he rhetorically asked, "In the long run, what's more important to America: Afghanistan or China?" issues such as a rising China and an aggressive Russia are more important to America's long-term interests than either Iraq or Afghanistan.[32] Unfortunately, the post-9/11 fear of terrorism has resulted in Afghanistan and Iraq receiving priority, and the post–Desert Storm prioritization of intelligence support to the military has resulted in the CIA assuming a greater operational role to the detriment of strategic analysis.

Over time, CIA support to military operations could lead to subordination to the military, and the CIA's dual focus on military support and counterterrorism operations could leave existential threats such as China and Russia insufficiently covered: two realities that would leave the United States without an adequate independent intelligence organization to inform foreign policy and strategy development.[33] The CIA and the DoD are the organizations immediately affected by this evolving relationship, but policy maker preference for military force to "shape the environment" and the militarization of foreign policy have led both organizations down this path.[34] In this regard, the evolved DoD/CIA partnership is both a symptom and a cause of the militarization of US foreign policy. Although there are definite short-term operational benefits to an improved DoD/CIA partnership, the long-term repercussions are not yet known, but they could be significant.

ACKNOWLEDGMENTS

Many people have mentored and supported me throughout the years. Although I cannot identify all of them, I would like to recognize some who helped make possible the research, writing, and publication of this book. First, I thank David Edger, Dale Herspring, Michael Krysko, and David Stone, who helped me throughout the research process, for their mentorship and continued friendship. Thanks to Doug Wise for his continued friendship and mentorship and for sharing his wisdom and connecting me with numerous interviewees. Thanks to the archives that supported my research efforts and the numerous interviewees who generously gave of their time so I could better understand the DoD/CIA relationship (a list of these individuals can be found in the bibliography). Thanks to Hassan Abbas, R. E. Burnett, James Carafano, Craig Deare, Geoffrey Gresh, Tom Marks, Sean McFate, Jay Parker, Tino Perez, Paul Pope, Pat Proctor, and David Ucko for their sage advice as I developed the manuscript into a book. Thanks to National Defense University's College of International Security Affairs, under the leadership of Mike Bell and Chuck Cushman. I appreciate the many friendships and the opportunity to work with such a great faculty and staff. Thanks to the Department of War and Conflict Studies (Kirklin Bateman, David Beans, Bonnie Calabria, Ad Godinez, Zach Hennessa, Jennifer Jung, Ted Larsen, Chuck Moore, Carlos Ospina, Mike Sullivan, Kyle Taylor, and David Ucko) for providing friendship, guidance, and support during the publication process.

Thanks to Joint Special Operations University and the Arthur D. Simons Center, which published my original research, and to David Aitchison, Beth Bochtler, and Alice Butler-Smith, whose support and friendship provided the initial research opportunity. Thanks to the Kansas State University Security

Studies Program and its director, Andrew Long, for supporting my research efforts.

Thanks to David Cobb, Melissa Hammer, Jackie Wilson, Natalie O'Neal, and the rest of the team at the University Press of Kentucky, along with copy editor Annie Barva, for their support and the opportunity to publish my work.

Finally, thanks to my wife and children for their encouragement and patience in dealing with my research trips and the long hours I spent in the basement in front of a computer screen. Thanks to my parents, Don and Pat Oakley; to my brother, Chris, and his family; and to my in-laws, aunts, uncles, extended family, and friends who have always been there to provide support and words of encouragement.

NOTES

Preface

1. David Oakley, "Partners or Competitors? The Evolution of the Department of Defense/Central Intelligence Agency Relationship since Desert Storm and Its Prospects for the Future," Joint Special Operations University, May 2014, at http://jsou.libguides.com/ld.php?content_id=2876951.

2. Admiral (ret.) William O. Studeman, former CIA deputy director and former NSA director, interview by the author, Severna Park, MD, November 24, 2015.

Introduction

1. Leon Panetta, interviewed by Jim Lehrer, *Newshour,* PBS, May 3, 2011, at http://www.pbs.org/newshour/bb/terrorism/jan-june11/panetta_05-03.html.

2. Admiral (ret.) William McRaven, former commander of SOCOM and former commander, Joint Special Operations Command, telephone interview by the author, June 5, 2015.

3. Doug Wise, DIA deputy director, interview by the author, Washington, DC, area, August 28, 2012, and September 3, 2105; Lieutenant General Kurt A. Cichowski, CIA associate director for military affairs, interview by the author, Langley, VA, August 29, 2012.

4. Garry Reid, principal deputy ASD for special operations and low-intensity conflict, telephone interview by the author, September 19, 2012; Oakley, "Partners or Competitors?"

5. For a description of the ADMA mission, see https://www.cia.gov/offices-of-cia/military-affairs/history.html.

6. Alyssa G., military liaison to the CIA Office of the Associate Director of Military Affairs, interview by the author, Langley, VA, August 28. 2012.

7. Wise interview, August 28, 2012, and September 3, 2015.

8. Oakley, "Partners or Competitors?" Historians in the CIA Center for the Study

of Intelligence stated that interviews with CIA personnel highlight significant improvement in the CIA's relationship with other government organizations since 9/11. These improved partnerships have resulted in less parochialism and increased mission success. Most important, the officers recognize the value of these partnerships and are now more receptive to engaging their interagency colleagues instead of operating alone.

9. Thomas. L Ahearn Jr., *Vietnam Declassified: The CIA and Counterinsurgency* (Lexington: University Press of Kentucky, 2010). During Vietnam, elements of the military and the CIA did work together. For example, US Air Force colonel Edward Lansdale ran the CIA's Saigon Military Mission in Vietnam, but the CIA–military interaction was not common and was usually limited to military officers who were working for the CIA on specific programs. These paramilitary-type programs were much different from the CIA support to military operations that occurred after Desert Storm.

10. Chris Kojm, former chairman of the National Intelligence Council, telephone interview by the author, October 14, 2015; General (ret.) David Petraeus, former CIA director and former commander of US CENTCOM, interview by the author, Washington, DC, October 23, 2015.

11. George H. W. Bush, *National Security Strategy of the United States* (Washington, DC: US White House, August 1991).

12. Lieutenant General (ret.) Ronald L. Burgess, former DIA director, telephone interview by the author, September 17, 2015.

13. The DoD defines "area of operations" as "an operational area defined by the joint force commander for land and maritime forces that should be large enough to accomplish their missions and protect their forces" (US DoD, *Joint Publication 1-02*: *Department of Defense Dictionary of Military and Associated Terms* [Washington, DC: US DoD, November 8, 2010], 14).

14. Michael Nelson and Barbara A. Perry, *41: Inside the Presidency of George H. W. Bush* (Ithaca, NY: Cornell University Press, 2014), 20. Nelson and Perry indicate that the first mention of a "peace dividend" was in William Safire, "Is Peace Bullish?" *New York Times,* June 8, 1989.

15. George H. W. Bush, *National Security Review 29: National Security Review of Intelligence* (Washington, DC: White House, November 15, 1991).

16. George H. W. Bush, *National Security Directive 67: Intelligence Capabilities: 1992–2005* (Washington, DC: White House, March 30, 1992).

17. William Jefferson Clinton, "Remarks Announcing the National Performance Review," March 3, 1993, American Presidency Project, at http://www.presidency.ucsb.edu/ws/?pid=46291.

18. William Jefferson Clinton, *Presidential Decision Directive 35: Intelligence Requirements* (Washington, DC: US Government Printing Office, March 2, 1995).

19. Loch K. Johnson, *The Threat on the Horizon: An Inside Account of America's Search for Security after the Cold War* (Oxford: Oxford University Press, 2011), 65, 125, 237. Johnson states that Anthony Lake, Bill Studeman, and John Deutch discussed the importance of intelligence support to military operations. Lake discussed how PDD-35 "made support to military operations" the top priority "wherever U.S. forces are

deployed." Studeman called "support to military operations" the "defining mission" for the Intelligence Community. Deutch was the most assertive, saying there was "not enough" support to military operations, despite acknowledging that support to military operations took up "about 90% of the intelligence budget."

20. Richard N. Haas, *Making Intelligence Smarter,* Task Force Report (Washington, DC: Council on Foreign Relations, January 1996), at http://www.cfr.org/intelligence/making-intelligence-smarter/p127; John Hollister Hedley, *Checklist for the Future of Intelligence* (Washington, DC: Institute for the Study of Diplomacy, Georgetown University, 1995).

21. US Senate and House, Select Committee on Intelligence and Permanent Select Committee on Intelligence, *Joint Inquiry into Events Surrounding September 11,* 107th Cong., 2nd sess., October 3, 2002, at http://fas.org/irp/congress/2002_hr/100302hamilton.html; Johnson, *Threat on the Horizon,* 237–38.

22. Wise interview, August 28, 2012, and September 3, 2015; "U.S. Intelligence Official Acknowledges Missed Arab Spring Signs," *Los Angeles Times,* July 19, 2012, at http://latimesblogs.latimes.com/world_now/2012/07/us-intelligence-official-acknowledges-missed-signs-ahead-of-arab-spring-.html.

23. Petraeus interview, October 23, 2015; General (ret.) Michael V. Hayden, former CIA director and former NSA director, interview by the author, Washington, DC, September 18, 2015. Petraeus somewhat disagreed with my argument, saying that Desert Storm might have had a "catalytic effect," but 9/11 was the actual catalyst. General Hayden advised the incoming DCIA David Petraeus not to let the CIA become just another OSS.

24. Jennifer Kibbe, "The Military, the CIA, and America's Shadow Wars," in *Mission Creep: The Militarization of US Foreign Policy,* ed. Gordon Adams and Shoon Murray (Washington, DC: Georgetown University Press, 2014), 210–34; Melvin Goodman, *Failure of Intelligence: The Decline and Fall of the CIA* (New York: Rowman and Littlefield, 2008), 312, 331–36. Kibbe describes the two organizations taking on the same type of missions. Goodman describes the dominance of the DoD within the Intelligence Community.

25. Vice Admiral (ret.) Michael McConnell, former director of national intelligence, former NSA director, and former JCS J2, interview by the author, Leesburg, VA, August 8, 2015.

26. Kojm telephone interview, October 14, 2015. Kojm described intelligence as information required to enable decision making.

27. "A Look Back . . . the National Security Act of 1947," CIA, News & Information, July 7, 2008, at https://www.cia.gov/news-information/featured-story-archive/2008-featured-story-archive/national-security-act-of-1947.html. During an interview, Rich Haver discussed the influence of the Roberts Commission's review of Pearl Harbor on establishing an independent intelligence agency (Richard Haver, former ASD for intelligence and former intelligence adviser to the secretary of defense [Cheney and Rumsfeld], interview by the author, Great Falls, VA, December 1, 2015, and email exchange with the author, January 4, 2016). Haver conducted research on the Roberts Commission for Secretary Rumsfeld when they were considering intelligence reform.

1. Change on the Horizon

1. Cichowski interview, August 2002. Lieutenant General Cichowski compared the evolutionary path of the DoD/CIA partnership to the path the military service relationships took following Goldwater-Nichols.

2. US House of Representatives, Committee on the Armed Services, *Hearings on Military Posture and H. R. 5968 Department of Defense Appropriations for 1983,* 97th Cong., 2nd sess., February–March 1983; James Locher, *Victory on the Potomac: The Goldwater-Nichols Act Unifies the Pentagon* (College Station: Texas A&M University Press, 2002). In chapter 2, "Jones Breaks Ranks," Locher goes into detail on General Jones's actions to initiate reform.

3. David C. Jones, "Why the Joint Chiefs of Staff Must Change," *Presidential Studies Quarterly* 12, no. 2 (Spring 1982): 138–49.

4. Ronald Reagan, "Remarks on Central America and El Salvador," speech at the Annual Meeting of the National Association of Manufacturers, Washington, DC, March 10, 1983, American Presidency Project, at http://www.presidency.ucsb.edu/ws/?pid=41034; Benjamin Beede, *The Small Wars of the United States 1899–2009* (New York: Routledge, 2010), 327.

5. Ronald Reagan, "Peace: Restoring the Margin of Safety," speech given at the Veterans of Foreign Affairs Convention, Chicago, August 18, 1980, at http://www.reagan.utexas.edu/archives/reference/8.18.80.html.

6. Reagan, "Remarks on Central America and El Salvador."

7. US House of Representatives and Senate, *Caribbean Economic Initiative* (Pub. L. 98-67), 98th Cong., 1st sess., August 5, 1983; US House of Representatives, Committee on Ways and Means, *Hearing on HR 2769: Caribbean Basin Economic Recovery Act,* 98th Cong., 1st sess., June 9, 1983.

8. Russell Crandall, *Gunboat Diplomacy: U.S. Intervention in the Dominican Republic, Grenada, and Panama* (Oxford: Rowman and Littlefield, 2006), 111–12, 126.

9. Robert Cole, *Operation Urgent Fury: Grenada* (Washington, DC: Joint History Office of the Chairman of the Joint Chiefs of Staff, 1997), 9–10.

10. Dennis Hevesi, "Wesley McDonald, Who Planned for Grenada, Dies at 84," *New York Times,* February 23, 2009, at http://www.nytimes.com/2009/02/23/us/23mcdonald.html?_r=0.

11. Jeffrey J. Clarke, *Operation Urgent Fury: The Invasion of Grenada, October 1983* (Washington, DC: US Army Center for Military History, 2008), 11.

12. US House of Representatives, Committee on the Armed Services, *Lessons Learned as a Result of the U.S. Military Operations in Grenada,* 98th Cong., 2nd sess., January 24, 1984, 11; Cole, *Operation Urgent Fury,* 6.

13. Clarke, *Operation Urgent Fury,* 11. Clarke lays out a roughly forty-eight-hour time lapse between when the announcement that Vice Admiral Metcalf would be the commander until the actual invasion.

14. Samuel D. Ward, "The Operational Leadership of Vice Admiral Joseph P. Metcalf, III," 2012, at http://www.dtic.mil/dtic/tr/fulltext/u2/a564017.pdf., 6; Cole, *Operation Urgent Fury,* 52, 56.

15. US House of Representatives, Defense Appropriations Subcommittee of the Committee on Appropriations, *Situation in Lebanon and Grenada* (Washington, DC: US Government Printing Office, November 8, 1983), 38–40.

16. US House of Representatives, Committee on the Armed Services, *Lessons Learned,* 27–28, 33–34; Ted Shackley, with Richard A. Finney, *Spymaster: My Life in the CIA* (Dulles, VA: Potomac Books, 2005), 91, 292.

17. US House of Representatives, Committee on the Armed Services, *Lessons Learned,* 27–28, 33–34.

18. US DoD, *Joint Overview of Operation Urgent Fury* (Washington, DC: US DoD, May 1, 1985), 48, 55, 78.

19. Defense attachés provide valuable overt information through their foreign engagements and contacts, but overt collection, although valuable, cannot cover all the information requirements, and DoD's clandestine capability is not sufficient (as the request to build up the DCS in 2012 highlighted).

20. Peter Huchthausen, *America's Splendid Little Wars: A Short History of U.S. Engagement from the Fall of Saigon to Baghdad* (New York: Penguin, 2003), 49–50.

21. Ronald Reagan, *Communication from the President of the United States: Use of United States Armed Forces in Lebanon* (Washington, DC: US Government Printing Office, September 8, 1982), 2.

22. US House of Representatives, Committee on the Armed Services, *The Use of Military Personnel in Lebanon and Consideration of Report from September 24–25 Committee Delegation to Lebanon,* 98th Cong., 1st sess., September 27 and 28, 1983, 5.

23. Timothy J. Geraghty, *Peacekeepers at War: Beirut 1983—the Marine Commander Tells His Story* (Washington, DC: Potomac Books, 2009), 19–20.

24. Glen Hastedt, "Intelligence Failure and Terrorism: The Attack on the Marines in Beirut," *Journal of Conflict Studies* 8, no. 2 (1988): 17–18; Geraghty, *Peacekeepers at War,* 143.

25. US House of Representatives, Committee on the Armed Services, *Use of Military Personnel in Lebanon,* 1.

26. US House of Representatives, Committee on the Armed Services, *Use of Military Personnel in Lebanon,* 1, 20–21.

27. Locher, *Victory on the Potomac,* 129–31.

28. US Senate, Committee on Armed Services, *Hearings before the Committee on Armed Services: The Situation in Lebanon,* 98th Cong., 1st sess., October 25 and 31, 1983, 51, 92–93, 107.

29. Senator Warner did ask General Rogers whether any of the flag officers who visited Beirut following the embassy bombing in April 1983 were terrorist experts who reported to him and if any of them "express[ed] concern with the adequacy or inadequacy of the preventative measures" (for Warner's full statement, see US Senate, Committee on Armed Services, *Hearings before the Committee on Armed Services,* 97).

30. US House of Representatives, Committee on the Armed Services, *Use of Military Personnel in Lebanon,* 31.

31. US Senate, Committee on Armed Services, *Hearings before the Committee on Armed Services,* 56.

32. US DoD, *Report of the DoD Commission on Beirut International Airport Terrorist Act* (Washington, DC: US DoD, December 10, 1983), 2.

33. US DoD, *Report of the DoD Commission on Beirut International Airport Terrorist Act,* 8. General Rogers, a former army chief of staff and highly regarded officer, was a native Kansan who attended Kansas State University for one year before he went to West Point. He was never officially reprimanded, even though he held the command that was ultimately responsible for the security at the marine barracks. The Long Commission also found "that there was a series of circumstances beyond the control of these commands that influenced their judgment and their actions relating to the security of the USMNF" (quoted in Geraghty, *Peacekeepers at War,* 143).

34. US DoD, *Report of the DoD Commission on Beirut International Airport Terrorist Act,* 10.

35. White House, Office of the Press Secretary, "Biography of Bobby Ray Inman," press release, December 16, 1993, at http://fas.org/irp/news/1993/931216i.htm; Admiral (ret.) Bobby Ray Inman, former CIA deputy director, interview by the author, Austin, TX, August 27, 2014.

36. US Department of State, Bureau of Diplomatic Security, *History of the Bureau of Diplomatic Security of the United States Department of State* (Washington, DC: Global Publishing Solutions, 2011), 285–89; Alex Tiersky and Susan B. Epstein, *Securing U.S. Diplomatic Facilities and Personnel Abroad: Background and Policy Issues* (Washington, DC: Congressional Research Service, July 30, 2014), at https://www.fas.org/sgp/crs/row/R42834.pdf.

37. Locher, *Victory on the Potomac,* 305–14, 424–25.

38. During congressional hearings on defense reform, Senator Goldwater spoke of the importance of identifying the different roles and responsibilities of American national security organizations during war. See US Senate, Committee on Armed Services, *Hearings on the Reorganization of the Department of Defense,* 98th Cong., 1st sess., October–December 1985, 31.

39. Locher, *Victory on the Potomac,* 124–25.

40. US Senate, Committee on Armed Services, *Hearings on the Reorganization of the Department of Defense,* 118, 149, 495, 559.

41. Richard Lock-Pullan, *US Intervention Policy and Army Innovation: From Vietnam to Iraq* (New York: Routledge, 2006), 61.

42. Christopher Paul, Isaac R. Porche III, and Elliott Axelband, *The Other Quiet Professionals: Lessons for Future Cyber Professionals from the Evolution of Special Forces* (Santa Monica, CA: RAND, 2014), 9.

43. US Special Operations Command, "United States Special Operations Command History," April 16, 1987, at http://www.fas.org/irp/agency/dod/socom/ 2007history.pdf.

44. US Senate, Committee on Armed Services, *Hearings on the Reorganization of the Department of Defense,* 5. For further details, see "*Achille Lauro* Hijacking Ends" (October 8, 1985), *This Day in History,* History Channel, n.d., at http://www.history.com/this-day-in-history/achille-lauro-hijacking-ends for further details (accessed March 18, 2016).

45. Ronald Reagan, *Executive Order 12526: President's Blue Ribbon Commission on*

Defense Management (Washington, DC: US Government Printing Office, July 15, 1985). Four issues were of concern: (1) the adequacy of the current authority and control of the secretary of defense in the oversight of the military departments as well as the efficiency of the decision-making apparatus of the Office of the Secretary of Defense; (2) the responsibilities of the Organization of the Joint Chiefs of Staff in providing for joint military advice and force development within a resource-constrained environment; (3) the adequacy of the Unified and Specified Command system in providing for the effective planning for and use of military forces; and (4) the value and continued role of intervening layers of command on the direction and control of military forces in peace and in war.

46. Richard A. Hunt, "Melvin Laird and the Foundation of the Post-Vietnam Military, 1969–1973," 2015, at http://history.defense.gov/Portals/70/Documents/secretaryofdefense/OSDSeries_V017.pdf; Locher, *Victory on the Potomac*, 294. Locher states that "Packard believed the two [Reagan and Weinberger] 'wanted the commission to come in, look things over, and tell everybody that everything was fine and not to worry." According to Locher, Packard had a different view of his role and did not want to be a rubber stamp.

47. Walter Pincus, "Defense Procurement Problems Won't Go Away," *Washington Post*, May 2, 2012. President Reagan implemented some of the recommendations after the release of the Packard Commission's initial report and just prior to the release of its final report by issuing National Security Decision Directive 219 (Ronald Reagan, *National Security Decision Directive 219: Implementation of the Recommendations of the President's Commission on Defense Management* [Washington, DC: US Government Printing Office, April 1, 1986]). Its implementation guidance included the requirement that DoD report back to the president regarding various policy changes that would empower the chairman of the JCS and the combatant commanders.

48. US Blue Ribbon Commission on Defense Management, *A Quest for Excellence* (Washington, DC: US Government Printing Office, June 1986), 38.

49. Dana Priest, *The Mission: Waging War and Keeping Peace with America's Military* (New York: Norton, 2003), 94–96. Priest explains the rise of the combatant commanders and how Goldwater-Nichols helped lead to their rise in power. See also Wise interview, September 3, 2105.

50. US House of Representatives and Senate, *Goldwater-Nichols Reorganization Act of 1986* (Pub. L. 99-53), 99th Cong., 2nd sess., October 1, 1986.

51. Andrew Feickert, *The Unified Command Plan and Combatant Commands: Background and Issues for Congress* (Washington, DC: Congressional Research Service, January 3, 2013), at https://www.fas.org/sgp/crs/natsec/R42077.pdf.

52. In 2006, US military joint doctrine introduced a six-phase "phasing model." *Joint Publication 3-0* states that Phase 0-Shape is "executed continuously with the intent to enhance international legitimacy and gain both adversaries and allies, developing allied and friendly military capabilities for self-defense and coalition operations, improving information exchange and intelligence sharing, and providing US forces with peacetime and contingency access" (US DoD, *Joint Publication 3-0: Doctrine for Joint Operations* [Washington, DC: US DoD, February 1, 2008], IV-27).

53. US Senate, Select Committee on Intelligence, *Authorizing Appropriations for Fiscal Year 1992 for the Intelligence Activities of the U.S. Government, the Intelligence Community Staff, the Central Intelligence Agency Retirement and Disability System, and for Other Purposes,* 102nd Cong., 1st sess., July 8, 1991, 7.

54. US Senate, Committee on Armed Services, *Hearings on the Reorganization of the Department of Defense,* 5; US Blue Ribbon Commission, *A Quest for Excellence,* 20. The Packard Commission recommended that the DCI work with DoD leadership to "prepare a military net assessment" that would inform strategies (US Blue Ribbon Commission, *A Quest for Excellence,* 20).

55. US Special Operations Command, "United States Special Operations Command History," 6–7.

56. For information on the abduction and murder of William Buckley, see CIA, "Remembering CIA's Heroes: William F. Buckley," CIA, News & Information, n.d., at https://www.cia.gov/news-information/featured-story-archive/2015-featured-story-archive/william-buckley.html (accessed February 10, 2017), and "Body Believed to Be CIA Agent and Hostage Is Found in Lebanon," *New York Times,* December 27, 1991, at http://www.nytimes.com/1991/12/27/world/ bodybelieved-to-be-cia-agent-and-hostage-is-found-in-lebanon.html. See also Robert Baer, *See No Evil: The True Story of a Ground Soldier in the CIA's War on Terrorism* (New York: Crown, 2002), in which Baer discusses the early days of the CTC in chapter 7.

57. Henry A. Crumpton, *The Art of Intelligence: Lessons from a Life in the CIA's Clandestine Service* (New York: Penguin, 2012), 122.

58. Colin Powell to Secretary of Defense, "Report on the Role and Functions of the Armed Forces," memo with attachment, November 2, 1989, File 218-93-0010, Doc. CM-44-89, Colin Powell Collection, National Defense University Archives, Washington, DC.

59. US Senate, Subcommittee on Western Hemisphere Affairs of the Committee on Foreign Relations, *Situation in Panama* (Hearing 99-832), 99th Cong., 2nd sess., March 10 and April 21, 1986.

60. Frederick Kempe, *Divorcing the Dictator: America's Bungled Affair with Noriega* (London: Putnam's, 1990), 94, 176.

61. US Senate, Subcommittee on Western Hemisphere Affairs of the Committee on Foreign Relations, *Situation in Panama,* 4–5, 48.

62. Scott Rosenberg, "Panama and Noriega: Our SOB," Emory University, 2007, at http://history.emory.edu/home/documents/endeavors/volume1/Scotts.pdf.

63. Phillip Shenon, "Noriega Indicted by U.S. for Link to Illegal Drugs," *New York Times,* February 6, 1988, at http://www.nytimes.com/1988/02/06/world/noriega-indicted-by-us-for-links-to-illegal-drugs.html?_r=0.

64. Rosenberg, "Panama and Noriega."

65. Cole, *Operation Urgent Fury,* 12.

66. "US Expands Its Sanctions against Panama," *New York Times,* September 13, 1989, at http://www.nytimes.com/1989/09/13/world/us-expands-its-sanctions-against-panama.html; Andrew Rosenthal and Michael R. Gordon, "A Failed Coup: The

Bush Team and Noriega," *New York Times,* October 8, 1989, at http://www.nytimes.com/1989/10/08/world/failed-coup-bush-team-noriega-special-report-panama-crisis-disarray-hindered.html?pagewanted=all; Kempe, *Divorcing the Dictator,* 273, 281 283, 293.

67. "Central America, 1981–93," Office of the Historian, Milestones 1981–1988, n.d., at https://history.state.gov/milestones/1981-1988/central-america (accessed March 18, 2016).

68. Linda Wallace and Mark Fazlollah, "The Man Whose Death Led to Warfare," *Philadelphia Inquirer,* December 22, 1989, at http://articles.philly.com/1989-12-22/news/26158426_1_jaime-paz-animal-science-panamanians.

69. Kempe, *Divorcing the Dictator,* 363, 374.

70. US House of Representatives, *Operation Just Cause: Preliminary Session,* 101st Cong., 2nd sess., February 5, 1990; Emily Langer, "Ike Skelton, Congressman, Who Led House Armed Services Committee, Dies at 81," *Washington Post,* October 29, 2013, at https://www.washingtonpost.com/politics/ike-skelton-congressman-who-led-house-armed-services-committee-dies-at-81/2013/10/29/ba8ae458-40ad-11e3-9c8b-e8deeb3c755b_story.html.

71. US DoD, Secretary, Joint Staff Directive, *Permanent Select Committee on Intelligence Hearing to Address Intelligence Planning and Support to Operation Just Cause,* January 31, 1990, File 218-93-0010, Doc. SJS 1778/1424, Colin Powell Collection, National Defense University Archives, Washington, DC.

72. US DoD, Secretary, Joint Staff Directive, *Intelligence Support to Special Operations and Low-Intensity Conflict Activities. Congressional Report,* File 218-93-0010, Doc. SJS 1927/266, Colin Powell Collection, National Defense University Archives, Washington, DC. This document included two attachments, a memo from the ASD for special operations and low-intensity conflicts and the actual request from the senators.

73. US Senate, Committee on Armed Services, *Nominations before the Armed Services Committee,* 101st Cong., 1st sess., March–November 1989, 689.

74. US Senate, Committee on Armed Services, *Nominations before the Armed Services Committee,* March–November 1989, 689, 99.

75. NSR 27 followed George H. W. Bush, *National Security Review 12: Review of National Defense Strategy* (Washington, DC: White House, March 1989), which looked at how DoD had to adapt to the changing global environment in consideration of the reduced budgets.

76. George H. W. Bush, *National Security Review 27: National Security Review of Low Intensity Conflict* (Washington, DC: White House, June 11, 1990).

77. US House of Representatives, *Operation Just Cause.* The full quote is: "Militarily, I think we earned a good A-minus for our forces. As I said, the shortcoming was in the intelligence area. And we did learn, as the gentleman from Mississippi knows, we did learn from the mistakes made in Grenada. The communication mistakes were horrendous, but we did well despite that; but none of those Grenada mistakes reoccurred. As long as our military, with its capable leadership—and particular I want to give applause to General Max Thurman down in Panama—as long as our military learns from the past,

they will do better in the days ahead. This is a prime example of learning from the mistakes of the past and doing a good job. We achieved our objective, and now we go on to the civilian side of the coin."

78. US Senate, Committee on Armed Services, *Nominations before the Armed Services Committee,* March–November 1989.

2. The Gulf War

1. McConnell interview, August 8, 2015.

2. US Senate, Select Committee on Intelligence, *Authorizing Appropriations for Fiscal Year 1992,* 5–6.

3. George H. W. Bush, *National Security Directive 26: U.S. Policy towards the Persian Gulf* (Washington, DC: US Government Printing Office, October 2, 1989).

4. George H. W. Bush and Brent Scowcroft, *A World Transformed* (New York: Vintage Books, 1999), 306; Richard M. Swain, *Lucky War: Third Army in Desert Storm* (Fort Leavenworth, KS: US Army Command and General Staff College Press, 1991), 4–6; Andrew Bacevich, *America's War for the Greater Middle East* (New York: Random House, 2016), 44; Michael R. Gordon and Bernard E. Trainor, *The General's War* (New York: Little, Brown, 1995), 12. Some dispute that the United States was looking to improve the relationship with Iraq. For example, Swain describes how Schwarzkopf focused more on the Iraqi threat beginning in 1989 and changed the US operations plan so that the "Iraqi threat to Saudi Arabia . . . [would] be made the priority for Central Command planning" (*Lucky War,* 4). Bacevich's book adds to Swain's perspective by arguing that CENTCOM embraced Iraq as a threat in order to remain relevant and justify budgets. Gordon and Trainor make an argument similar to Bush and Scowcroft's, that the Bush administration tried to improve the relationship with Iraq after the Iraq-Iran War, citing as evidence Schwarzkopf's proposal in 1989 to do military officer exchanges with Iraq.

5. Gordon and Trainor, *The General's War,* 14–16.

6. Bush and Scowcroft, *A World Transformed,* 312.

7. Gordon and Trainor, *The General's War,* 14–16, 27.

8. Bush and Scowcroft, *A World Transformed,* 302, 310.

9. George H. W. Bush, "Remarks and an Exchange with Reporters on the Iraqi Invasion of Kuwait," August 5, 1990, American Presidency Project, at http://www.presidency.ucsb.edu/ws/?pid=18741.

10. United Nations Security Council Resolution 661, August 6, 1990, at https://documents-dds-ny.un.org/doc/RESOLUTION/GEN/NR0/575/11/IMG/NR057511.pdf?OpenElement.

11. US DoD, *Final Report to Congress on the Conduct of the Persian Gulf War* (Washington, DC: US DoD, April 1992), 70.

12. Stuart Lockwood, "That's Me in the Picture: Stuart Lockwood with Saddam Hussein, 24 August 1990 Baghdad, Iraq," *Guardian,* June 5, 2015, at https://www.theguardian.com/artanddesign/2015/jun/05/that's-me-picture-stuart-lockwood-saddam-hussein-iraq; see also the news conference at https:www.youtube.com/watch?v=7q5KMe7LPRI (accessed December 29, 2015).

13. US DoD, *Final Report to Congress on the Conduct of the Persian Gulf War*, 693.

14. Gordon and Trainor, *The General's War*, ix, 205.

15. "The Senate Passed S.J. Res. 2, to Authorize the Use of United States Armed Forces Pursuant to United Nations Security Council Resolution 678," C-Span, January 12, 1991, at http://www.c-span.org/video/?15665-1/senate-session&start=11899.

16. US Senate, *Authorization for Use of Military Force against Iraq Resolution,* 102nd Cong., 1st sess., January 11, 1991, 8.

17. Congressman Thomas Foley to President George H. W. Bush, October 30, 1990, Staff and Office Files, Correspondence Re: Persian Gulf 1990–1991, George H. W. Bush Library Archives, Texas A&M University, College Station. John Diamond discusses the casualty debate and says that Nunn had mentioned the estimate of 10,000–20,000 casualties (*The CIA and the Culture of Failure: U.S. Intelligence from the End of the Cold War to the Invasion of Iraq* [Stanford, CA: Stanford University Press, 2008], 149).

18. Bush and Scowcroft, *A World Transformed,* 417. Bush and Scowcroft discuss the hearings and how Bush believed the "witness list had been stacked in favor of individuals who favored sanctions as the only option." For the hearings, see US Senate, Committee on Armed Services, *Crisis in the Persian Gulf Region: U.S. Policy Options and Implications,* 101st Cong., 2nd sess., September–December 1991, 464.

19. US DoD, *Final Report to Congress on the Conduct of the Persian Gulf War.*

20. Hew Strachan's book *Clausewitz's* On War: *A Biography* (London: Atlantic Books, 2007) discusses Carl von Clausewitz's influence on General Powell and how Powell's reading of Michael Eliot Howard and Peter Paret's translation (Carl von Clausewitz, *On War,* ed. and trans. Michael Eliot Howard and Peter Paret, paperback ed. [Princeton, NJ: Princeton University Press, 1989]), coupled with Powell's Vietnam experience, helped him frame the policy–war link.

21. One retired military officer recalled Schwarzkopf, a lieutenant general at the time, addressing an auditorium full of junior officers at Fort Lewis, Washington, during an I-Corp Officer Professional Development session. As Schwarzkopf, who was not known for his slender build, berated the audience of officers about height and weight, this young officer sat amazed and disgusted at the hypocrisy.

22. Mark Crispin Miller, "Operation Desert Sham," *New York Times,* June 24, 1992, at http://www.nytimes.com/1992/06/24/opinion/operation-desert-sham.html; see video of the press conference at http://www.c-span.org/video/?16102-1/us-centcom-military-news-briefing (accessed December 29, 2015).

23. Rick Atkinson, *Crusade: The Untold Story of the Persian Gulf War* (New York: Houghton Mifflin Harcourt, 1993), 232; McConnell interview, August 8, 2015. Atkinson describes a CIA analyst discovering that the supposed Scuds were actually Jordanian fuel trucks and a DIA analyst saying they might have been milk trucks. McConnell remembered one of his analysts giving him the news that the reported Scuds were Jordanian fuel trucks.

24. McConnell, interview, August 8, 2015.

25. Gordon and Trainor, *The General's War,* 178–79.

26. Atkinson, *Crusade,* 234–35.

27. US House of Representatives, Oversight and Investigations Subcommittee of the Committee on the Armed Services, *Intelligence Successes and Failures in Operations Desert Storm/Shield* (Washington, DC: US Government Printing Office, August 16, 1993), 18–19.

28. US DoD, *Final Report to Congress on the Conduct of the Persian Gulf War*, 192.

29. Robert Vickers, "Desert Storm and the BDA Controversy," n.d., approved for release September 10, 2014, http://www.foia.cia.gov/sites/default/files/DOC_0006122350.pdf (accessed April 5, 2016).

30. Atkinson, *Crusade*, 346.

31. McConnell interview, August 8, 2015.

32. Atkinson, *Crusade*, 346–47.

33. "Lieutenant General Brent Scowcroft," US Air Force, current as of July 15, 1975, at http://www.af.mil/AboutUs/Biographies/Display/tabid/225/Article/104997/ lieutenant-general-brent-scowcroft.aspx (accessed April 2, 2018).

34. Atkinson, *Crusade*, 346–47.

35. McConnell interview, August 8, 2015.

36. Atkinson, *Crusade*, 346–47.

37. John F. Stewart Jr., "Operation Desert Storm, the Military Intelligence Story: A View from the G-2 3D U.S. Army," April 1991, National Security Archive, George Washington University, Washington, DC, at http://nsarchive.gwu.edu/NSAEBB/NSAEBB39/document5.pdf. The ARCENT G2 report argued that the ease of the invasion proved that ARCENT assessments were accurate. The final congressional report argues they were greatly exaggerated and inaccurate (US DoD, *Final Report to Congress on the Conduct of the Persian Gulf War*).

38. US DoD, *Final Report to Congress on the Conduct of the Persian Gulf War*, 276.

39. McConnell interview, August 8, 2015.

40. Studeman, interview, November 24, 2015.

41. Gregory Vistica, *Fall from Glory: The Men Who Sank the U.S Navy* (New York: Simon and Schuster, 1997), 47. Team Charlie was a group of navy personnel tasked with researching Soviet submarine doctrine. The team was led by Rich Haver and included future admirals Studeman and McConnell (Haver interview, December 1, 2015, and email exchange, January 4, 2016). According to Haver, "[Chief of Naval Operations] Tom Hayward held a meeting in the special navy spaces in the Pentagon in February 1981. He wanted a broad look at the rational for a strong navy. He complained intel was giving great details on how long, how wide, how well armed and laid out the new Soviet nuclear cruiser was. However, we provided nothing about why it was being built, what [it] was intended to do for them, or more important why he should care. I was the briefer, and I provided a view quite different from the prevailing wisdom. He was engaged and at the end asked me what I needed. I told him I needed a customer. Line naval officers who had the clearances needed to see all the special material I had access to. Admiral Ken McKee was there, OP-95; he said he would create such a group of middle-grade officers headed for flag rank to create such a group. The [vice chief of naval operations], Jim Watkins, was also there and said he knew who those officers were. Team Charlie was born that morn-

ing. I was the briefer because three months earlier Admiral Hayward held a conference in Newport, RI, with all the living former chiefs of naval operations. I was the intel briefer at the meeting, along with my boss, Admiral Tom Brooks. Brooks had raised the strategy issue and was not treated well. At the end of the day Hayward surprised me by asking the others how he was doing. Arleigh Burke spoke up, gave him big grades for cleaning up drugs and other problems, then hit him with a comment that he had failed to justify the role of the navy in national security. The next week I was removed as technical director of the Navy Field Operational Intelligence Office, placed on the staff of the DNI in the Pentagon, and designated the chief of the Soviet Strategy Branch, OP-009J. Hence the briefing two months later. The [Special Studies Group] at the Naval War College came about six months later."

42. William O. Studeman, "Farewell," memo, April 8, 1992, National Security Archive, George Washington University, Washington, DC, at http://nsarchive.gwu.edu/ NSAEBB/NSAEBB23/docs/doc10.pdf; Studeman interview, November 24, 2015. Some influential congressmen wanted Inman as DCI when Reagan selected Casey. Although they did not get their nominee, they got him nominated for the deputy position, a position Inman was not thrilled about after being the NSA chief.

43. McConnell interview, August 8, 2015. For a history of the JIC, see "The Evolution and Relevance of Joint Intelligence Centers," CIA, Library, n.d., at https://www. cia.gov/library/center-for-the-study-of-intelligence/csi-publications/csi-studies/studies/ vol49no1/html_files/the_evolution_6.html (accessed April 20, 2018). Admiral McConnell was credited with using the term *fusion center* in this article.

44. US DoD defines the Military Intelligence Board as " the senior board of governors for the military [intelligence community] and works to develop cooperation and consensus on cross-agency, Service, and command issues. The [board] is chaired by the Director of DIA" (*Joint Publication 2-01: Joint and National Intelligence Support to Military Operations* [Washington, DC: US DoD, January 5, 2012], A-4). See also US Defense Intelligence Agency, "A Brief History: Committed to Excellence in Defense of the Nation," 1996, at http://fas.org/irp/dia/dia_history.pdf. The Military Intelligence Board was originally established as the Defense Intelligence Board in 1975 when the ASD for intelligence was established as the director of military intelligence. The ASD for intelligence position was later consolidated during the Carter administration into the ASD for command, control, and communication.

45. Brian G. Shellum, "Defense Intelligence Crisis Response Procedures and the Gulf War," National Security Archive, George Washington University, Washington, DC, 1996, at http://nsarchive.gwu.edu/NSAEBB/NSAEBB39/document14.pdf.

46. Brigadier General Charles W. Thomas, "Inside a J-2 Joint Intelligence Center," approved for release September 10, 2014, at http://www.foia.cia.gov/sites/default/files/ DOC_0006122143.pdf (accessed May 10, 2018).

47. McConnell interview, August 8, 2015

48. Major General Leide also had significant experience with the Eighty-Second Airborne Division and Special Operations. See Atkinson, *Crusade,* 234, for more detail on Leide's background.

49. Atkinson, *Crusade*, 64; McConnell interview, August 8, 2015.

50. "Lieutenant General Buster C. Glosson," US Air Force, current as of October 1993, at http://www.af.mil/AboutUs/Biographies/Display/tabid/225/Article/106980/lieutenant-general-buster-c-glosson.aspx (accessed April 10, 2016).

51. McConnell interview, August 8, 2015; John Olsen Andres, *Strategic Air Power in Desert Storm* (Oxford: Routledge, 2003), 128.

52. Eric Schmitt, "General Is Scolded in Ethics Inquiry," *New York Times*, December 4, 1993, at http://www.nytimes.com/1993/12/04/us/general-is-scolded-in-ethics-inquiry.html; Suzanne M. Schafer, "Desert Storm General Volunteers for Lower Rank Retirement," Associated Press, July 7, 1994, at http://www.apnewsarchive.com/1994/Desert-Storm-General-Volunteers-for-Lower-Rank-Retirement/id-633995e095fc5db2694d3e47711c8b03.

53. Gordon and Trainor, *The General's War*, 234; McConnell interview, August 8, 2015.

54. Edward Mann, "Desert Storm: The First Information War?" *Airpower Journal*, Winter 1994, 11, at http://www.airpower.maxwell.af.mil/airchronicles/apj/apj94/win94/man1.html. This article mentions that Brigadier General Glosson reached out and grabbed imagery from Rear Admiral McConnell, and the same imagery came down later via normal dissemination channels.

55. Studeman interview, November 24, 2015.

56. McConnell interview, August 8, 2015.

57. Lamont Wood, *Datapoint: The Lost Story of the Texans Who Invented the Personal Computer Revolution* (Englewood, CO: Hugo House, 2010), 224. The inventors of the personal computer founded Datapoint (originally Computer Terminal Corporation) in the late 1960s.

58. Gregory J. Allen, "The Feasibility of Implementing Videoconferencing Systems aboard Afloat Naval Units," Calhoun, Naval Postgraduate School, March 1990, 48, at http://calhoun.nps.edu/bitstream/handle/ 10945/30671/90Mar_Allen.pdf?sequence=1.

59. MINX was not the only system utilized for intelligence dissemination during Desert Storm. The army built the DoD Intelligence Information System to help with the transmission of intelligence reports to forces on the ground. See Stewart, "Operation Desert Storm," for more information on the technology developed during Desert Storm.

60. McConnell interview, August 8, 2015; Tom Carhart's book *Iron Soldiers: How America's 1st Armored Division Crushed Iraq's Elite Republican Guard* (New York: Pocket, 1994) highlights Alexander's adversarial relationship with his division commander.

61. McConnell interview, August 8, 2015; White House, Office of the Press Secretary, "Statement by General Michael Carns Withdrawing His Nomination to Be Director of CIA," press release, March 11, 1995, at https://fas.org/irp/news/1995/950311carns.htm. In 1995, President Clinton would nominate Carns for the position of DCI, but a controversy involving Carns's family's relationship with a Filipino national convinced Carns to withdraw his name from consideration.

62. McConnell interview, August 8, 2015. McConnell's recollection was that the individual was a former senior officer within the CIA DO's Near East Division.

63. US House, Oversight and Investigations Subcommittee of the Committee on the Armed Services, *Intelligence Successes and Failures in Operations Desert Storm/Shield*; CIA, Gulf War Task Force, "CIA Support to the US Military During the Persian Gulf War," National Security Archive, George Washington University, Washington, DC, June 16, 1997, 1, at http://nsarchive.gwu.edu/NSAEBB/NSAEBB63/doc6.pdf.

64. Gordon and Trainor, *The General's War,* 4–6; Diamond, *The CIA and the Culture of Failure,* 125. According to Diamond, Kenneth Pollack, a CIA analyst at the time, "attempted to warn senior administration and military decision-makers about potential Iraqi aggression" the same day Saddam met with Glaspie. Again according to Diamond, Thomas Keaney and Eliot A. Cohen mentioned Pollack's warning in a draft of the *Gulf War Air Power Survey,* but "U.S. security censors who reviewed the *Survey* before its release in 1993 deleted any further discussion of this analyst's minority view, identifying neither the analyst nor his agency" (125).

65. CIA, Gulf War Task Force, "CIA Support to the US Military during the Persian Gulf War."

66. Janet A. McDonnell, *Adopting to a Changing Environment: The Defense Intelligence Agency in the 1990s* (Washington, DC: Historical Office, Defense Intelligence Agency, 2013), 14; US DoD, Secretary, Joint Staff Directive, *Intelligence Support to Military Operations,* File 218-93-0020, Doc. SJS 2031/884, Box 1, Folder 4, National Defense University Archives, Washington, DC.

3. The Gulf War's Aftermath

1. Haver interview, December 1, 2015, and email exchange, January 4, 2016.

2. Although Cheney directed this intelligence review, he was looking beyond the DoD and was particularly concerned with the CIA's HUMINT support to military operations. His statement in the DoD's *Final Report to Congress on the Conduct of the Persian Gulf War* that "the morale and intentions of Iraqi forces and leaders were obscure to us" (vii) highlights this point. The only way to truly understand intentions is through HUMINT means. Imagery can capture actions, and signals intelligence can capture communication, but to appreciate intentions you need someone who can provide context to the recordings and photographs.

3. Sara Fritz and William J. Eaton, "Congress Authorizes Gulf War: Historic Act: The Vote in Both Houses, Supporting Bush and Freeing Troops to Attack Iraq, Is Decisive and Bipartisan. It Is the Strongest Move since Tonkin Gulf," *Los Angeles Times,* January 13, 1991, at http://articles.latimes.com/1991-01-13/news/mn-374_1_persian-gulf.

4. L. Britt Snider, "Sharing Secrets with Lawmakers: Congress as a User of Intelligence," in *Intelligence and the National Security Strategist: Enduring Issues and Challenges,* ed. Roger Z. George and Robert D. Kline (New York: Rowman and Littlefield, 2006), 98.

5. Quoted in L. Britt Snider, *The Agency and the Hill: CIA's Relationship with Congress, 1946–2004* (Washington, DC: CIA Center for the Study of Intelligence, 2008), 209.

6. Diamond, *The CIA and the Culture of Failure,* 143–44.

7. Admiral Studeman called Haver one of the best community managers there has been (Studeman interview, November 24, 2015). In an interview, Haver told the story of how Ambrose advised him to memorize details to exercise the brain for memory recall (Haver interview, December 1, 2015).

8. Haver interview, December 1, 2015, and email exchange, January 4, 2016; Vistica, *Fall from Glory,* 47. Vistica mentions Admiral Inman identifying Haver's talent and recruiting him to stay in the navy as a civilian intelligence analyst.

9. Haver interview, December 1, 2015, and email exchange, January 4, 2016.

10. John Prados, "The Navy's Biggest Betrayal," *Naval History Magazine* 24, no. 3 (June 2010), at http://www.usni.org/magazines/navalhistory/2010-06/navys-biggest-betrayal; Pete Earley, *Family of Spies* (New York: Bantam Books, 1988), 358.

11. Haver interview, December 1, 2015, and email exchange January 4, 2016. According to Haver, the failure to recognize Saddam's intentions was not just an intelligence issue because multiple people, including leaders from other countries, were discussing the issue with President Bush and trying to determine Iraq's motivations and future actions. Haver said that "everybody has an opinion, and in the absence of exquisite knowledge, that is all it is, an opinion."

12. *Human intelligence* is a broad and contentious term that can describe both clandestinely acquired and overtly acquired information. Some classify the information collected by diplomats and military foreign-area officers as HUMINT. Many in the CIA, however, would question whether these activities are HUMINT because they view HUMINT collection as a clandestine activity. Although overt collection is important, certain characteristics distinguish intelligence from information, and in many CIA DO officers' view clandestine acquisition is one of those characteristics.

13. Major General (ret.) Michael Ennis, former CIA deputy director of HUMINT, interview by the author, Leesburg, VA, November 17, 2015; Donald Rumsfeld to Steve Cambone, "Defense HUMINT Service," memo, January 27, 2004, National Security Archive, George Washington University, Washington, DC, at https://nsarchive2.gwu.edu/NSAEBB/NSAEBB520-the-Pentagons-Spies/EBB-PS35.pdf; Greg Miller, "Senate Moves Blocks to Block Pentagon Plans to Increase Number of Spies Overseas," *Washington Post,* December 10, 2012, at http://articles.washingtonpost.com/2012-12-10/world/35745387_1_defense-clandestine-service-pentagon-dia. For more information on the Great Skills Program, see http://asamra.hqda.pentagon.mil/nco/DA%20Pam%20600–25%20(Approved)%20CMF%2035–09L.pdf.

14. Lowell Jacoby, "Message to the Workforce—DH Strategic Support Teams," January 27, 2005, National Security Archive, George Washington University, Washington, DC, at http://nsarchive.gwu.edu/NSAEBB/NSAEBB520-the-Pentagons-Spies/. Jeffrey T. Richelson, a prolific writer on intelligence issues, has a page on the National Security Archive website that describes some of the DoD's HUMINT history. One of the page's sections, with supporting sources, describes the closing of Navy HUMINT TF-157 in the mid-1970s, and another covers Rumsfeld's "snowflake" on fixing DoD's HUMINT-management issues (at https://nsarchive2.gwu.edu/NSAEBB/NSAEBB520-the-Pentagons-Spies/ [accessed April 21, 2018]). Ennis described the army cutting HUMINT billets in

the 1990s to provide space for field artillery capability and how this cut hurt the army following 9/11 (interview, November 17, 2015).

15. Ennis interview , November 17, 2015.

16. President George H. W. Bush's *National Security Strategy for 1990* was one of the first documents that signaled the shift to a regional focus that the United States would take following the collapse of the Soviet Union (James R. FitzSimonds, "Intelligence and the Revolution in Military Affairs," in *U.S. Intelligence at the Crossroads: Agendas for Reform*, ed. Roy Godson, Ernest R. May, and Gary Schmit [Washington, DC: Brassey's, 1995], 265–87). FitzSimonds's article discusses the influence of the Revolution in Military Affairs on intelligence requirements. Although focused on the military, he specifically mentions HUMINT's important role in enabling the Revolution in Military Affairs.

17. John M. Collins, *Desert Shield and Desert Storm: Implications for Future Force Requirements* (Washington, DC: Congressional Research Service, April 19, 1991), at http://www.hsdl.org/?view&did=712698, 13, 14. An example of using HUMINT to establish networks and relationships in peacetime is the establishment of liaison elements that ran HUMINT networks throughout Iraq in the early to mid-1990s. See Patrick Tyler, *A World of Trouble: The White House and the Middle East—from the Cold War to the War on Terror* (New York: Farrar, Straus and Giroux, 2009), 428–66.

18. US House of Representatives, Committee on the Armed Services, *Lessons Learned as a Result of the U.S. Military Operations in Grenada*, 27–28, 33–34; US DoD, *Report of the DoD Commission on Beirut International Airport Terrorist Act*, 8.

19. Alex Heard, "The Schwarzkopf File," *New York Times,* August 11, 1991, at http://www.nytimes.com/1991 /08/11/magazine/the-schwarzkopf-filet.html.

20. Major General (ret.) Roland Lajoie, former/first CIA associate DDO/MA, telephone interview by the author, November 10, 2015. During the interview, Lajoie mentioned Schwarzkopf's "war hero" status as a reason for the reform initiated at the CIA to increase support to the military.

21. Snider, *The Agency and the Hill,* 243; Norman H. Schwarzkopf, *It Doesn't Take a Hero* (New York: Bantam Books, 1992), 376.

22. Diamond, *The CIA and the Culture of Failure,* 113.

23. Schwarzkopf, *It Doesn't Take a Hero,* 376.

24. Richard K. Betts, *Enemies of Intelligence: Knowledge and Power in American National Security* (New York: Columbia University Press, 2007), 358–62.

25. McConnell interview, August 8, 2015. During an SSCI meeting in early March (a few weeks after Desert Storm), Senator Warner said, "Now, to the extent, that reference has been made to the Gulf, I would like to add my perspective. If that is a news hook, I hope it is a positive news hook, because the record will show what we employed our intelligence assets very skillfully throughout that operation. Just a week ago today— or tomorrow to be exact—I was in General Schwarzkopf's office when that question was put directly to him about intelligence, and he said unequivocally that intelligence played a great role, it was well—professionally –and certainly we have some lessons learned. But I think that in any situation, you have some lessons learned" (US Senate, Select Commit-

tee on Intelligence, *Review of Intelligence Organization* [Hearing 102-91], 102nd Cong., 1st sess., March 12, 1991, 9).

26. US House of Representatives, Permanent Select Committee on Intelligence, *IC21: The Intelligence Community in the 21st Century,* 104th Cong., 1st sess., May 22–December 19, 1995, 43.

27. Molly Moore, "Schwarzkopf: War Intelligence Flawed; General Reports to Congress on Desert Storm," *Washington Post,* June 13, 1991.

28. US DoD, *Final Report to Congress on the Conduct of the Persian Gulf War,* 388.

29. US Senate, Select Committee on Intelligence, *Report on the U.S. Intelligence Community's Prewar Intelligence Assessments on Iraq,* 108th Cong., 2nd sess., July 7, 2004 (Washington, DC: US Government Printing Office, 2004), 18.

30. US Department of the Army, Office of the Deputy Chief of Staff for Intelligence, *Annual Historical Review 1 October 1990–30 September 1991* (Washington, DC: US Department of the Army, 1991), 4–10.

31. Stewart, "Operation Desert Storm."

32. Collins, *Desert Shield and Desert Storm.*

33. Keaney and Cohen, *Gulf War Air Power Survey Summary Report,* 182, 288, 392.

34. Frank J. Smist, *Congress Oversees the United States Intelligence Community 1947–1989* (Knoxville: University of Tennessee Press, 1990), 104.

35. Douglas F. Garthoff, *Directors of Central Intelligence as Leaders of the U.S. Intelligence Community 1946–2005* (Washington, DC: Center for the Study of Intelligence, 2005), 188.

36. US DoD, *Final Report to Congress on the Conduct of the Persian Gulf War,* 387.

37. US Senate, Select Committee on Intelligence, *Authorizing Appropriations for Fiscal Year 1992,* 5–6.

38. "Taskings" is a principle of combatant command authority: "nontransferable command authority, which cannot be delegated, of a combatant commander to perform those functions of command over assigned forces involving organizing and employing commands and forces; assigning tasks; designating objectives; and giving authoritative direction over all aspects of military operations, joint training, and logistics necessary to accomplish the missions assigned to the command" (US DoD, *Joint Publication 1-02,* 37); *Joint Publication 1-02* defines "unity of effort" as "coordination and cooperation toward common objectives, even if the participants are not necessarily part of the same command or organization, which is the product of successful unified action" (252). The ability to task is directly related to authority over an organization, whereas unity of effort takes into consideration the absence of any authority over an organization.

39. US Senate, Select Committee on Intelligence, *Authorizing Appropriations for Fiscal Year 1992,* 6–7.

40. US House of Representatives, Oversight and Investigations Subcommittee of the Committee on the Armed Services, *Intelligence Successes and Failures in Operations Desert Storm/Shield.*

41. US DoD, "Lessons Learned from the Persian Gulf," memo with attachments,

March 29, 1993, slide 2, File 218-93-0018, Doc. SJS 2588/456, Box 4, Folder 3, Colin Powell Collection, National Defense University Archives, Washington, DC.

42. US House of Representatives, Oversight and Investigations Subcommittee of the Committee on the Armed Services, *Intelligence Successes and Failures in Operations Desert Storm/Shield,* 6.

43. US House of Representatives, Oversight and Investigations Subcommittee of the Committee on the Armed Services, *Intelligence Successes and Failures in Operations Desert Storm/Shield,* 24.

44. David Oakley, "Taming the Rogue Elephant?" *American Intelligence Journal* 26, no. 2 (2008–2009): 61.

45. US Senate, Select Committee on Intelligence, *Hearings before the Select Committee on Intelligence: U.S. Intelligence Agencies and Activities: Intelligence Cost and Fiscal Procedures,* 94th Cong., 1st sess., July–August 1975, 173.

46. Persian Gulf War Illness Task Force, *CIA Support to the US Military during the Persian Gulf War* (Washington, DC: US Central Intelligence Agency, 1997).

47. US Senate, Committee on Veterans Affairs, *Report of the Special Investigation Unit on Gulf War Illnesses,* 105th Cong., 2nd sess. (Washington, DC: US Government Printing Office, 1998), 9, 20, 29, 30.

48. US DoD, *Report of the DoD Commission on Beirut International Airport Terrorist Act,* 66, 136.

49. US DoD, Assistant Secretary of Defense for Command, Control, Communications, and Intelligence, *Plan for Restructuring Defense Intelligence* (Washington, DC: US DoD, March 15, 1991).

50. US Senate and House of Representatives, Select Committee on Intelligence and Permanent Select Committee on Intelligence, *S. 2198 and S.421 to Reorganize the United States Intelligence Community,* 102nd Cong., 2nd sess., April 1, 1992, 2, 8.

51. US Senate, Select Committee on Intelligence, *Review of Intelligence Organization,* 8.

52. US House of Representatives, *National Defense Authorization Act for Fiscal Year 1991,* 101st Cong., 2nd sess., November 5, 1990, 284.

53. Rear Admiral (ret.) Rosanne M. LeVitre, national intelligence manager for military issues, deputy DNI for intelligence integration, interview by the author, Washington, DC, November 4, 2015.

54. Vice Admiral (ret.) Lowell E. Jacoby, former DIA director and former JCS J2, interview by the author, Ashburn, VA, November 18, 2015.

55. US DoD, Assistant Secretary of Defense for Command, Control, Communications, and Intelligence, "Strengthening Defense Intelligence—DIA HUMINT Plan," memo, August 6, 1991, National Security Archive, George Washington University, Washington, DC, at https://nsarchive2.gwu.edu/NSAEBB/NSAEBB46/document15.pdf.

56. US DoD, *Centralized Management of Department of Defense Human Intelligence (HUMINT) Operations,* Directive 5200-37 (Washington, DC: US DoD, December 18, 1992).

57. Collins, *Desert Shield and Desert Storm*, 13, 14.

58. Michael Warner, *The Rise and Fall of Intelligence: An International Security History* (Washington, DC: Georgetown University Press, 2014), 261.

4. End of the Cold War and the Continuation of Reform

1. Bush, *National Security Review 29*.

2. Michelle R. Garfinkel, "The Economic Consequences of Reducing Military Spending," *Federal Reserve Bank of St. Louis Review* 72, no. 6 (November–December 1990): 49.

3. Christopher Andrew, *For the President's Eyes Only: Secret Intelligence and the American Presidency from Washington to Bush* (New York: Harper Perennial, 1996), 5, 532–33.

4. Robert M. Gates, *From the Shadows: The Ultimate Insider's Story of Five Presidents and How They Won the Cold War* (New York: Simon and Schuster, 2006), 137. The CIA held a reception to celebrate the DCI as the leader of the Intelligence Community not long after the Intelligence Reform and Terrorism Prevention Act of 2004 created the position of DNI. The living former DCIs and the widows of others participated in the ceremony. Each former DCI was given the opportunity to speak to the CIA workforce. It was interesting to see how warmly or not the CIA workforce received each DCI. Bush and Tenet were warmly received, but the reception of Turner and Tenet was a little colder.

5. "Flashback: April 26, 1999: CIA Headquarters Named George Bush Center for Intelligence," CIA, News & Information, 2014, at https://www.cia.gov/news-information/featured-story-archive/2014-featured-story-archive/flashback-cia-headquarters-named-george-bush-center-for-intelligence.html.

6. Quoted in Jon Meacham, *Destiny and Power: The American Odyssey of George Herbert Walker Bush* (New York: Random House Books, 2015), 580.

7. Garthoff, *Directors of Central Intelligence*, 122.

8. Garthoff, *Directors of Central Intelligence*, 122, 114.

9. US DoD, "Defense Intelligence Board," memo, December 16, 1976, Donald Rumsfeld Papers Online, at http://library.rumsfeld.com/doclib/sp/4361/1976-12-16%20From%20Robert%20Ellsworth%20re%20Defense%20Intelligence%20Board%20(569-7).pdf#search="defense%20intelligence%20board".

10. Garthoff, *Directors of Central Intelligence,* 114.

11. US Commission on the Organization of the Government for the Conduct of Foreign Policy, *Report by the Commission on the Organization of the Government for the Conduct of Foreign Policy: Background and Principal Recommendations,* CRS 9-11 (Washington, DC: Congressional Research Service, n.d.), at research.policyarchive.org/20213.pdf (accessed January 12, 2016).

12. Bush, *National Security Review 29*.

13. Tim Weiner, "Rewiring the CIA for a Post-Cold-War World," *Rolling Stone,* June 27, 1991, at http://www.rollingstone.com/politics/news/rewiring-the-cia-for-a-post-cold-war-world-19910627.

14. "Robert Gates: Government Official (1943–)," *Biography*, n.d., at http://www. biography.com/people/robert-gates-40993#early-career (accessed April 3, 2018).

15. During congressional testimony, Inman gave his former mentee a ringing endorsement when he said, "I believe even if we weren't in the troubled world that we are going to be in, that [Robert Gates] is the best candidate for the job and that he is now ready to provide the leadership and the management, not only of the CIA, but for the Intelligence Community that the country needs and that CIA needs" (US Senate, Select Committee on Intelligence, *Nomination of Robert M. Gates to Be Director of Central Intelligence* [Hearing 102-799], 102nd Cong., 1st sess., September 16, 17, 19, 20, 1991, 938).

16. US Senate, Select Committee on Intelligence, *Nomination of Robert M. Gates to Be Director of Central Intelligence*, 927; Gates, *From the Shadows*, 221, 224–25. Admiral Inman stood up for Gates during the latter's unsuccessful nomination hearings, telling a *New York Times* reporter when asked about his own status as a potential nominee, "There is no set of circumstances under which I would accept the job. . . . Gates was exactly right" (quoted in Gerald M. Boyd, "Reagan Retracts Gates Nomination to Head the C.I.A.," *New York Times*, March 3, 1987, at http://www.nytimes.com/1987/03/03/world/ reagan-retracts-gates-nomination-to-head-the-cia.html). Inman was so angry about how Gates was treated that he told reporters, "I will never come back to government. I have zero Potomac fever. I don't have the patience anymore. Watching this process has absolutely locked that in concrete" (quoted in Elaine Sciolino, "Change at the Pentagon: Man in the News—Bobby Ray Inman; an Operator for the CIA," *New York Times*, December 17, 1993, at http://www.nytimes.com/1993/12/17/us/change-pentagon-man-bobby-ray-inman-operator-for-pentagon.html?pagewanted=all).

17. Garthoff, *Directors of Central Intelligence*, 168.

18. US Senate, *Nomination of Robert M. Gates to Be Director of Central Intelligence*, Executive Report, 102nd Cong., 1st sess., January 3, 1991 (Washington, DC: US Government Printing Office, 1991), 2, 4–5. The October Surprise was the allegation that members of the Reagan campaign team (including Casey and Bush) and others had conducted backdoor negotiations with Iran to hold the hostages until after the campaign in 1980 to weaken Carter's chances of reelection. These allegations, driven largely by Gary Sick, a Carter national security adviser, led to a congressional task force. The task force chair, Lee Hamilton, found that "there was virtually no credible evidence to support the allegations" (Lee Hamilton, "Dialogue: Last Word on the October Surprise? Case Closed," *New York Times*, January 24, 1993, at http://www.nytimes.com/1993/01/24/ opinion/dialogue-last-word-on-the-october-surprise-case-closed.html). Compare the vote on Gates as DCI in 1991 to the vote on Gates to be secretary of defense in 2006, which was 95–2.

19. US Senate, *Nomination of Robert M. Gates to Be Director of Central Intelligence*, 191.

20. During Gates's confirmation hearings, both Senator Boren and Dr. Gates argued for improving support to the military and the link for tactical and national intelligence. Senator Boren also cautioned that the DoD should not control the intelligence com-

munity, an issue he would raise twenty-one years later when responding to questions. In 2008, when Gates was departing as secretary of defense, he discussed his concern regarding the DoD's power and influence in foreign policy, a concern he said he had during his career as an intelligence officer.

21. Haver interview, December 1, 2015, and email exchange, January 4, 2016; US Senate, Select Committee on Intelligence, *Nomination of Robert M. Gates to Be Director of Central Intelligence*, 443–44. Inman conducted a review of intelligence capabilities in the early 1980s to determine intelligence requirements that Gates highlighted as informing his push for the review outlined in NSR-29.

22. Haver interview, December 1, 2015, and email exchange, January 4, 2016.

23. Robert Gates, former secretary of defense and former DCI, telephone interview by the author, March 29, 2016.

24. Haver interview, December 1, 2015, and email exchange, January 4, 2016; Haver noted that during close-door congressional testimony Cheney advocated for imagery and drones. Haver stated that capacity for war, which included both the equipment and the "gray matter," had to be developed during peace. He also mentioned as examples of the cost of unpreparedness language shortfalls during Desert Storm and the inability to interrogate prisoners of war.

25. US Senate and House of Representatives, Select Committee on Intelligence and Permanent Select Committee on Intelligence, *S. 2198 and S.421 to Reorganize the United States Intelligence Community*, 14.

26. US Senate, Select Committee on Intelligence, *Nomination of Robert M. Gates to Be Director of Central Intelligence*, 640.

27. US Senate and House of Representatives, Select Committee on Intelligence and Permanent Select Committee on Intelligence, *S. 2198 and S.421 to Reorganize the United States Intelligence Community*, 14.

28. Haver interview, December 1, 2015, and email exchange, January 4, 2016.

29. US Senate and House of Representatives, Select Committee on Intelligence and Permanent Select Committee on Intelligence, *S. 2198 and S.421 to Reorganize the United States Intelligence Community*.

30. US Senate and House of Representatives, Select Committee on Intelligence and Permanent Select Committee on Intelligence, *S. 2198 and S.421 to Reorganize the United States Intelligence Community*, 14.

31. US Senate and House of Representatives, Select Committee on Intelligence and Permanent Select Committee on Intelligence, *S. 2198 and S.421 to Reorganize the United States Intelligence Community*, 15–16. Red Teams and Team A/B provide alternative analysis and often serve as a kind of "devil's advocate" to help ensure all angles are considered.

32. Robert M. Gates, "Secretary Gates Speech at National Defense University," September 2008, at http://www.cfr.org/defense-strategy/ secretary-gates-speech-national-defense-university-september-2008/p17411.

33. US Senate and House of Representatives, Select Committee on Intelligence and Permanent Select Committee on Intelligence, *S. 2198 and S.421 to Reorganize the United States Intelligence Community*, 16.

34. US Senate and House of Representatives, Select Committee on Intelligence and Permanent Select Committee on Intelligence, *S. 2198 and S.421 to Reorganize the United States Intelligence Community,* 16.

35. Andrew, *For the President's Eyes Only,* 533.

36. "Creating the National Imagery and Mapping Agency," CIA, Library, n.d., at http://www.foia.cia.gov/sites/default/files/DOC_0000619983.pdf (accessed February 9, 2016).

37. Gates telephone interview, March 29, 2016. During the interview, Gates referred to the establishment of the Central Imagery Office as a "half-step."

38. Anne Daugherty Miles, *The Creation of the National Imagery and Mapping Agency: Congress's Role as Overseer* (Washington, DC: Joint Military Intelligence College, 2002), 5.

39. Bruce Berkowitz, *The National Reconnaissance Office at 50 Years: A Brief History* (Chantilly, VA: Center for the Study of National Reconnaissance, 2011), 18.

40. DCI Task Force on the National Reconnaissance Office, "Report to the Director of Central Intelligence," April 1992, National Security Archive, George Washington University, Washington, DC, at http://nsarchive.gwu.edu/NSAEBB/NSAEBB35/ docs/ doc14.pdf.

41. Berkowitz, *National Reconnaissance Office at 50 Years,* iii, 13. There was a fourth program, "Program D, the Air Force and CIA aerial reconnaissance program, comprising all national assets, including the U-2 and A-12/SR-71 programs. (This program was dissolved and its assets were transferred to the Air Force when the CIA's A-12s were deactivated on 1 October 1974)" (Berkowitz, *The National Reconnaissance Office at 50 Years,* 13).

42. DCI Task Force on the National Reconnaissance Office, "Report to the Director of Central Intelligence."

43. Berkowitz, *National Reconnaissance Office at 50 Years,* 20.

44. Walter Pincus, "Secret Agency Reportedly Salted Away $1-Billion Fund: Finances: The National Reconnaissance Office Did Nothing Illegal, but CIA Director Orders a Restructuring," *Los Angeles Times,* September 24, 1995, at http://articles. latimes.com/1995-09-24/news/mn-49643_1_national-reconnaissance-office. The controversy had to do with the NRO using "unspent funds" set aside to build a new headquarters without properly notifying Congress.

45. US Senate and House of Representatives, Select Committee on Intelligence and Permanent Select Committee on Intelligence, *S. 2198 and S.421 to Reorganize the United States Intelligence Community,* 18–19.

46. Gates telephone interview, March 29, 2016.

47. Office of the Chief of Military History, "Unit History 1964—United States Military Liaison Mission to Commander in Chief, Group of Soviet Force in Germany," n.d., at http://www.coldwarspies.com/resources/uh1964cpr.pdf (accessed April 22, 2016), 1; Lajoie telephone interview, November 10, 2015.

48. Lajoie telephone interview, November 10, 2015.

49. "Soldiers Rammed by the Soviets Not in the Wrong, U.S. Says," *Pittsburgh Press,*

July 17, 1985, at https://news.google.com/newspapers?nid=1144&dat=19850717&id=1N
QbAAAAIBAJ&sjid=CWMEAAAAIBAJ&pg=4947,203827&hl=en.

50. Lajoie telephone interview, November 10, 2015; "U.S. Major Killed by Soviet
Sentry: Accused of Photographing E. German Military Installation," UPI, *Los Angeles
Times,* March 25, 1985, at http://articles.latimes.com/1985-03-25/news/mn-21307_1_
soviet-union; White House, Office of the Press Secretary, "Principal Deputy Press
Secretary Speaks on the Death of Major Arthur D. Nicholson, Jr., in the German
Democratic Republic," April 23, 1985, at http://www.reagan.utexas.edu/archives/
speeches/1985/42385d.htm.

51. Michael Wines, "Washington at Work; after 30 Years in Shadows, a Spymaster
Emerges," *New York Times,* November 20, 1990.

52. Lajoie telephone interview, November 10, 2015.

53. Lajoie telephone interview, November 10, 2015.

54. US House of Representatives, *Intelligence Authorization Act, Fiscal Year 1991,*
Report 102-166, 102nd Cong., 1st sess., July 25, 1991 (Washington, DC: US Government Printing Office, 1991), 16.

55. US Senate, Select Committee on Intelligence, *Authorizing Appropriations for Fiscal Year 1991 for the Intelligence Activities of the U.S. Government, the Intelligence Community Staff, the Central Intelligence Agency Retirement and Disability System, and for Other
Purposes,* 102nd Cong., 1st sess., June 19, 1991, 7.

56. US Senate, *National Intelligence Reorganization Act,* 102nd Cong., 1st sess., February 19, 1991.

57. Senator Specter had previously introduced S. Bill 1820, passed as the National
Intelligence Reorganization Act of 1987, and S. Bill 175, passed as the National Intelligence Reorganization Act of 1989.

58. US Senate, Select Committee on Intelligence, *Review of Intelligence Organization,* 5; George J. Tenet to National Security Adviser Samuel R. Berger, "Meeting with
the President's Foreign Intelligence Advisory Board," memo, April 16, 1993, Box 10:
White House Staff and Office Files, Clinton Presidential Records, William J. Clinton
Presidential Library Archives, Little Rock, AR. During Inman's tenure, the President's
Foreign Intelligence Advisory Board would publish a report titled *Intelligence Support to
the Persian Gulf Crisis* (as indicated in Tenet's memo). This report argued that "the failure of U. S. intelligence to provide strategic warning of Saddam Hussein's intentions to
invade Kuwait, the paucity of human intelligence we had collected on Iraq, and the real
problems between military and civilian intelligence in providing unified support, in the
initial stages of the Desert Shield deployment, to our commanders on the ground" (as
quoted in Tenet's memo).

59. US Senate, Select Committee on Intelligence, *Authorizing Appropriations for Fiscal Year 1992,* 6.

60. US Senate, Select Committee on Intelligence, *Review of Intelligence Organization,* 18, 17–35. Morton Abramowitz also argued for a bottom-up review on intelligence
needs during his testimony to the SSCI in March 1992 (US Senate, Select Committee

on Intelligence, *S. 2198 and S. 421 to Reorganize the United States Intelligence Community* [Hearing 894], 102nd Cong., 2nd sess., February 20 and March 4, 12, 19, 1992, 221).

61. US Senate, Select Committee on Intelligence, *Review of Intelligence Organization,* 17–35.

62. See the William E. Odom Papers at the Library of Congress for personal correspondence covering Odom's opposition to the Iraq War. The finding aid and an overview of the content can be accessed at http://rs5.loc.gov/service/mss/eadxmlmss/eadpd-fmss/2009/ms009006.pdf (accessed April 24, 2018).

63. US Senate, Foreign Relations Committee, *Security Situation in Iraq,* 110th Cong., 2nd sess., April 2, 2008; Matt Schudel, "William E. Odom, 75; Military Adviser to 2 Administrations," *Washington Post,* May 31, 2008, at http://www.washingtonpost.com/wp-dyn/content/article/2008/05/31/AR2008053102193.html.

64. US Senate, Select Committee on Intelligence, *Review of Intelligence Organization,* 36–52.

65. US Senate, Select Committee on Intelligence, *Review of Intelligence Organization,* 53–66.

66. US Senate, Select Committee on Intelligence, *Review of Intelligence Organization,* 59.

67. US Senate, Select Committee on Intelligence, *Review of Intelligence Organization,* 37.

68. Representative Dave McCurdy, "Democratic Convention Seconding Speech," July 15, 1992, C-Span, http://www.c-span.org/video/?27124-1/democratic-convention-seconding-speech.

69. Robert Shogan, "Centrist Ally Calls Clinton 'Old Democrat,'" *Los Angeles Times,* December 7, 1994, at http://articles.latimes.com/1994-12-07/news/mn-5990_1_leadership-council.

70. R. W. Apple Jr., "The 1994 Campaign; in Oklahoma's Senate Race, Both Candidates Are Running against Clinton," *New York Times,* October 5, 1994, at http://www.nytimes.com/1994/10/05/us/1994-campaign-oklahoma-s-senate-race-both-candidates-are-running-against-clinton.html?pagewanted=all.

71. US Senate, *Intelligence Reorganization Act of 1992,* 102nd Cong., 2nd sess., February 5, 1992, 7.

72. This was not the first time a proposal mandating that either the head of the Intelligence Community or his deputy be a military officer had been made. General Gorman mentioned previous legislation during his testimony on March 12, 1992 (US Senate, Select Committee on Intelligence, *S. 2198 and S. 421 to Reorganize the United States Intelligence Community,* 286).

73. US Senate, *Intelligence Reorganization Act of 1992,* 10.

74. US Senate, *Intelligence Reorganization Act of 1992;* Robert David Steele, "The National Security Act of 1992," *American Intelligence Journal,* Winter–Spring 1992, 31–33.

75. Steele, "The National Security Act of 1992," 35; US House of Representatives, *National Security Act of 1992* (H.R. 165), 102nd Cong., 2nd sess., February 5, 1992.

76. US Senate, Select Committee on Intelligence, *S. 2198 and S. 421 to Reorganize the United States Intelligence Community,* 252.

77. William Odom, *On Internal War: American and Soviet Approaches to Third World Clients and Insurgents* (Durham, NC: Duke University Press, 1991).

78. Odom, *On Internal War,* 215.

79. Odom, *On Internal War,* 33, 215.

80. Odom argued that analytical support to policy makers often did not provide them any valuable insight or help determining policy actions, whereas analytic support to the military at all levels provided the commander more clarity and understanding (US Senate, Select Committee on Intelligence, *S. 2198 and S. 421 to Reorganize the United States Intelligence Community,* 202–15). Although Odom's analytical argument focused on the importance of decentralization of analysis, his opinion on the value of tactical analysis compared to strategic analysis highlighted where he thought intelligence provided the most value—at the policy-implementation level (i.e., military operations).

81. Paul F. Gorman, "Preparing for Low-Intensity Conflict: Four Fundamentals," in *Essays on Strategy* (Washington, DC: National Defense University Press, 1988), at http:// usacac.army.mil/cac2/csi/docs/Gorman/06_Retired/01_Retired_1985_90/30_88_ NDUPreparing_LowIntensityConflict_Four%20Fundamentals_Aug.pdf, 4.

82. US Senate, Select Committee on Intelligence, *S. 2198 and S. 421 to Reorganize the United States Intelligence Community,* 260, 262.

83. US Senate, Select Committee on Intelligence, *S. 2198 and S. 421 to Reorganize the United States Intelligence Community,* 289.

84. Robert M. Cassidy, *Counterinsurgency and the Global War on Terror: Military Culture and Irregular War* (Westport, CT: Praeger Security International, 2006), 121.

85. US Senate, Select Committee on Intelligence, *S. 2198 and S. 421 to Reorganize the United States Intelligence Community,* 183. Schlesinger further argued that most of the "prospective savings" should come from cuts in the DoD's collection capabilities and manpower as part of the drive toward jointness initiated with Goldwater-Nichols.

86. US Senate, Select Committee on Intelligence, *S. 2198 and S. 421 to Reorganize the United States Intelligence Community.* Vice Admiral McConnell offered a similar opinion during an interview in 2015 when he stated that the value in intelligence was identifying the "guy behind the door" (McConnell interview, August 8, 2015).

87. Secretary of Defense Richard Cheney to Representative Les Aspin, with attachments, March 17, 1992, quoted in Amy Zegart, *Spying Blind: The CIA, the FBI, and the Origins of 9/11* (Princeton, NJ: Princeton University Press, 1999), 72 n. 40, where Zegart provides the following link to this document: https://fas.org/irp/congress/1992_ cr/cheney1992.pdf.

88. Cheney to Aspin, with attachments, March 17, 1992.

89. US Senate, Committee on Armed Services, *Operation Desert Shield/Desert Storm,* 102nd Cong., 1st sess., April–June 1991, 341.

90. Cheney to Aspin, March 17, 1992.

91. McConnell interview, August 8, 2015. McConnell mentioned that Secretary

of Defense Cheney knew that intelligence provided great support to the military during Desert Storm.

92. Studeman interview, November 24, 2015; Vice Admiral McConnell spoke about a meeting he later had with General Paul Funk, who had been the Third Armored Division commander during Desert Storm. When Admiral McConnell mentioned to Funk the "great" intelligence support provided to commanders on the ground in Desert Storm, Funk disagreed and told McConnell that his division was not receiving tactical intelligence from higher up the military chain. McConnell concluded that not all the unit G2s used the intelligence being pushed down the line and that many commanders remained unaware of the products available.

93. Bush, *National Security Directive 67*.

94. White House, Office of the Press Secretary, "Statement by Press Secretary Fitz-water on Organizational Changes in the Intelligence Community," April 1, 1992, American Presidency Project, at http://www.presidency.ucsb.edu/ws/?pid=20786.

95. Haver interview, December 1, 2015, and email exchange, January 4, 2016.

96. Haver interview, December 1, 2015, and email exchange, January 4, 2016.

97. "The 1992 Campaign: On the Trail; Poll Gives Perot a Clear Lead," *New York Times*, June 11, 1992, at http://www.nytimes.com/1992/06/11/us/the-1992-campaign-on-the-trail-poll-gives-perot-a-clear-lead.html.

98. Haver interview, December 1, 2015, and email exchange, January 4, 2016.

99. Haver interview, December 1, 2015, and email exchange, January 4, 2016.

100. Glenn Kessler, "Cutting the Defense Budget," *Washington Post*, January 25, 2011, at http://voices.washingtonpost.com/fact-checker/2011/01/cutting_the_defense_budget.html.

101. US Commission on the Roles and Capabilities of the United States Intelligence Community, *Preparing for the 21st Century: An Appraisal of U.S. Intelligence* (Washington, DC: US Government Printing Office, 1996), 131.

102. Gallup, "Presidential Approval Ratings—Gallup Historical Statistics and Trends," n.d., at http://www.gallup.com/poll/116677/presidential-approval-ratings-gallup-historical-statistics-trends.aspx (accessed January 28, 2016).

5. "It's the Economy, Stupid"

1. Federal Elections Commission, *Federal Elections 92: Election Results for the U.S. President, the U.S. Senate, and the U.S. House of Representatives* (Washington, DC: Federal Elections Commission, June 1993), at http://www.fec.gov/pubrec/fe1992/federalelections92.pdf.

2. George H. W. Bush, "Remarks at the Aspen Institute Symposium in Aspen Colorado," August 2, 1990, at http://www.presidency.ucsb.edu/ws/?pid=18731; Michael R. Gordon, "Cheney Gives Plan to Reduce Forces by 25% in 5 Years," *New York Times*, June 20, 1990, http://www.nytimes.com/1990/06/20/us/cheney-gives-plan-to-reduce-forces-by-25-in-5-years.html?pagewanted=all.

3. US General Accounting Office, "Military Downsizing: Balancing Accessions

and Losses Is Key to Shaping the Future Force," September 1993, at http://www.gao.gov/assets/160/153782.pdf.

4. US Congressional Budget Office, *The Drawdown of the Military Officer Corps* (Washington, DC: US Government Printing Office, November 1999), at http://fas.org/irp/congress/1993_cr/index.html.

5. Burton Gerber, "Managing HUMINT: The Need for a New Approach," in *Transforming U.S. Intelligence,* ed. Jennifer E. Sims and Burton Gerber (Washington, DC: Georgetown University Press, 2005), 180; US General Accounting Office, *Military Personnel: High Aggregate Personnel Levels Maintained throughout Drawdown* (Washington, DC: US General Accounting Office, June 1995), 10.

6. Gates telephone interview, March 29, 2016.

7. Robert M. Gates, *Duty: Memoirs of a Secretary at War* (New York: Penguin Random House, 2014), 23.

8. McDonnell, *Adopting to a Changing Environment,* 19.

9. US DoD, *Centralized Management of Department of Defense Human Intelligence (HUMINT) Operations;* "Plans for Consolidation of Defense HUMINT," n.d., National Security Archive, George Washington University, Washington, DC, at http://nsarchive.gwu.edu/NSAEBB/NSAEBB46/document18.pdf (accessed February 9, 2016).

10. US Department of the Army, Office of the Deputy Chief of Staff for Intelligence, *Annual Historical Review 1 October 1990–30 September 1991,* 4–19.

11. "Plans for Consolidation of Defense HUMINT."

12. "Plans for Consolidation of Defense HUMINT," 2.

13. US DoD, Deputy Secretary of Defense, "Consolidation of Defense HUMINT," memo, November 2, 1993, National Security Archive, George Washington University, Washington, DC, at https://nsarchive2.gwu.edu/NSAEBB/NSAEBB46/document18.pdf.

14. "Plans for Consolidation of Defense HUMINT."

15. Clinton, "Remarks Announcing the National Performance Review."

16. "A Brief History of Vice President Al Gore's National Partnership for Reinventing Government during the Administration of President Bill Clinton, 1993–2001," National Performance Review, n.d., at http://govinfo.library.unt.edu/npr/whoweare/historyofnpr.html (accessed June 26, 2016).

17. Reagan, *Executive Order 12526.*

18. "Al Gore and the Office of the Vice President, 1993–2001," n.d., Clinton Digital Library Archives, at http://clinton.presidentiallibraries.us/items/show/5043 (accessed January 28, 2016).

19. *1993 Report: From Red Tape to Results: Creating a Government That Works Better and Costs Less,* National Performance Review, September 7, 1994, at http://govinfo.library.unt.edu/npr/library/nprrpt/redtpe93/259e.html. The seven objectives were: Intel 01, Enhance Intelligence Community Integration; Intel 02, Enhance Community Responsiveness to Customers; Intel 03, Reassess Information Collection to Meet New Analytical Challenges; Intel 04, Integrate Intelligence Community Information Management Systems; Intel 05, Develop Integrated Personnel and Training Systems;

Intel 06, Merge the President's Intelligence Oversight Board with the President's Foreign Intelligence Advisory Board; Intel 07, Improve Support to Ground Troops during Combat Operations.

20. US Senate, Select Committee on Intelligence, *S. 2198 and S. 421 to Reorganize the United States Intelligence Community*, 183.

21. PDD-35 also established a tiered intelligence collection/support system that prioritized efforts for the Intelligence Community (see Clinton, *Presidential Decision Directive 35*). PDD-35 would be replaced in 2003 with the National Intelligence Priorities Framework, which would require a review of intelligence priorities every six months to identify changing requirements and ensure proper resource allocation based on collection requirements. Around 2006, Lieutenant General Michael Maples, the DIA director, and Lieutenant General Ronald Burgess, the JCS J2, established the Defense Intelligence Priorities Framework to ensure that DoD's collection priorities were in line with the national collection priorities (Burgess telephone interview, September 17, 2015).

22. Michael Warner, "Central Intelligence: Origin and Evolution," in *Intelligence and the National Security Strategist*, ed. George and Kline, 50.

23. Mark Bowden, *Black Hawk Down: A Story of Modern War* (New York: Atlantic Monthly Press, 1999), 335; Bacevich, *America's War for the Greater Middle East*, 157, where Bacevich describes Aspin as a fall guy; Richard H. P. Sia, "Embattled Les Aspin Steps Down," *Baltimore Sun*, December 16, 1993, at http://articles.baltimoresun.com/1993-12-16/news/1993350006_1_les-aspin-clinton-oval; David E. Rosenbaum, "Les Aspin, 56, Dies: Member of Congress and Defense Chief," *New York Times*, May 22, 1995, at http://www.nytimes.com/1995/05/22/obituaries/les-aspin-56-dies-member-of-congress-and-defense-chief.html?pagewanted=all; John Barry, "The Collapse of Les Aspin," *Newsweek*, December 26, 1993, at http://www.newsweek.com/collapse-les-aspin-190744.

24. Loch Johnson, a leading intelligence scholar, who served on both the Church Committee and the Aspin-Brown Commission, has written extensively about the Aspin-Brown Commission and the events leading up to its establishment. According to Johnson, it was the "confluence of events" in the early 1990s that brought about the push for an intelligence review (*Threat on the Horizon*, 3).

25. US House of Representatives, *Intelligence Authorization Act, Fiscal Year 1995*, H. R. 4299. 103rd Cong., 2nd sess., September 30, 1994.

26. US Commission on the Roles and Capabilities of the United States Intelligence Community, *Preparing for the 21st Century*, 149; Diamond, *The CIA and the Culture of Failure*, 21.

27. Kathryn S. Olmstead, *Challenging the Secret Government: The Post-Watergate Investigations of the CIA and FBI* (Chapel Hill: University of North Carolina Press, 1996), 170; Smist, *Congress Oversees the United States Intelligence Community*, 160.

28. Smist, *Congress Oversees the United States Intelligence Community*, 228.

29. US Commission on the Roles and Capabilities of the United States Intelligence Community, *Preparing for the 21st Century*, 54–57.

30. US Commission on the Roles and Capabilities of the United States Intelligence Community, *Preparing for the 21st Century*, 33.

31. Johnson, *Threat on the Horizon,* 324, 320–21.

32. US House of Representatives, Permanent Select Committee on Intelligence, *IC21* (hearings), 2.

33. US House of Representatives, Permanent Select Committee on Intelligence, *IC21* (hearings), 373.

34. US House of Representatives, Permanent Select Committee on Intelligence, *IC21* (hearings), 340, 215.

35. US House of Representatives, Permanent Select Committee on Intelligence, *IC21* (hearings), 2, 96, 120, 215, 310, 369–70, 373.

36. US House of Representatives, Permanent Select Committee on Intelligence, *IC21: The Intelligence Community in the 21st Century,* Staff Study Report, 104th Cong., 2nd sess., June 5, 1996 (Washington, DC: US Government Printing Office, 1996), at https://www.gpo.gov/fdsys/pkg/GPO-IC21/html/ic21001.htm; Jeffrey Cooper, "Dominant Battlespace Awareness and Future Warfare," in *Dominant Battlespace Knowledge,* ed. Stuart E. Johnson and Martin C. Libicki (Washington, DC: National Defense University Press, 1995), 39–46; Frederick W. Kagan, *Finding the Target: The Transformation of American Military Policy* (New York: Encounter Books, 1997), 212–18. Cooper's article describes Dominant Battlefield Awareness as the ability to know more about the battlefield because technology allows the collection, organization, and understanding of larger amounts of data than was before possible. Kagan's book discusses the history of Dominant Battlefield Awareness and critiques the promises and expectations of those who developed it.

37. US House of Representatives, Permanent Select Committee on Intelligence, *IC21,* Staff Study Report.

38. US House of Representatives, Permanent Select Committee on Intelligence, IC21, Staff Study Report.

39. US House of Representatives, Permanent Select Committee on Intelligence, *IC21,* Staff Study Report.

40. McDonnell, *Adopting to a Changing Environment,* 29–31, 226.

41. Garthoff, *Directors of Central Intelligence,* 226–27; Hayden interview, September 18, 2015. General Hayden discussed how the existence of the USD for information could take away power from the DNI.

42. Johnson, *Threat on the Horizon,* 357.

43. US House of Representatives, *National Defense Authorization Act for Fiscal Year 1997,* 104th Cong., 2nd sess., September 10, 1996.

44. Randall B. Woods, *Shadow Warrior: William Egan Colby and the CIA* (New York: Basic Books, 2013), 397, 1.

45. John Judis, "The Case for Abolishing the CIA," *New Republic Online,* December 20, 2005, at http://carnegieendowment.org/2005/12/20/case-for-abolishing-cia.

46. Michael J. Sulick, *American Spies: Espionage against the United States from the Cold War to the Present* (Washington, DC: Georgetown University Press, 2013), 201.

47. US Senate, Select Committee on Intelligence, *An Assessment of the Aldrich H.*

Ames Espionage Case and Its Implication for U.S. Intelligence, 103rd Cong., 2nd sess., November 1, 1994 (Washington, DC: US Government Printing Office, 1994), 126.

48. Garthoff, *Directors of Central Intelligence,* 231–32.

49. US Senate, Select Committee on Intelligence, *Nomination of John Deutch* (Hearing 104-160), 104th Cong., 1st sess., April 26 and May 3, 1995, 67, 14.

50. Quoted in Johnson, *Threat on the Horizon,* 237

51. Johnson, *Threat on the Horizon,* 163; David Edger, former CIA associate DDO, telephone interview by the author, December 7, 2015. Edger explained that Deutch made it clear that he preferred the DoD over the CIA when he first arrived at Langley.

52. Edger telephone interview, December 7, 2015.

53. Garthoff, *Directors of Central Intelligence,* 237–38.

54. "Military Affairs/History," CIA, n.d., at https://www.cia.gov/offices-of-cia/military-affairs/history.html (accessed November 18, 2012).

55. The Intelligence Reform Terrorism Prevention Act of 2005 replaced the director of central intelligence (DCI) with the director of national intelligence (DNI). Prior to 2005, the DCI was the head of both the CIA and the Intelligence Community. Now the head of the CIA is referred to as the director of the Central Intelligence Agency (DCIA).

56. "Military Affairs/History."

57. Blair argued that he, as the DNI, should be the one who assigned the senior intelligence officer in each country. Panetta argued that the CIA chief of station should be the senior intelligence officer in each country. The issue was eventually taken to President Obama, who sided with Panetta. Numerous interviewees commented on this debate, some arguing that it was a nonissue because in the majority of cases the chief of station would be the senior intelligence officer and would not be so only in unique circumstances (e.g., warzones). Some believed Panetta fought the issue because senior CIA officers got to him early on and convinced him of the need for the CIA to retain the senior intelligence officer position. Some believed the president's siding with Panetta over Blair further weakened the DNI because the DCIA is supposed to be a subordinate to the DNI. Panetta describes his perspective in Leon Panetta and Jim Newton, *Worthy Fights: A Memoir of Leadership in War and Peace* (New York: Penguin, 2015), 229–31.

58. Gregory C. McCarty, "Congressional Oversight of Intelligence," PhD diss., Catholic University of America, 2009, 171; Mark M. Lowenthal, *Intelligence: From Secrets to Policy* (Los Angeles: Sage, 2012), 323.

59. CIA, *Report of Investigation: Guatemala Volume IV: Michael Devine* (Washington, DC: US Government Printing Office, July 15, 1995).

60. Studeman interview, November 24, 2015. Before Studeman walked into the SSCI hearing on April 5, he was unaware that Jennifer Hardbury was going to be present (Johnson, *Threat on the Horizon,* 118). Johnson mentions Studeman testifying and is also critical of Torricelli's actions, stating, "Torricelli had no right to reveal Alpirez's name or the identity of another CIA asset" (*Threat on the Horizon,* 119).

61. CIA, *Report of Investigation;* Melissa Boyle Mahle, *Denial and Deception: An Insider's View of the CIA from Iran Contra to 9/11* (New York: Nations Books, 2004), 175.

62. Johnson, *Threat on the Horizon,* 317–18.

63. Edger telephone interview, December 7, 2015. Senior CIA DO officers eventually briefed Deutch on a still classified case that had produced significant results for the CIA and the United States.

64. David Kocieniewski, "Challenger to Toricelli Attacks Curbs on the CIA," *New York Times,* September 17, 2002, at http://www.nytimes.com/2002/09/17/nyregion/challenger-to-torricelli-attacks-curbs-on-the-cia.html.

65. Edger telephone interview, December 7, 2015.

66. John L. Mitchell and Nora Zamichow, "CIA Head Speaks in L.A. to Counter Crack Claims," *Los Angeles Times,* November 16, 1996, at http://articles.latimes.com/1996-11-16/news/mn-65300_1_cia-crack-cocaine; Snider, *The Agency and the Hill,* 245–46, 326.

67. US Senate, Select Committee on Intelligence, *Nomination of James Woolsey* (Hearing 103-296), 103rd Cong., 1st sess., February 2–3, 1993, 76.

68. "The Cost of Intelligence," n.d., at http://www.gpo.gov/fdsys/pkg/GPO-INTELLIGENCE/html/int017.html (accessed January 7, 2013).

69. National Commission on Terrorist Attacks, "The Performance of the Intelligence Community: Staff Statement No. 11," n.d., at https://9-11commission.gov/staff_statements/staff_statement_11.pdf (accessed November 27, 2012).

70. Vernon Loeb, "After Action Report," *Washington Post,* February 27, 2000, at https://www.washingtonpost.com/archive/lifestyle/magazine/2000/02/27/after-action-report/3c474a43-ea21-4bf5-afc5-02820b8579e5/.

71. Edger telephone interview, December 7, 2015; Loeb, "After Action Report."

72. Donna Jackson, *Jimmy Carter and the Horn of Africa: Cold War Policy in Ethiopia and Somalia* (Jefferson, NC: McFarland, 2007), 7.

73. Peter J. Schraeder, "From Ally to Orphan: Understanding U.S. Policy toward Somalia after the Cold War," in *After the End: Making U.S. Foreign Policy in the Post–Cold War World,* ed. Paul James M. Scott (Durham, NC: Duke University Press, 2000), 332.

74. Huchthausen, *America's Splendid Little Wars,* 161.

75. Benis Frank, *U.S. Marines in Lebanon: 1982–1984* (Washington, DC: History and Museum Division Headquarters, US Marine Corps, 1987), 10.

76. Eric Schmitt, "War in the Gulf: Commanders; Top Brass in Gulf: Profiles in Uniformed Authority," *New York Times,* February 12, 1991, at http://www.nytimes.com/1991/02/12/world/war-in-the-gulf-commanders-top-brass-in-gulf-profiles-in-uniformed-authority.html?pagewanted=all.

77. US DoD, *Joint Publication 2-01,* II-22; Loeb, "After Action Report"; Lajoie telephone interview, November 10, 2015. Major General Lajoie mentioned the deployment of CIA operators in support of the CIA.

78. "CIA Holds Annual Memorial Ceremony to Honor Fallen Colleagues," CIA, News & Information, May 22, 2012, https://www.cia.gov/news-information/press-releases-statements/2012-press-releasese-statements/2012-memorial-ceremony.html.

79. Ted Gup, *The Book of Honor: The Secret Lives and Deaths of CIA Operatives* (New York: First Anchor Books, 2001), 359–60.

80. Vernon Loeb, "Warlords, Peacekeepers, and Spies," *Washington Post,* February

27, 2000, at http://www.somaliawatch.org/archivejuly/000927601.htm; US Army, Center of Military History, *United States Forces, Somalia after Action Report and Historical Overview: The United States Army in Somalia 1992–1994* (Washington, DC: US Army Center of Military History, 2003), 8.

81. US Senate, Committee on Armed Services, Senator John Warner and Senator Carl Levin to Chairman Strom Thurmond, "Review of the Circumstances Surrounding the Ranger Raid on October 3–4, 1993, in Mogadishu Somalia," memo, September 29, 1995, 42, at https://fas.org/irp/congress/1995_rpt/mogadishu.pdf (accessed on April 24, 2018). Major General William Garrison stated that he "was totally satisfied with the intelligence effort—never saw anything better from the intelligence community or architecture. It was totally fused—we got everything we asked for. It was a superb intelligence effort and architecture" ("Review of the Circumstances Surrounding the Ranger Raid").

82. Position identified on Lieutenant General Boykin's official army résumé.

83. Jerry Boykin, *Never Surrender: A Soldier's Journey to the Crossroads of Faith and Freedom* (New York: Hachette Book Group, 2008). Boykin's book covers his career in the military.

84. US Senate, Committee on Armed Services, *Review of the Circumstances Surrounding the Ranger Raid on October 3–4, 1993 in Mogadishu, Somalia,* 104th Cong., 1st sess., September 29, 1995, 42.

85. Mahle, *Denial and Deception,* 148. Mahle discusses how the "CIA abandoned its position as a 'world-wide' intelligence organization" during the 1990s, pointing out that the CIA reduced or "closed large numbers of stations and bases." She also points out that the "Africa Division was the hardest hit."

86. Huchthausen, *America's Splendid Little Wars,* 197.

87. *Bosnia, Intelligence, and the Clinton Presidency: The Role of Intelligence and Political Leadership in Ending the Bosnian War* (Little Rock, AR: William J. Clinton Presidential Library, October 1, 2013), at https://www.cia.gov/library/publications /international-relations/bosnia-intelligence-and-the-clinton-presidency/Clinton_Bosnia_Booklet.pdf.

88. Larry K. Wentz, "Bosnia: Setting the Stage," in *Lessons from Bosnia: The IFOR Experience,* ed. Larry Wentz (Washington, DC: National Defense University Press, 1997), 9–34.

89. Federation of American Scientists, *2018 Nuclear Posture Review Resource,* n.d., at http://fas.org/irp/news/1996/x011996_x0118je.html (accessed April 4, 2018).

90. Craig R. Nation, *A History of the War in the Balkans* (Carlisle, PA: Strategic Studies Institute, 2015), 223.

91. Derek Chollet, *The Road to the Dayton Accords: A Study of American Statecraft* (New York: Palgrave, 2005), 191.

92. David L. Phillips, *Liberating Kosovo: Coercive Diplomacy and U.S. Intervention* (Cambridge, MA: MIT Press, 2012), 68.

93. Nation, *A History of the War in the Balkans,* 251; Phillips, *Liberating Kosovo,* 107.

94. Wesley K. Clark, *Waging Modern War* (New York: PublicAffairs, 2002), 425.

95. "DCI Statement on the Belgrade Chinese Embassy Bombing," CIA, News & Information, n.d., at https://www.cia.gov/news-information/speeches-testimony/1999/dci_speech_072299.html (accessed February 24, 2016).

96. Steven Lee Myers, "Chinese Embassy Bombing: A Wide Net of Blame," *New York Times*, April 17, 2000, at http://www.nytimes.com/2000/04/17/world/chinese-embassy-bombing-a-wide-net-of-blame.html?pagewanted=all; "DCI Statement on the Belgrade Chinese Embassy Bombing" (quotations from Tenet).

97. Steven Coll, *Ghost Wars: The Secret History of the CIA, Afghanistan, and bin Laden, from the Soviet Invasion to September 10, 2001* (New York: Penguin, 2004), 529.

98. Inman interview, August 27, 2014.

99. Wentz, *Lessons from Bosnia*, 228–29. George Tenet, *At the Center of the Storm: My Years at the CIA* (New York: Harper Collins E-Book, 2007), 503. David D. Perkins discusses how HUMINT and counterintelligence experiences during other operations informed operations in Bosnia ("Counterintelligence and HUMINT," in *Lessons from Bosnia*, ed. Wentz, 225–54).

100. Reid telephone interview, September 19, 2012.

101. Janine Davidson, *Lifting the Fog of Peace: How Americans Learned to Fight Modern War* (Ann Arbor: University of Michigan Press, 2010), 134. Davidson discusses the absence of MOOTW in most military doctrine in the early 1990s and the introduction of it in 1993.

102. US DoD, *Joint Publication 3-0: Doctrine for Joint Operations* (Washington, DC: US DoD, February 1, 1995), I-3. Andrew Bacevich credits Wolfowitz with introducing the concept of "shaping" in the Defense Planning Guidance of 1992: "Shaping now became the military's primary job. Back in 1992, the Defense Planning Guidance drafted under the aegis of Paul Wolfowitz had spelled out this argument in detail. Pointing proudly to the 'new international environment' that had already 'been shaped by the victory' over Saddam Hussein the year before, that document provided a blueprint explaining how American power could 'shape the future.' The sledgehammer was to become a sculptor's chisel" (*America's War for the Greater Middle East*, 361).

103. US Joint Chiefs of Staff, *National Military Strategy* (Washington, DC: US Government Printing Office, February 1995), at http://www.au.af.mil/au/awc/awcgate/nms/nms_feb95.htm#CS.

104. Find the transcript at http://www.cfr.org/homeland-security/national-security-21st-century-findings-hart-rudman-commission/p4049 (accessed March 16, 2016).

105. US Commission on National Security/21st Century, *New World Coming: American Security in the 21st Century. The Phase I Report on the Emerging Global Security Environment* (Washington, DC: US Government Printing Office, September 15, 1999).

106. US Commission on National Security/21st Century, *New World Coming: American Security in the 21st Century. The Phase II Report. Seeking a National Strategy: A Concert for Preserving Security and Promoting Freedom* (Washington, DC: US Government Printing Office, April 15, 2000), 8–11.

107. US Commission on National Security/21st Century, *New World Coming: American Security in the 21st Century. The Phase III Road Map for National Security: Imperative for Change* (Washington, DC: US Government Printing Office, February 15, 2001), 82–83.

108. The Hart-Rudman Commission also recommended establishing a "National Homeland Security Agency with responsibility for planning, coordinating, and integrat-

ing various U. S. government activities involved in homeland security" (US Commission on National Security/21st Century, *New World Coming: American Security in the 21st Century. The Phase III Road Map,* 124).

109. National Commission on Terrorism, *Countering the Changing Threat of International Terrorism* (Washington, DC: US Government Printing Office, August 2, 2000), 8.

110. Haas, *Making Intelligence Smarter.*

111. Hedley, *Checklist for the Future of Intelligence.*

6. A New Administration

1. John F. Troxell, "Sizing the Force for the 21st Century," in *Revising the Two MTW Force Shaping Paradigm,* ed. Steven Metz (Carlisle, PA: Strategic Studies Institute, 2001), 10–12.

2. US House, Committee on the Armed Services, *Military Service, Posture, Readiness, and Budget Issues,* 106th Cong., 1st sess., October 21, 1999.

3. Tom Raum, "CIA Recruiting Drive Paying Off," Associated Press, January 17, 2000, at http://fas.org/sgp/news/2000/01/ ap011700.html; Coll, *Ghost Wars,* 317.

4. Morris Fiorina, Samuel Abrams, and Jeremy Pope, "The 2000 Presidential Election: Can Retrospective Voting Be Saved?" *British Journal of Political Science* 33 (2003): 163–87, at http://www.uvm.edu/~dguber/POLS234/articles/fiorina.pdf; James E. Campbell, "The Curious and Close Presidential Campaign of 2000," in *America's Choice 2000,* ed. William Crotty (Boulder, CO: Westview Press, 2001), 115–37.

5. "2000 Republican Party Platform," July 31, 2000, American Presidency Project, at http://www.presidency.ucsb.edu/ws/?pid=25849. Bush's vision for the role of US military power during his presidency did include a focus on the Middle East, but this focus was directed instead toward nation-states, in particular Iraq, which was one of his administration's top priorities when he entered office. Candidate Bush's more traditional approach emphasized protecting the homeland through missile defense and deploying the US military in conventional wars.

6. "Al Gore 2000 on the Issues," n.d., at http://www.4president.us/issues/gore2000/gore2000foreignpolicy.htm (accessed February 26, 2016).

7. Both Fleischer and Rice quoted in Steven A. Holmes, "The 2000 Campaign: Foreign Policy; Gore Assails Bush on Plan to Recall U.S. Balkan Force," *New York Times,* October 22, 2000, at http://www.nytimes.com/2000/10/22/world/2000-campaign-for-eign-policy-gore-assails-bush-plan-recall-us-balkan-force.html.

8. *National Strategy for Combating Terrorism* (Washington, DC: White House, September 2006), 9 and 16.

9. James Mann, *Rise of the Vulcans: History of Bush's War Cabinet* (New York: Penguin, 2004), xi.

10. Haver interview, December 1, 2015, and email exchange, January 4, 2016. Also present at this meeting were Barbara Olson, who would tragically die on September 11, 2001, aboard American Airlines Flight 77, and Scooter Libby, the loyal Cheney aide who would be found guilty of leaking a CIA officer's identity in 2007.

11. Quoted in Janet A. McDonnell, *Defense Intelligence Coming of Age: The Office*

of the Undersecretary of Defense for Intelligence 2002–2012 (Washington, DC: Historical Office, Defense Intelligence Agency, 2014), 22.

12. Dick Cheney, *In My Time* (New York: Simon and Schuster, 2011), 141–42, 160.

13. Haver interview, December 1, 2015, and email exchange, January 4, 2016; Donald Rumsfeld, *Known and Unknown, a Memoir* (New York: Sentinel, 2011), 292. Rumsfeld describes Armitage as "brusque" in his first meeting with him.

14. Haver interview, December 1, 2015, and email exchange, January 4, 2016; see also Vernon Loeb, "Rumsfeld's Man on the Intelligence Front," *Washington Post,* February 10, 2003.

15. Jim Garamone, "Rumsfeld Attacks Pentagon Bureaucracy, Vows Changes," American Foreign Press Service, September 10, 2001, at http://archive.defense.gov/news/newsarticle.aspx?id=44916.

16. Dale R. Herspring, *Rumsfeld's Wars: The Arrogance of Power* (Lawrence: University of Kansas Press, 2008), 31.

17. Roberta Wohlstetter, *Pearl Harbor: Warning and Decision* (Stanford, CA: Stanford University Press, 1962).

18. US Senate, Committee on Armed Services, *Nominations before the Armed Services Committee,* 107th Cong., 1st sess., January–December 2001.

19. Herspring, *Rumsfeld's Wars,* 21.

20. US Senate, Committee on Armed Services, *Nominations before the Armed Services Committee,* January–December 2001 .

21. Donald Rumsfeld, "Intelligence," snowflake with attachment: "Visualizing the Intelligence System of 2025," February 23, 2001, Donald Rumsfeld Papers Online, at http://papers.rumsfeld.com/library/default.asp?zoom_sort=0&zoom_query=visualizing+the+intelligence&zoom_per_page=10&zoom_and=0&Tag+Level+1=-1%7E0&Tag+Level+2=-1%7E0.

22. Director of the Program Analysis Staff, National Security Council (Lynn), to the President's Assistant for National Security Affairs (Kissinger), Washington, DC, August 7, 1970, in US Department of State, *Foreign Relations of the United States, 1969–1976,* vol. 2: *Organization and Management of U.S. Foreign Policy, 1969–1972,* ed. David C. Humphrey (Washington, DC: US Government Printing Office, 2006), at https://history.state.gov/historicaldocuments/frus1969-76v02/d211; Robert Ellsworth to Secretary of Defense, "DoD Intelligence Restructuring," May 7, 1976, Donald Rumsfeld Papers Online, at http://papers.rumsfeld.com/library/default.asp?zoom_sort=0&zoom_query=DoD+Intelligence+Restructuring&zoom_per_page=10&zoom_and=0&Tag+Level+1=-1%7E0&Tag+Level+2=-1%7E0 (accessed April 25, 2018).

23. Historical Office, Office of the Secretary of Defense, *Department of Defense Key Officials: September 1947–June 2017* (Washington, DC: US DoD, 2016), 61, at http://history.defense.gov/Portals/70/Documents/key_officials/KEYOFFICIALS-JUN2017Final.pdf.

24. George W. Bush, *National Security Presidential Directive 5: Intelligence* (Washington, DC: US Government Printing Office, May 9, 2001).

25. Philip Zelikow, "The Evolution of Intelligence Reform, 2002–2004," *Studies in Intelligence* 56, no. 3 (September 2012): 6.

7. 9/11 and the Global War on Terrorism

1. Heidi Urben, "Civil–Military Relations in a Time of War," unpublished paper, April 14, 2010, 11; Ole R. Holsti, "Of Chasms and Convergences: Attitudes and Beliefs of Civilians and Military Elites at the Start of a New Millennium," in *Soldiers and Civilians: The Civil–Military Gap and American National Security,* ed. Peter D. Feaver and Richard H. Kohn (Cambridge, MA: Belfer Center for Science and International Affairs, John F. Kennedy School, Harvard University, 2001), 31.

2. George W. Bush, *National Security Presidential Directive 2: Improving Military Quality of Life* (Washington, DC: White House, February 15, 2001).

3. Paul Richter, "For the Military, Bush Is Not Yet All That He Can Be," *Los Angeles Times,* February 10, 2001, at http://articles.latimes.com/2001/feb/10/news/mn-23691.

4. Frank Pellegrini, "Defense: Rumsfeld's Lonely, Losing Battle," *Time,* August 9, 2001, at http://content.time.com/time/nation/article/0,8599,170605,00.html.

5. Quoted in James Kitfield, *War and Destiny: How the Bush Revolution in Foreign and Military Affairs Redefined American Power* (Washington, DC: Potomac Books, 2007), 31.

6. Herspring, *Rumsfeld's Wars,* 41.

7. "Text: President Bush Addresses the Nation," *Washington Post,* September 20, 2001, at http://www.washingtonpost.com/wp-srv/nation/specials/attacked/transcripts/bushaddress_092001.html.

8. Hugh Shelton, *Without Hesitation: The Odyssey of an American Warrior* (New York: St. Martin's Press, 2010), 443.

9. Gary Schroen, *First In: An Insider's Account of How the CIA Spearheaded the War on Terror in Afghanistan* (New York: Ballantine Books, 2005), 87.

10. Ennis interview, November 17, 2015.

11. Jacoby interview, November 18, 2015; Rumsfeld, *Known and Unknown,* 391. Rumsfeld describes a conversation he had with General Tommy Franks in which he said, "My goodness, Tommy, I repeatedly said to Franks. The Department of Defense is many times bigger than the CIA, and yet we are sitting here like little birds in a nest, waiting for someone to drop food in our mouths."

12. US Senate, Committee on Armed Services, *Nominations before the Armed Services Committee,* January–December 2001, 52.

13. Donald Rumsfeld, "JITF-CT," with attachment: "JITF-CT: Supporting a Unified National CT Campaign," snowflake, September 26, 2001, Donald Rumsfeld Papers Online, at http://library.rumsfeld.com/doclib/sp/1508/2001-09-26%20to%20George%20Tenet%20re%20JITF-CT.pdf#search="JITF-CT".

14. Jacoby interview, November 18, 2015.

15. CIA, *Support to Military Operations* (Washington, DC: CIA, posted May 1, 2007, last updated January 3, 2012), at https://www.cia.gov/library/reports/archived-reports-1/Ann_Rpt_2001/smo.html.

16. Haver interview, December 1, 2015, and email exchange, January 4, 2016.

17. Haver interview, December 1, 2015, and email exchange, January 4, 2016.

18. US House of Representatives and Senate, *Bob Stump National Defense Authori-zation Act for Fiscal Year 2003*, Pub. L. No. 107-314, 107th Cong., 2nd sess., December 2, 2002. In 2010, President Obama changed the order of precedence and moved the USD for information position to number nine.

19. Quoted in Noah Shachtman, "Rumsfeld's Intel Chief: Iraq War 'Great-est Decision of the Century,'" *Wired,* July 2012, at http://www.wired.com/2012/07/cambone-iraq/.

20. "Who Is Steve Cambone? A Look at Rumsfeld's Right-Hand Man," *Armed Forces Journal,* April 1, 2006, , at http://www.armedforcesjournal.com/who-is-steve-cambone/.

21. Pete Ogden, "Who Is Stephen Cambone?" Center for American Progress, July 20, 2004, at https://www.americanprogress.org/issues /security/news/2004/07/20/941/who-is-stephen-cambone/.

22. Boykin, *Never Surrender,* 7.

23. Barton Gellman, "Secret Unit Expands Rumsfeld's Domain," *Washington Post,* January 23, 2005; Eric Schmitt, "Pentagon Sends Its Spies to Join Fight on Terror," *New York Times,* January 24, 2005, at http://www.nytimes.com/2005/01/24/politics/penta-gon-sends-its-spies-to-join-fight-on-terror.html.

24. Donald Rumsfeld to Steve Cambone, "Defense HUMINT Service," memo, January 27, 2004, Donald Rumsfeld Papers Online, at http://papers.rumsfeld.com/library/default.asp?zoom_sort=0&zoom_query=defense+humint+service&zoom_per_page=100&zoom_and=0&Tag+Level+1=-1%7E0&Tag+Level+2=-1%7E0.

25. Ennis interview by author, November 17, 2015.

26. Lowell Jacoby, "Message to the Workforce–DH Strategic Support Teams," Jan-uary 27, 2005, National Security Archive, George Washington University, Washington, DC, at http://nsarchive.gwu.edu/NSAEBB520-the-Pentagons-Spies/EBB-PS36.pdf.

27. US Senate, Committee on Armed Forces, "Statement for the Record—Dr. Ste-phen Cambone [Undersecretary of Defense for Intelligence]," 109th Cong., 1st sess., April 28, 2005, https://fas.org/irp/congress/2005_hr/042805cambone.pdf.

28. Ennis interview, November 17, 2015.

29. Jacoby, "Message to the Workforce–DH Strategic Support Teams."

30. Gellman, "Secret Unit Expands Rumsfeld's Domain."

31. Jeremy Scahill, *Dirty Wars: The World Is a Battlefield* (New York: Nation Books, 2013), 95.

32. US Special Operations Command, "United States Special Operations Com-mand History."

33. George W. Bush, "President Bush Delivers Graduation Speech at West Point," June 1, 2002. at https://georgewbush-whitehouse.archives.gov/news/releases/2002/06/20020601-3.html. The National Security Strategy of 2002 says, "We will disrupt and destroy terrorist organizations by . . . defending the United States, the American people, and our interests at home and abroad by identifying and destroying the threat before it reaches our borders. While the United States will constantly strive to enlist the support of the international community, we will not hesitate to act alone, if necessary, to exercise our right of self-defense by acting preemptively against such terror-

ists, to prevent them from doing harm against our people and our country" (George W. Bush, *National Security Strategy of the United States* [Washington, DC: US Government Printing Office, September 2002], 6).

34. US House of Representatives, *Intelligence Authorization Act, Fiscal Year 1991,* 29. This act clarified the definition of "traditional military activities," and that definition is given later in this chapter. Jeremy Scahill mentions in his book *Dirty Wars* a memo from Rumsfeld where he declares, "The entire world is the battlespace" (quoted on 172).

35. Jose Rodriguez, former director of the CIA National Clandestine Service, telephone interview by the author, September 21, 2015; Ennis interview, November 17, 2015.

36. Jacoby interview, November 18, 2015.

37. US House of Representatives, Permanent Select Committee on Intelligence, *R. 111-186 to Intelligence Authorization Act for Fiscal Year 2010,* 111th Cong., 1st sess., June 26, 2009, 48–49. In *Joint Publication 2-01.3: Joint Intelligence Preparation of the Operational Environment* (Washington, DC: US DoD, May 21, 2014), the US DoD states that "the purpose of JIPOE (joint intelligence preparation of the operational environment) is to support the JFC (Joint Force Commander) by determining the probable intent and most likely COA (courses of action) for the adversary and other relevant actors throughout the OE (operating environment)" (I-5).

38. Marshall Curtis Erwin, *Covert Action: Legislative Background and Policy Questions* (Washington, DC: Congressional Research Service, April 10, 2013), at http://www.fas.org/sgp/crs/intel/RL33715.pdf. In response to a question on covert action, Senator Pat Roberts commented, "The CRS report is misleading. It was the concern of one member, Vice Chairman Kit Bond, about the United States Director of Intelligence's expansion of 'military source operations' authority to 'Committee concerns.' The CRS also erroneously stated these questions were for Jim Clapper's confirmation hearing when they were in fact for Dennis Blair. Since leaving the committee in 2006, it is my understanding that Members of the Committee continue to work closely with the military to ensure that all military intelligence activities are reported to the intelligence oversight committees" (Pat Roberts, US senator and former chairman of the Senate Select Committee on Intelligence, email interview by the author, January 9, 2013).

39. Baer, *See No Evil,* 186–217; Mahle, *Denial and Deception,* 216–17; Cambone's memo is discussed in Donald Rumsfeld, "Paramilitary," snowflake, September 30, 2004, Donald Rumsfeld Papers Online, at http://papers.rumsfeld.com/library/default.asp?zoom_query=paramilitary&zoom_page=1&zoom_per_page=10&zoom_cat%5B%5D=0&zoom_and=0&zoom_sort=0.

40. Rumsfeld, "Paramilitary," snowflake, September 30, 2004; Richard Helms, *A Look over My Shoulder: A Life in the Central Intelligence Agency* (New York: Random House, 2003); Woods, *Shadow Warrior,* 177; Thomas Powers, "The Rise and Fall of Richard Helms: Survival and Sudden Death in the CIA," *Rolling Stone,* December 16, 1976, at http://www.rollingstone.com/culture/features/the-rise-and-fall-of-richard-helms-19761216?page=3. Helms looked at covert action with a jaundiced eye and believed other avenues should be attempted prior to resorting to its use, whereas Colby was more supportive of its use.

41. Stephen Knott, *Secret and Sanctioned: Covert Operations and the American Presidency* (New York: Oxford University Press, 1996), 3–4.

42. Oakley, "Taming the Rogue Elephant?" 63.

43. Helms, *A Look over My Shoulder,* 107.

44. "50 U.S. Code §3093: Presidential Approval and Reporting of Covert Actions," Legal Information Institute, n.d., https://www.law.cornell.edu/uscode/text/50/3093 (accessed July 6, 2016).

45. US House of Representatives, *Intelligence Authorization Act, Fiscal Year 1991,* 29; Erwin, *Covert Action.* Erwin says that Congress also clarified that "traditional military activities" would not include the "clandestine" recruitment of individuals in third-party countries who have access to the targeted country or the recruitment of target-country citizens to "take certain actions" when military operations are initiated. He also states that the "clandestine efforts" to influence foreign populations to support war efforts is not a "traditional military activity."

46. "50 U.S. Code §3093."

47. Roberts interview, January 9, 2013.

48. During an interview on September 19, 2012, Garry Reid, the principal deputy ASD for special operations/low-intensity conflict, provided the most compelling reason for maintaining CIA's covert-action capability when he said that shifting paramilitary covert action to the DoD might run counter to the American public's image of the military as the "doer of good things." Reid accurately pointed out that "black-bag dirty stuff does not fit" the image America has of the military and that the CIA is doing a "perfectly fine job of conducting [covert activity]." Although often forgotten, the narrative of American institutions is very important in ensuring continued support from the American populace. Although the narrative of the American military as always being a force of good in the world is a simplistic and contestable notion, it is important to remember that in a democracy the military requires the support of its population.

49. Stanley McChrystal, *My Share of the Task* (London: Penguin, 2013), 156; Greg Miller, "DIA to Send Hundreds More Spies Overseas," *Washington Post,* December 1, 2012, at https://www.washingtonpost.com/world/national-security/dia-to-send-hundreds-more-spies-overseas/2012/12/01/97463e4e-399b-11e2-b01f-5f55b193f58f_story.html.

50. Wise interview, August 28, 2012, and September 3, 2015; Jennifer Sims, "More Military Spies: Why the CIA Is Applauding the Pentagon's Intelligence Grab," *Foreign Affairs,* May 18, 2012, at https://www.foreignaffairs.com/articles/2012-05-18/more-military-spies. Sims argues that the CIA liked the DCS concept because it would professionalize the defense HUMINT, reduce the number of short-term assignments in the field, improve integration and cooperation, and allow the CIA to use DoD resources outside the war zone to enable its operations as part of a "networked team." Although there is probably some truth to Sims's observations, the relief from military collection requirements seems to be what garnered the most support from the individuals I spoke with.

51. Ennis interview, November 17, 2015.

52. Wise interview, August 28, 2012, and September 3, 2015; Greg Miller, "Penta-

gon's Plans for a Spy Service to Rival the CIA Have Been Pared Back," *Washington Post,* November 1, 2014, at https://www.washingtonpost.com/world/national-security/pentagons-plans-for-a-spy-service-to-rival-the-cia-have-been-pared-back/2014/11/01/1871bb9 2-6118-11e4-8b9e-2ccdac31a031_story.html; Oakley, "Partners or Competitors?"

53. Miller, "Senate Moves to Block Pentagon Plans to Increase Number of Spies Overseas."

54. Hayden interview, September 18, 2015; Jacoby interview, November 18, 2015.

55. Wise interview, August 28, 2012, and September 3, 2105.

56. National Commission on Terrorist Attacks upon the United States, *The 9/11 Commission Report* (Washington, DC: US Government Printing Office, July 2004), xv.

57. George W. Bush, *Executive Order 13354: National Counterterrorism Center* (Washington, DC: US Government Printing Office, August 27, 2004), 2.

58. The DoD is one of the only organizations in the US government that develops and trains planners. Although other organizations have made efforts to lessen the divide, as an institution the DoD is far better at planning. It can be problematic when the DoD becomes the only element involved in the exertion of national power simply because other institutions are not organized to contribute to planning efforts.

59. US House of Representatives and Senate, *Intelligence Reform and Terrorism Prevention Act of 2004* (Pub. L. No. 108-458), 108th Cong., 2nd sess., December 17, 2004.

60. National Commission on Terrorist Attacks upon the United States, *The 9/11 Commission Report,* 104.

61. Donald Rumsfeld, "Intelligence," snowflake, December 9, 2002; "Moving DoD Intelligence Capabilities," snowflake, June 21, 2004; and "Intelligence Reorganization," snowflake, October 5, 2002: all in Donald Rumsfeld Papers Online, at http://papers.rumsfeld.com/library/default.asp?zoom_page=1&zoom_ per_page=10&zoom_and=0&zoom_sort=0&zoom_query=moving%20DoD%20 intelligence.

62. Quoted in Michael Allen, *Blinking Red: Crisis and Compromise in Intelligence after 9/11* (Lincoln: University of Nebraska Press, 2013), 69.

63. James Joyce, *Ulysses* (London: Not So Noble Books, 2013), 295.

64. Richard A. Best and Andrew Flicker, *Special Operations Forces (SOF) and CIA Paramilitary Operations: Issues for Congress,* Report for Congress (Washington, DC: Congressional Research Service, August 3, 2009), at http://www.fas.org/sgp/crs/natsec/ RS22017.pdf.

65. National Commission on Terrorist Attacks upon the United States, *The 9/11 Commission Report,* 415–16.

66. Roberts email interview, January 9, 2013. It is not clear why the SSCI possessed this opinion even after the CIA performed well in the early days of Afghanistan, providing the United States the ability to quickly enter the country and link up with indigenous forces. Despite this success, according to Senator Roberts, the SSCI still had concerns with the CIA.

67. Best and Flicker, *Special Operations Forces (SOF) and CIA Paramilitary Operations,* 3; Reid telephone interview, September 19, 2012.

68. George W. Bush, *Executive Order 13328: Commission on the Intelligence Capabilities of the United States regarding Weapons of Mass Destruction* (Washington, DC: US Government Printing Office, February 6, 2004), 1.

69. US Commission on the Intelligence Capabilities of the United States regarding Weapons of Mass Destruction, *Report to the President* (Washington, DC: US Government Printing Office, March 31, 2005), 34.

70. Lowenthal, *Intelligence,* 60; White House, Office of the Press Secretary, "President Bush Administration Actions to Implement WMD Commission Recommendations," press release, July 29, 2005, at http://georgewbush-whitehouse.archives.gov/news/releases/2005/06/text/20050629-5.html.

71. Major General Michael Ennis, "Transcript of Interview of Major General Michael E. Ennis," CIA, News & Information, February 28, 2007, at https://www.cia.gov/news-information/press-releases-statements/press-release-archive-2007/february-28-2007.html.

72. LeVitre interview, November 4, 2015.

73. Ennis interview, November 17, 2015. Major General Ennis commented that JIOCs did not provide anything additional, and Jacoby did not support establishment of them, but Cambone was insistent on their being established.

74. US Senate, Committee on Armed Forces, "Statement for the Record—Dr. Stephen Cambone," 5, 7.

75. US Senate, Committee on Armed Forces, "Statement for the Record—Dr. Stephen Cambone."

76. Major General (ret.) David Baratto, former CIA ADMA, telephone interview by the author, January 23, 2013. Baratto commented that he saw a vast difference in the DoD/CIA relationship from his time as the commanding general of the US Army Special Warfare Center and School from 1988 to 1992 compared to his time as the ADMA in 1994–1995.

77. Reid telephone interview, September 19, 2012.

78. Schroen, *First In*, and Eric Blehm, *The Only Thing Worth Dying For: How Eleven Green Berets Forged a New Afghanistan* (New York: Harper Collins E-Books, 2010). Schroen describes a largely positive relationship between the CIA and the DoD, whereas Blehm focuses more on the friction in the relationship.

79. Crumpton, *The Art of Intelligence,* 122.

80. US Special Operations Command, "United States Special Operations Command History," 6–7.

81. McChrystal, *My Share of the Task,* 117.

82. Tenet, *At the Center of the Storm,* 386, 394, 395.

83. Colonel David Perkins, "Interview: Col. David Perkins," *Frontline,* PBS, n.d., at http://www.pbs.org/wgbh/pages/frontline/shows/invasion/interviews/perkins.html (accessed March 15, 2016); Greg Fontenot, E. J. Degen, and David Tohn, *On Point: The United States Army in Operation Iraqi Freedom* (Fort Leavenworth, KS: Combat Studies Institute Press, 2004), 336.

84. Lieutenant General David G. Perkins, commander, US Army Combined Arms

Center, interview by the author, Fort Leavenworth, KS, October 3, 2012; Oakley, "Partners or Competitors?"

85. Douglas Jehl, "2 CIA Reports Offer Warnings on Iraq's Path," *New York Times,* December 7, 2004, at http://www.nytimes.com/2004/12/07/international/middleeast/07intell.html?_r=0, and Greg Miller, "CIA Expanding Presence in Afghanistan," *Los Angeles Times,* September 20, 2009, at http://articles.latimes.com/2009/sep/20/world/fg-afghan-intel20.

86. Crumpton, *The Art of Intelligence,* 180, 314. Crumpton highlights Cofer Black's dislike of Rumsfeld.

87. Richard Perle, "Iraq: Saddam Unbound," in *Present Dangers: Crisis and Opportunity in American Foreign and Defense Policy,* ed. Robert Kagan and William Kristol (New York: Encounter Books, 2000), 99–110. During an interview, Vice Admiral Jacoby relayed a story that he described as "third-hand information from an impeccable information flow." The event occurred on September 12, 2001, as the fire department was still trying to get access to and extinguish a fire in the fifth-floor attic area of the Pentagon that threatened the building's communication lines. On that day, an officer found an "incomprehensible" celebratory mood in Feith's outer office because they now had a reason to go to Iraq (Jacoby interview, November 18, 2015).

88. Jacoby interview, November 18, 2015. A detailed background on Feith's efforts can be found in Jeffrey T. Richelson, *Special Plans and Double Meanings: Controversies over Deception, Intelligence, and Policy Counterterrorism,* National Security Archive Electronic Briefing Book No. 456, posted February 20, 2014, National Security Archive, George Washington University, Washington, DC, at http://nsarchive.gwu.edu/NSAEBB/NSAEBB456/.

89. Walter Pincus and Dana Priest, "Bush Orders the CIA to Hire More Spies," *Washington Post,* November 23, 2004, at http://www.washingtonpost.com/wp-dyn/articles/A8650-2004Nov23.html; Garthoff, *Directors of Central Intelligence,* 283, 287.

90. Daniel Klaidman, "Broken Furniture at the CIA," *Newsweek,* November 28, 2004, at http://www.newsweek.com/broken-furniture-cia-124599; David Ignatius, "How the CIA Came Unglued," *Washington Post,* May 12, 2006, at http://www.washingtonpost.com/wp-dyn/content/article/2006/05/11/AR2006051101947.html; Jerry Markon, "Former Top CIA Official Sentenced to 37 Months," *Washington Post,* February 27, 2009, at http://www.washingtonpost.com/wp-dyn/content/article/2009/02/26/AR2009022601742.html; "Feds: CIA Boss Had History of Bad Behavior," Associated Press, February 25, 2009, at http://www.nbcnews.com/id/29391260/ns/us_news-crime_and_courts/t/feds-cia-boss-had-history-bad-behavior/#.V3Kfd1d-t8. Tyler Drumheller, a former senior CIA officer, writes about the friction with Goss in his book *On the Brink: An Insider's Account of How the White House Compromised American Intelligence* (New York: Carroll & Graf, 2006).

91. Gates, *Duty,* 4–6.

92. Ann Scott Tyson, "Gates Warns of Militarized Policy," *Washington Post,* July 16, 2008, at http://www.washingtonpost.com/wp-dyn/content/article/2008/07/15/AR2008071502777.html; Robert M. Gates, "U.S. Global Leadership Campaign,"

Washington, DC, July 15, 2008, US DoD Online Archive, at http://archive.defense.gov/
Speeches/Speech.aspx?SpeechID=1262.

93. Gates, *Duty,* 93.

94. Hayden interview, September 18, 2015. General Hayden described how the creation of the USD for information position and placing an individual in charge of 80
percent of the capabilities within the Intelligence Community could weaken the DNI's
authority.

95. Gates, *Duty,* 92.

96. Crumpton, *The Art of Intelligence,* 187; McChrystal, *My Share of the Task,* 116.
All of these individuals mention leaders who helped strengthen the partnership and highlight how personalities matter.

97. Hayden interview, September 18, 2015.

98. "McCain Defends '100 Years in Iraq' Statement," CNN, February 15, 2008,
at http://www.cnn.com/2008/POLITICS/02/14/mccain.king/; "Election of 2008,"
American Presidency Project, n.d., at http://www.presidency.ucsb.edu/showelection.
php?year=2008 (accessed March 7, 2016).

8. Everything Comes with a Cost

1. US House of Representatives and Senate, Joint Committee on the Investigation of the Pearl Harbor Attack, *Pearl Harbor Attack,* 79th Cong., 1st sess., January 14,
1946, 141.

2. US House of Representatives and Senate, *National Security Act of 1947,* Pub. L.
253, 80th Cong., 1st sess., July 26, 1947.

3. Richard A. Best, *Proposals for Intelligence Reorganization, 1949–2004* (Washington, DC: Congressional Research Service, September 24, 2004), 3–11, at https://fas.org/
irp/crs/RL32500.pdf. A flag officer could remain on active duty, but the DoD could have
not authority over that individual.

4. Ahearn, *Vietnam Declassified,* 95, 228–29; John Prados, *Vietnam: The History of
an Unwinnable War* (Lawrence: University of Kansas Press, 2009), 320, and *Lost Crusader: The Secret Wars of CIA Director William Colby* (New York: Oxford University Press,
2003), 213–14. Both Ahearn and Prados discuss how the CIA initially led the pacification efforts, but, encouraged by Robert Komer, the efforts were placed under Military
Assistance Command Vietnam to gain more resources and instill a unity of effort. In his
book about Colby, Prados discusses Colby's and Ted Shackley's desire to focus the CIA
"more on traditional intelligence functions" (213) in Vietnam.

5. US House of Representatives, *Operation Just Cause.*

6. Lajoie telephone interview, November 10, 2015.

7. Karl Eikenberry, "The Militarization of US Foreign Policy," *American Foreign Policy Interests,* February 2013, at https://www.ncafp.org/2016/wp-content/
uploads/2013/02/Amb.-Eikenberry-Mil-USFP.pdf.

8. Michael Mandelbaum, *Mission Failure: America and the World in the Post–Cold
War World* (New York: Oxford University Press, 2016). Mandelbaum argues that the end
of the Cold War resulted in the United States neglecting the concept of national sover-

eignty over internal affairs and becoming involved in numerous MOOTWs to change the characteristics of a particular state and not in response to what a state did outside its borders.

9. Shoon Murray and Anthony Quainton, "Combatant Commanders, Ambassadorial Authority, and the Conduct of Diplomacy," in *Mission Creep*, ed. Adams and Murray, 169; Bacevich, *America's War for the Greater Middle East*, 36, where Bacevich describes the increasing militarization of foreign policy; Priest, *The Mission*, 97, where Priest mentions a "Clinton administration's National Security Strategy" that "directed the CINC's [*sic*] to 'shape, prepare, respond' all over the globe."

10. US DoD, *Joint Publication 3-0: Doctrine for Joint Operations* (Washington, DC: US DoD, September 17, 2006, with changes from February 13, 2008), IV-27.

11. Reid telephone interview, September 19, 2012.

12. Candace B., CIA analyst, interview by the author, Ft. Leavenworth, KS, August 10, 2012. Both the after-action review and the interview highlighted officers' willingness and creativity to break down barriers to accomplish mission objectives.

13. Wise interview, August 28, 2012, and September 3, 2015.

14. John McLaughlin, former deputy DCIA, telephone interview by the author, September 19, 2012.

15. David L. Boren, president of the University of Oklahoma and former chairman of the SSCI, email interview by the author, November 20, 2012.

16. Boren email interview, November 20, 2012; Richard L. Russell, professor in the Department of Near East–South Asia, Center for Strategic Studies, National Defense University, telephone interview by the author, September 14, 2012.

17. Gates telephone interview, March 29, 2016; Allen, *Blinking Red*, 154. In the interview, Gates said he thought it used to be important for the deputy DCIA to be a military officer. Now with the DNI, he believed this requirement was less important.

18. Quoted in Johnson, *Threat on the Horizon*, 237.

19. Studeman interview, November 24, 2015.

20. Ennis interview, November 17, 2015. Ennis relayed a story about when marine general Peter Pace was commander of the Southern Command: Pace had such a distrust and misunderstanding of HUMINT collection that he would not allow certain defense attachés in meetings with foreign officers—a shortsighted view for a senior leader in the DoD.

21. Gates telephone interview, March 29, 2016.

22. Inman interview, August 27, 2014.

23. Hayden interview, September 18, 2015.

24. Recent changes in the CIA might encourage a further tactical focus and operationalization of intelligence. In 2014, DCIA John Brennan announced a reorganization that will create more CTC-like facilities, where CIA operations officers and analysts will work closely together identifying collection requirements and then targeting collection efforts. In 2014, the *Washington Post* quoted Hayden commenting that centers can be "consumed with the operational challenges of the moment," and another former senior intelligence official raised concern that placing analysts and case officers in

the same organizations risks compromising independent analysis (Greg Miller, "CIA Director John Brennan Considering Sweeping Organizational Changes," *Washington Post,* November 19, 2014, at https://www.washingtonpost.com/world/national-security/cia-director-john-brennan-considering-sweeping-organizational-changes/2014/11/19/fa85b320-6ffb-11e4-ad12-3734c461eab6_story.html).

25. Quoted in Tyson, "Gates Warns of Militarized Policy."

26. Johnson, *Threat on the Horizon,* 238.

27. Eikenberry, "The Militarization of US Foreign Policy."

28. Michael Mullen, speech given at Kansas State University, March 2010, at http://www.cfr.org/defense-strategy/admiral-mullens-speech-military-strategy-kansas-state-university-march-2010/p21590.

29. Gordon Adams and Shoon Murray, "An Introduction to Mission Creep." in *Mission Creep,* ed. Adams and Murray, 4.

30. Wise interview, August 28, 2012, and September 3, 2015.

31. Kibbe, "The Military, the CIA, and America's Shadow Wars," 229. Kibbe mentions news articles by journalist Greg Miller and Julie Tate that discuss the rise of CIA "targeters" focused on tactical operations that concerned even DCIA Brennan, who said the CIA's role in counterterrorism operations were an "aberration from its traditional role" (quoted on 229).

32. Quoted in Greg Miller, "Secret Report Raises Alarms on Intelligence Blind Spots because of AQ Focus," *Washington Post,* March 20, 2013, at https://www.washingtonpost.com/world/national-security/secret-report-raises-alarms-on-intelligence-blind-spots-because-of-aq-focus/2013/03/20/1f8f1834-90d6-11e2-9cfd-36d6c9b5d7ad_story.html?hpid=z1.

33. Wise interview, August 28, 2012, and September 3, 2015.

34. At the same time, the US government has lacked a long-term vision and become obsessed with tactical actions in the erroneous belief that military force can solve a number of crises and shape the world to America's likening.

BIBLIOGRAPHY

Archives

Clinton Digital Library Archives. At http://clinton.presidentiallibraries.us.

Donald Rumsfeld Papers Online. At http://papers.rumsfeld.com and http://library.rumsfeld.com.

George H. W. Bush Presidential Library Archives. Texas A&M University, College Station.

National Defense University Archives. Washington, DC.

National Security Archive. George Washington University, Washington, DC. Some items available online at http://nsarchive.gwu.edu.

US Department of Defense Online Archive. At http://archive.defense.gov.

William J. Clinton Presidential Library Archives. Little Rock, AR.

Government Documents

"50 U.S. Code §3093: Presidential Approval and Reporting of Covert Actions." Legal Information Institute, n.d. At https://www.law.cornell.edu/uscode/text/50/3093. Accessed July 6, 2016.

1993 Report: From Red Tape to Results: Creating a Government That Works Better and Costs Less. National Performance Review. Washington, DC: US Government Printing Office, September 7, 1994. At http://govinfo.library.unt.edu/npr/library/nprrpt/annrpt/redtpe93/259e.html.

Best, Richard A. *Proposals for Intelligence Reform 1949–2004.* Washington, DC: Congressional Research Service, September 24, 2004. At http://www.fas.org/irp/crs/RL32500.pdf.

Best, Richard A., and Andrew Feickert. *Special Operations Forces (SOF) and CIA Paramilitary Operations: Issues for Congress.* Report for Congress. Washington, DC: Congressional Research Service, August 3, 2009. At http://www.fas.org/sgp/crs/natsec/RS22017.pdf.

Bosnia, Intelligence, and the Clinton Presidency: The Role of Intelligence and Political Leadership in Ending the Bosnian War. Little Rock, AR: William J. Clinton Presidential Library, October 1, 2013. At https://www.cia.gov/library/publications/international-relations/bosnia-intelligence-and-the-clinton-presidency/Clinton_Bosnia_Booklet.pdf.

Bush, George H. W. *National Security Directive 26: U.S. Policy towards the Persian Gulf.* Washington, DC: White House, October 2, 1989.

———. *National Security Directive 67: Intelligence Capabilities: 1992–2005.* Washington, DC: White House, March 30, 1992.

———. *National Security Review 12: Review of National Defense Strategy.* Washington, DC: White House, March 1989.

———. *National Security Review 27: National Security Review of Low Intensity Conflict.* Washington, DC: White House, June 11, 1990.

———. *National Security Review 29: National Security Review of Intelligence.* Washington, DC: White House, November 15, 1991.

———. *National Security Strategy of the United States.* Washington, DC: White House, August 1991.

———. "Remarks and an Exchange with Reporters on the Iraqi Invasion of Kuwait." August 5, 1990. American Presidency Project. At http://www.presidency.ucsb.edu/ws/?pid=18741.

———. "Remarks at the Aspen Institute Symposium in Aspen Colorado." August 2, 1990. At http://www.presidency.ucsb.edu/ws/?pid=18731.

Bush, George W. *National Security Presidential Directive 2: Improving Military Quality of Life.* Washington, DC: White House, February 15, 2001.

———. *National Security Presidential Directive 5: Intelligence.* Washington, DC: White House, May 9, 2001.

———. *Executive Order 13328: Commission on the Intelligence Capabilities of the United States regarding Weapons of Mass Destruction.* Washington, DC: US Government Printing Office, February 6, 2004.

———. *Executive Order 13354: National Counterterrorism Center.* Washington, DC: US Government Printing Office, August 27, 2004.

———. "President Bush Delivers Graduation Speech at West Point." June 1, 2002. At https://georgewbush-whitehouse.archives.gov/news/releases/2002/06/20020601-3.html.

Clinton, William Jefferson. *Presidential Decision Directive 35: Intelligence Requirements.* Washington, DC: US Government Printing Office, March 2, 1995.

———. "Remarks Announcing the National Performance Review." March 3, 1993. American Presidency Project. At http://www.presidency.ucsb.edu/ws/?pid=46291.

Collins, John M. *Desert Shield and Desert Storm: Implications for Future Force Requirements.* Washington, DC: Congressional Research Service, April 19, 1991. At http://www.hsdl.org/?view&did=712698.

"The Cost of Intelligence." N.d. At http://www.gpo.gov/fdsys/pkg/GPO-INTELLIGENCE/html/int017.html. Accessed January 7, 2013.

Erwin, Marshall Curtis. *Covert Action: Legislative Background and Policy Questions.* Washington, DC: Congressional Research Service, April 10, 2013. At http://www.fas.org/sgp/crs/intel/RL33715.pdf.

Federal Elections Commission. *Federal Elections 92: Election Results for the U.S. President, the U.S. Senate, and the U.S. House of Representatives.* Washington, DC: Federal Elections Commission, June 1993. At http://www.fec.gov/pubrec/fe1992/federalelections92.pdf.

Feickert, Andrew. *The Unified Command Plan and Combatant Commands: Background and Issues for Congress.* Washington, DC: Congressional Research Service, January 3, 2013. At https://www.fas.org/sgp/crs/natsec/R42077.pdf.

Gates, Robert M. "Secretary Gates Speech at National Defense University." September 2008. At http://www.cfr.org/defense-strategy/secretary-gates-speech-national-defense-university-september-2008/p17411.

Haas, Richard M. *Making Intelligence Smarter.* Task Force Report. Washington, DC: Council on Foreign Relations, January 1996. At http://www.cfr.org/intelligence/making-intelligence-smarter/p127.

Historical Office, Office of the Secretary of Defense. *Department of Defense Key Officials: September 1947–June 2017.* Washington, DC: US DoD, 2016. At http://history.defense.gov/Portals/70/Documents/key_officials/KEYOFFICIALS-JUN2017Final.pdf.

Hunt, Richard A. "Melvin Laird and the Foundation of the Post-Vietnam Military, 1969–1973." 2015. At http://history.defense.gov/Portals/70/Documents/secretaryofdefense/OSDSeries_Vol7.pdf.

Keaney, Thomas, and Eliot A. Cohen. *Gulf War Air Power Survey Summary Report.* Washington, DC: US Department of the Air Force, 1993.

Mann, Edward. "Desert Storm: The First Information War?" *Airpower Journal,* Winter 1994, 11. At http://www.airpower.maxwell.af.mil/airchronicles/apj/apj94/win94/man1.html.

McCurdy, Representative Dave. "Democratic Convention Seconding Speech." July 15, 1992. C-Span. At http://www.c-span.org/video/?27124-1/democratic-convention-seconding-speech.

National Commission on Terrorism. *Countering the Changing Threat of International Terrorism.* Washington, DC: US Government Printing Office, August 2, 2000.

National Commission on Terrorist Attacks upon the United States. *The 9/11 Commission Report.* Washington, DC: US Government Printing Office, July 2004.

———. "The Performance of the Intelligence Community: Staff Statement No. 11." N.d. At https://9-11commission.gov/staff_statements/staff_statement_11.pdf. Accessed November 27, 2012.

National Strategy for Combating Terrorism. Washington, DC: White House, September 2006.

Office of the Chief of Military History. "Unit History 1964—United States Military Liaison Mission to Commander in Chief, Group of Soviet Force in Germany." N.d. At http://www.coldwarspies.com/resources/uh1964cpr.pdf. Accessed April 22, 2016.

Persian Gulf War Illness Task Force. *CIA Support to the US Military during the Persian Gulf War.* Washington, DC: US Central Intelligence Agency, 1997.

Reagan, Ronald. *Communication from the President of the United States: Use of United States Armed Forces in Lebanon.* Washington, DC: US Government Printing Office, September 8, 1982.

———. *Executive Order 12526: President's Blue Ribbon Commission on Defense Management.* Washington, DC: US Government Printing Office, July 15, 1985.

———. *National Security Decision Directive 219: Implementation of the Recommendations of the President's Commission on Defense Management.* Washington, DC: US Government Printing Office, April 1, 1986.

———. "Peace: Restoring the Margin of Safety." Speech at the Veterans of Foreign Affairs Convention, Chicago, August 18, 1980. At http://www.reagan.utexas.edu/archives/reference/8.18.80.html.

———. "Remarks on Central America and El Salvador." Speech at the Annual Meeting of the National Association of Manufacturers, Washington, DC, March 10, 1983. American Presidency Project. At http://www.presidency.ucsb.edu/ws/?pid=41034.

"The Senate Passed S.J. Res. 2, to Authorize the Use of United States Armed Forces Pursuant to United Nations Security Council Resolution 678." C-Span, January 12, 1991. At http://www.c-span.org/video/?15665-1/senate-session&start=11899.

Thomas, Brigadier General Charles W. "Inside a J-2 Joint Intelligence Center." Approved for release September 10, 2014. At http://www.foia.cia.gov/sites/default/files/DOC_0006122143.pdf. Accessed May 10, 2018.

Tiersky, Alex, and Susan B. Epstein. *Securing U.S. Diplomatic Facilities and Personnel Abroad: Background and Policy Issues.* Washington, DC: Congressional Research Service, July 30, 2014. At https://www.fas.org/sgp/crs/row/R42834.pdf.

United Nations Security Council Resolution 661. August 6, 1990. At https://documents-dds-ny.un.org/doc/RESOLUTION/GEN/NR0/575/11/IMG/NR057511.pdf?OpenElement.

US Army. Center of Military History. *United States Forces, Somalia after Action Report and Historical Overview: The United States Army in Somalia 1992–1994.* Washington, DC: US Army Center of Military History, 2003.

US Blue Ribbon Commission on Defense Management. *A Quest for Excellence.* Washington, DC: US Government Printing Office, June 1986.

US Central Intelligence Agency (CIA). *Report of Investigation. Guatemala Volume IV: Michael Devine.* Washington, DC: US Government Printing Office, July 15, 1995.

———. *Support to Military Operations.* Washington, DC: CIA, posted May 1, 2007, last updated January 3, 2012. At https://www.cia.gov/library/reports/archived-reports-1/Ann_Rpt_2001/smo.html.

US Commission on the Intelligence Capabilities of the United States regarding Weapons of Mass Destruction. *Report to the President.* Washington, DC: US Government Printing Office, March 31, 2005.

US Commission on National Security/21st Century. *New World Coming: American Secu-*

rity in the 21st Century. The Phase I Report on the Emerging Global Security Environment. Washington, DC: US Government Printing Office, September 15, 1999.

———. *New World Coming: American Security in the 21st Century. The Phase II Report. Seeking a National Strategy: A Concert for Preserving Security and Promoting Freedom.* Washington, DC: US Government Printing Office, April 15, 2000.

———. *New World Coming: American Security in the 21st Century. The Phase III Road Map for National Security: Imperative for Change.* Washington, DC: US Government Printing Office, February 15, 2001.

US Commission on the Organization of the Government for the Conduct of Foreign Policy. *Report by the Commission on the Organization of the Government for the Conduct of Foreign Policy: Background and Principal Recommendations.* CRS-9-11. Washington, DC: Congressional Research Service, n.d. At research.policyarchive.org/20213.pdf. Accessed January 12, 2016.

US Commission on the Roles and Capabilities of the United States Intelligence Community. *Preparing for the 21st Century: An Appraisal of U.S. Intelligence.* Washington, DC: US Government Printing Office, 1996.

US Congressional Budget Office. *The Drawdown of the Military Officer Corps.* Washington, DC: US Government Printing Office, November 1999. At http://fas.org/irp/congress/1993_cr/index.html.

US Defense Intelligence Agency. "A Brief History: Committed to Excellence in Defense of the Nation." 1996. At http://fas.org/irp/dia/dia_history.pdf.

US Department of the Army. Office of the Deputy Chief of Staff for Intelligence. *Annual Historical Review 1 October 1990–30 September 1991.* Washington DC: US Department of the Army, 1991.

US Department of Defense (DoD). *Centralized Management of Department of Defense Human Intelligence (HUMINT) Operations.* Directive 5200-37. Washington, DC: US DoD, December 18, 1992.

———. *Final Report to Congress on the Conduct of the Persian Gulf War.* Washington, DC: US DoD, April 1992.

———. *Joint Overview of Operation Urgent Fury.* Washington, DC: US DoD, May 1, 1985.

———. *Joint Publication 1-0: Doctrine for the Armed Forces of the United States.* Washington, DC: US DoD, March 25, 2013.

———. *Joint Publication 1-02: Department of Defense Dictionary of Military and Associated Terms.* Washington, DC: US DoD, November 8, 2010.

———. *Joint Publication 2-01: Joint and National Intelligence Support to Military Operations.* Washington, DC: US DoD, January 5, 2012.

———. *Joint Publication 2-01.3: Joint Intelligence Preparation of the Operational Environment.* Washington, DC: US DoD, June 16, 2009.

———. *Joint Publication 3-0: Doctrine for Joint Operations.* Washington, DC: US DoD, February 1, 1995.

———. *Report of the DoD Commission on Beirut International Airport Terrorist Act.* Washington, DC: US DoD, December 10, 1983.

———. Assistant Secretary of Defense for Command, Control, Communications, and Intelligence. *Plan for Restructuring Defense Intelligence.* Washington, DC: US DoD, March 15, 1991.

US Department of State. *Foreign Relations of the United States, 1969–1976.* Vol. 2: *Organization and Management of U.S. Foreign Policy, 1969–1972,* edited by David C. Humphrey. Washington, DC: US Government Printing Office, 2006.

———. Bureau of Diplomatic Security. *History of the Bureau of Diplomatic Security of the United States Department of State.* Washington, DC: Global Publishing Solutions, 2011.

US Government Accounting Office. "Military Downsizing: Balancing Accessions and Losses Is Key to Shaping the Future Force." September 1993. At http://www.gao.gov/assets/160/153782.pdf.

———. *Military Personnel: High Aggregate Personnel Levels Maintained throughout Drawdown.* Washington, DC: US General Accounting Office, June 1995.

US House of Representatives. *Intelligence Authorization Act, Fiscal Year 1991.* Report 102-166. 102nd Cong., 1st sess., July 25, 1991. Washington, DC: US Government Printing Office, 1991.

———. *Intelligence Authorization Act, Fiscal Year 1995, H. R. 4299.* 103rd Cong., 2nd sess., September 30, 1994.

———. *National Defense Authorization Act for Fiscal Year 1991.* 101st Cong., 2nd sess., November 5, 1990.

———. *National Defense Authorization Act for Fiscal Year 1997.* 104th Cong., 2nd sess., September 10, 1996.

———. *National Security Act of 1992.* 102nd Cong., 2nd sess., February 5, 1992.

———. *Operation Just Cause: Preliminary Session.* 101st Cong., 2nd sess., February 5, 1990.

———. Committee on the Armed Services. *Hearings on Military Posture and H. R. 5968 Department of Defense Appropriations for 1983.* 97th Cong., 2nd sess., February–March 1983.

———. Committee on the Armed Services. *Lessons Learned as a Result of the U.S. Military Operations in Grenada.* 98th Cong., 2nd sess., January 24, 1984.

———. Committee on the Armed Services. *Military Service, Posture, Readiness, and Budget Issues.* 106th Cong., 1st sess., October 21, 1999.

———. Committee on the Armed Services. *The Use of Military Personnel in Lebanon and Consideration of Report from September 24–25 Committee Delegation to Lebanon.* 98th Cong., 1st sess., September 27 and 28, 1983.

———. Committee on Ways and Means. *Hearing on HR 2769: Caribbean Basin Economic Recovery Act.* 98th Cong., 1st sess., June 9, 1983.

———. Defense Appropriations Subcommittee of the Committee on Appropriations. *Situation in Lebanon and Grenada.* Washington, DC: US Government Printing Office, November 8, 1983.

———. Oversight and Investigations Subcommittee of the Committee on the Armed Services. *Intelligence Successes and Failures in Operations Desert Storm/Shield.* Washington, DC: US Government Printing Office, August 16, 1993.

———. Permanent Select Committee on Intelligence. *IC21: The Intelligence Community in the 21st Century.* 104th Cong., 1st sess., May 22–December 19, 1995.

———. Permanent Select Committee on Intelligence. *IC21: The Intelligence Community in the 21st Century.* Staff Study Report. 104th Cong., 2nd sess., June 5, 1996. Washington, DC: US Government Printing Office, 1996. At https://www.gpo.gov/fdsys/pkg/GPO-IC21/html/ic21001.htm.

———. Permanent Select Committee on Intelligence. *R. 111-186 to Intelligence Authorization Act for Fiscal Year 2010.* 111th Cong., 1st sess., June 26, 2009.

US House of Representatives and Senate. *Bob Stump National Defense Authorization Act for Fiscal Year 2003* (Pub. L. 107-314). 107th Cong., 2nd sess., December 2, 2002.

———. *Caribbean Economic Initiative* (Pub. L. 98-67). 98th Cong., 1st sess., August 5, 1983.

———. *Goldwater-Nichols Reorganization Act of 1986* (Pub. L. 99-53). 99th Cong., 2nd sess., October 1, 1986.

———. *Intelligence Reform and Terrorism Prevention Act of 2004* (Pub. L. 108-458). 108th Cong., XXth sess., 2nd sess., December 17, 2004.

———. *National Security Act of 1947* (Pub. L. 253). 80th Cong., 1st sess., July 26, 1947.

———. Joint Committee on the Investigation of the Pearl Harbor Attack. *Pearl Harbor Attack.* 79th Cong., 1st sess., January 14, 1946.

US Joint Chiefs of Staff. *National Military Strategy.* Washington, DC: US Government Printing Office, February 1995. At http://www.au.af.mil/au/awc/awcgate/nms/nms_feb95.htm#CS.

US Senate. *Authorization for Use of Military Force against Iraq Resolution.* 102nd Cong., 1st sess., January 11, 1991.

———. *Intelligence Reorganization Act of 1992.* 102nd Cong., 2nd sess., February 5, 1992.

———. *National Intelligence Reorganization Act.* 102nd Cong., 1st sess., February 19, 1991.

———. *Nomination of Robert M. Gates to Be Director of Central Intelligence.* Executive Report. 102nd Cong., 1st sess., January 3, 1991. Washington, DC: US Government Printing Office, 1991.

———. Committee on Armed Services. *Crisis in the Persian Gulf Region: U.S. Policy Options and Implications.* 101st Cong., 2nd sess., September–December 1991.

———. Committee on Armed Services. *Hearings before the Committee on Armed Services: The Situation in Lebanon.* 98th Cong., 1st sess., October 25 and 31, 1983.

———. Committee on Armed Services. *Hearings on the Reorganization of the Department of Defense.* 98th Cong., 1st sess., October–December 1985.

———. Committee on Armed Services. *Nominations before the Armed Services Committee.* 101st Cong., 1st sess., March–November 1989.

———. Committee on Armed Services. *Nominations before the Armed Services Committee.* 107th Cong., 1st sess., January–December 2001.

———. Committee on Armed Services. *Operation Desert Shield/Desert Storm.* 102nd Cong., 1st sess., April–June 1991.

———. Committee on Armed Services. *Review of the Circumstances Surrounding the*

Ranger Raid on October 3–4, 1993 in Mogadishu, Somalia. 104th Cong., 1st sess., September 29, 1995.

———. Committee on Armed Forces. "Statement for the Record—Dr. Stephen Cambone [Undersecretary of Defense for Intelligence]." 109th Cong., 1st sess., April 28, 2005. At https://fas.org/irp/congress/2005_hr/042805cambone.pdf.

———. Committee on Veterans Affairs. *Report of the Special Investigation Unit on Gulf War Illnesses.* 105th Cong, 2nd sess. Washington, DC: US Government Printing Office, 1998.

———. Foreign Relations Committee. *Security Situation in Iraq.* 110th Cong., 2nd sess., April 2, 2008.

———. Select Committee on Intelligence. *An Assessment of the Aldrich H. Ames Espionage Case and Its Implication for U.S. Intelligence.* 103rd Cong., 2nd sess., November 1, 1994. Washington, DC: US Government Printing Office, 1994.

———. Select Committee on Intelligence. *Authorizing Appropriations for Fiscal Year 1991 for the Intelligence Activities of the U.S. Government, the Intelligence Community Staff, the Central Intelligence Agency Retirement and Disability System and for other Purposes.* 102nd Cong., 1st sess., June 19, 1991.

———. Select Committee on Intelligence. *Authorizing Appropriations for Fiscal Year 1992 for the Intelligence Activities of the U.S. Government, the Intelligence Community Staff, the Central Intelligence Agency Retirement and Disability System, and for Other Purposes.* 102nd Cong., 1st sess., July 8, 1991.

———. Select Committee on Intelligence. *Hearings before the Select Committee on Intelligence: U.S. Intelligence Agencies and Activities: Intelligence Cost and Fiscal Procedures.* 94th Cong., 1st sess., July–August 1975.

———. Select Committee on Intelligence. *Nomination of James Woolsey* (Hearing 103-296).103rd Cong., 1st sess., February 2–3, 1993.

———. Select Committee on Intelligence. *Nomination of John Deutch* (Hearing 104-160). 104th Cong., 1st sess., April 26 and May 3, 1995.

———. Select Committee on Intelligence. *Nomination of Robert M. Gates to Be Director of Central Intelligence* (Hearing 102-799). 102nd Cong., 1st sess., September 16, 17, 19, 20, 1991.

———. Select Committee on Intelligence. *Report on the U.S. Intelligence Community's Prewar Intelligence Assessments on Iraq.* 108th Cong., 2nd sess., July 7, 2004. Washington, DC: US Government Printing Office, 2004.

———. Select Committee on Intelligence. *Review of Intelligence Organization* (Hearing 102-91). 102nd Cong., 1st sess., March 12, 1991.

———. Select Committee on Intelligence. *S. 2198 and S. 421 to Reorganize the United States Intelligence Community* (Hearing 894). 102nd Cong., 2nd sess., February 20 and March 4, 12, 19, 1992.

———. Subcommittee on Western Hemisphere Affairs of the Committee on Foreign Relations. *Situation in Panama* (Hearing 99-832). 99th Cong., 2nd sess., March 10 and April 21, 1986.

US Senate and House of Representatives. Select Committee on Intelligence and Permanent Select Committee on Intelligence. *Joint Inquiry into Events Surrounding September 11*. 107th Cong., 2nd sess., October 3, 2002.

———. Select Committee on Intelligence and Permanent Select Committee on Intelligence. *S. 2198 and S.421 to Reorganize the United States Intelligence Community*. 102nd Cong., 2nd sess., April 1, 1992.

US Special Operations Command. "United States Special Operations Command History." April 16, 1987. At http://www.fas.org/irp/agency/dod/socom/2007history.pdf.

Vickers, Robert. "Desert Storm and the BDA Controversy." N.d., approved for release September 10, 2014. At http://www.foia.cia.gov/sites/default/files/DOC_0006122350.pdf. Accessed April 5, 2016.

Ward, Samuel D. "The Operational Leadership of Vice Admiral Joseph P. Metcalf, III." 2012. At http://www.dtic.mil/dtic/tr/fulltext/u2/a564017.pdf.

White House. Office of the Press Secretary. "Biography of Bobby Ray Inman." Press release, December 16, 1993. At http://fas.org/irp/news/1993/931216i.htm.

———. Office of the Press Secretary. "President Bush Administration Actions to Implement WMD Commission Recommendations." Press release, July 29, 2005. At http://georgewbush-whitehouse.archives.gov/news/releases/2005/06/text/20050629-5.html.

———. Office of the Press Secretary. "Principal Deputy Press Secretary Speaks on the Death of Major Arthur D. Nicholson, Jr., in the German Democratic Republic." April 23, 1985. At http://www.reagan.utexas.edu/archives/speeches/1985/42385d.htm.

———. Office of the Press Secretary. "Statement by General Michael Carns Withdrawing His Nomination to Be Director of CIA." Press release, March 11, 1995. At https://fas.org/irp/news/1995/950311carns.htm.

———. Office of the Press Secretary. "Statement by Press Secretary Fitzwater on Organizational Changes in the Intelligence Community." April 1, 1992. American Presidency Project. At http://www.presidency.ucsb.edu/ws/?pid=20786.

Interviews

B., Candace. CIA analyst. Interview by the author, Fort Leavenworth, KS, August 10, 2012.

Baratto, Major General (ret.) David. Former CIA associate director for military affairs. Telephone interview by the author, January 23, 2013.

Boren, David L. President of the University of Oklahoma and former chairman of the Senate Select Committee on Intelligence. Email interview by the author, November 20, 2012.

Burgess, Lieutenant General (ret.) Ronald L. Former director of the Defense Intelligence Agency. Telephone interview by the author, September 17, 2015.

Cichowski, Lieutenant General Kurt A. CIA associate director for military affairs. Interview by the author, Langley, VA, August 29, 2012.

Edger, David. Former CIA associate deputy director of operations. Telephone interview by the author, December 7, 2015.

Ennis, Major General (ret.) Michael. Former CIA deputy director of human intelligence. Interview by the author, Leesburg, VA, November 17, 2015.

————. "Transcript of Interview of Major General Michael E. Ennis." CIA, News & Information, February 28, 2007. At https://www.cia.gov/news-information/press-releases-statements/press-release-archive-2007/february-28-2007.html.

G., Alyssa. Military liaison to the CIA Office of Military Affairs. Interview by the author, Langley, VA, August 28, 2012.

Gates, Robert. Former secretary of defense and former director of central intelligence. Telephone interview by the author, March 29, 2016.

Haver, Richard. Former assistant secretary of defense for intelligence and former intelligence adviser to the secretary of defense (Cheney and Rumsfeld). Interview by the author, Great Falls, VA, December 1, 2015, and email exchange with the author, January 4, 2016.

Hayden, General (ret.) Michael V. Former CIA director and former National Security Agency director. Interview by the author, Washington, DC, September 18, 2015.

Inman, Admiral (ret.) Bobby Ray. Former CIA deputy director. Interview by the author, Austin, TX, August 27, 2014.

Jacoby, Vice Admiral (ret.) Lowell E. Former director of the Defense Intelligence Agency and former Joint Chiefs of Staff J2. Interview by the author, Ashburn, VA, November 18, 2015.

Kojm, Chris. Former chairman of the National Intelligence Council. Telephone interview by the author, October 14, 2015.

Lajoie, Major General (ret.) Roland. Former CIA associate deputy director for operations and military affairs. Telephone interview by the author, November 10, 2015.

LeVitre, Rear Admiral (ret.) Rosanne M. National intelligence manager for military issues and deputy director of national intelligence for intelligence integration. Interview by the author, Washington, DC, November 4, 2015.

McConnell, Vice Admiral (ret.) Michael. Former director of national intelligence, former director of the National Security Agency, and former Joint Chiefs of Staff J2. Interview by the author, Leesburg, VA, August 8, 2015.

McLaughlin, John. Former CIA deputy director. Telephone interview by the author, September 19, 2012.

McRaven, Admiral (ret.) William H. Former commander Special Operations Command and former commander Joint Special Operations Command. Telephone interview by the author, June 5, 2015.

Panetta, Leon. Interviewed by Jim Lehrer. Newshour, PBS, May 3, 2011. At http://www.pbs.org/newshour/bb/terrorism/jan-june11/panetta_05-03.html.

Perkins, Lieutenant General David G. Commander of the US Army Combined Arms Center. Interview by the author, Fort Leavenworth, KS, October 3, 2012.

————. "Interview: Col. David Perkins." Frontline, PBS, n.d. At http://www.pbs.org/wgbh/pages/frontline/shows/invasion/interviews/perkins.html. Accessed March 15, 2016.

Petraeus, General (ret.) David. Former CIA director and commander of US Central Command. Interview by the author, Washington, DC, October 23, 2015.

Reid, Garry. Principal deputy assistant secretary of defense for special operations/low-intensity conflict. Telephone interview by the author, September 19, 2012.

Roberts, Pat. US senator and former chairman of the Senate Select Committee on Intelligence. Email interview by the author, January 9, 2013.

Rodriguez, Jose. Former director of the CIA National Clandestine Service. Telephone interview by the author, September 21, 2015.

Russell, Richard L. Professor in the Department of Near East–South Asia, Center for Strategic Studies, National Defense University. Telephone interview by the author, September 14, 2012.

Studeman, Admiral (ret.) William O. Former CIA deputy director and former National Security Agency director. Interview by the author, Severna Park, MD, November 24, 2015.

Wise, Doug. Deputy director of the Defense Intelligence Agency. Interview by the author, Washington, DC, area, August 28, 2012, and September 3, 2015.

Books

Adams, Gordon, and Shoon Murray, eds. *Mission Creep: The Militarization of US Foreign Policy*. Washington, DC: Georgetown University Press, 2014.

Ahearn, Thomas L., Jr. *Vietnam Declassified: The CIA and Counterinsurgency*. Lexington: University Press of Kentucky, 2010.

Allen, Michael. *Blinking Red: Crisis and Compromise in Intelligence after 9/11*. Lincoln: University of Nebraska Press, 2013.

Andres, John Olsen. *Strategic Air Power in Desert Storm*. Oxford: Routledge, 2003.

Andrew, Christopher. *For the President's Eyes Only: Secret Intelligence and the American Presidency from Washington to Bush*. New York: Harper Perennial, 1996.

Atkinson, Rick. *Crusade: The Untold Story of the Persian Gulf War*. New York: Houghton Mifflin Harcourt, 1993.

Bacevich, Andrew. *America's War for the Greater Middle East*. New York: Random House, 2016.

Baer, Robert. *See No Evil: The True Story of a Ground Soldier in the CIA's War on Terrorism*. New York: Crown, 2002.

Beede, Benjamin. *The Small Wars of the United States 1899–2009*. New York: Routledge, 2010.

Berkowitz, Bruce. *The National Reconnaissance Office at 50 Years: A Brief History*. Chantilly, VA: Center for the Study of National Reconnaissance, 2011.

Betts, Richard K. *Enemies of Intelligence: Knowledge and Power in American National Security*. New York: Columbia University Press, 2007.

Blehm, Eric. *The Only Thing Worth Dying For: How Eleven Green Berets Forged a New Afghanistan*. New York: Harper Collins E-Books, 2010.

Bowden, Mark. *Black Hawk Down: A Story of Modern War*. New York: Atlantic Monthly Press, 1999.

Boykin, Jerry. *Never Surrender: A Soldier's Journey to the Crossroads of Faith and Freedom*. New York: Hachette Book Group, 2008.

Bush, George H. W., and Brent Scowcroft. *A World Transformed*. New York: Vintage Books, 1999.

Carhart, Tom. *Iron Soldiers: How America's 1st Armored Division Crushed Iraq's Elite Republican Guard.* New York: Pocket, 1994.

Cassidy, Robert M. *Counterinsurgency and the Global War on Terror: Military Culture and Irregular War.* Westport, CT: Praeger Security International, 2006.

Cheney, Dick. *In My Time.* New York: Simon and Schuster, 2011.

Chollet, Derek. *The Road to the Dayton Accords: A Study of American Statecraft.* New York: Palgrave, 2005.

Clark, Wesley K. *Waging Modern War.* New York: PublicAffairs, 2002.

Clarke, Jeffrey J. *Operation Urgent Fury: The Invasion of Grenada, October 1983.* Washington, DC: US Army Center for Military History, 2008.

Clausewitz, Carl von. *On War.* Edited and translated by Michael Eliot Howard and Peter Paret. Paperback ed. Princeton, NJ: Princeton University Press, 1989.

Cole, Robert. *Operation Urgent Fury: Grenada.* Washington, DC: Joint History Office of the Chairman of the Joint Chiefs of Staff, 1997.

Coll, Steven. *Ghost Wars: The Secret History of the CIA, Afghanistan, and bin Laden, from the Soviet Invasion to September 10, 2001.* New York: Penguin, 2004.

Crandall, Russell. *Gunboat Diplomacy: U.S. Intervention in the Dominican Republic, Grenada, and Panama.* Oxford: Rowman and Littlefield, 2006.

Crotty, William, ed. *America's Choice 2000.* Boulder, CO: Westview Press, 2001.

Crumpton, Henry A. *The Art of Intelligence: Lesson from a Life in the CIA's Clandestine Service.* New York: Penguin, 2012.

Davidson, Janine. *Lifting the Fog of Peace: How Americans Learned to Fight Modern War.* Ann Arbor: University of Michigan Press, 2010.

Diamond, John. *The CIA and the Culture of Failure: U.S. Intelligence from the End of the Cold War to the Invasion of Iraq.* Stanford, CA: Stanford University Press, 2008.

Drumheller, Tyler. *On the Brink: An Insider's Account of How the White House Compromised American Intelligence.* New York: Carroll & Graf, 2006.

Earley, Pete. *Family of Spies.* New York: Bantam Books, 1988.

Essays on Strategy. Washington, DC: National Defense University Press, 1988.

Feaver, Peter D., and Richard H. Kohn, eds. *Soldiers and Civilians: The Civil–Military Gap and American National Security.* Cambridge, MA: Belfer Center for Science and International Affairs, John F. Kennedy School, Harvard University, 2001.

Federation of American Scientists. *2018 Nuclear Posture Review Resource.* N.d. At http://fas.org/irp/news/1996/x011996_x0118je.html. Accessed April 4, 2018.

Fontenot, Gregory, E. J. Degen, and David Tohn. *On Point: The United States Army in Operation Iraqi Freedom.* Fort Leavenworth, KS: Combat Studies Institute, 2004.

Frank, Benis. *U.S. Marines in Lebanon: 1982–1984.* Washington, DC: History and Museum Division Headquarters, US Marine Corps, 1987.

Garthoff, Douglas F. *Directors of Central Intelligence as Leaders of the U.S. Intelligence Community 1946–2005.* Washington, DC: Center for the Study of Intelligence, 2005.

Gates, Robert M. *Duty: Memoirs of a Secretary at War.* New York: Penguin Random House, 2014.

————. *From the Shadows: The Ultimate Insider's Story of Five Presidents and How They Won the Cold War.* New York: Simon and Schuster, 2006.

George, Roger Z., and Robert D. Kline, eds. *Intelligence and the National Security Strategist: Enduring Issues and Challenges.* New York: Rowman and Littlefield, 2006.

Geraghty, Timothy J. *Peacekeepers at War: Beirut 1983—the Marine Commander Tells His Story.* Washington, DC: Potomac Books, 2009.

Godson, Roy, Ernest R. May, and Gary Schmit, eds. *U.S. Intelligence at the Crossroads: Agendas for Reform.* Washington, DC: Brassey's, 1995.

Goodman, Melvin. *Failure of Intelligence: The Decline and Fall of the CIA.* New York: Rowman and Littlefield, 2008.

Gordon, Michael R., and Bernard E. Trainor. *The General's War.* New York: Little, Brown, 1995.

Gup, Ted. *The Book of Honor: The Secret Lives and Deaths of CIA Operatives.* New York: First Anchor Books, 2001.

Hedley, John Hollister. *Checklist for the Future of Intelligence.* Washington, DC: Institute for the Study of Diplomacy, Georgetown University, 1995.

Helms, Richard. *A Look over My Shoulder: A Life in the Central Intelligence Agency.* New York: Random House, 2003.

Herspring, Dale R. *Rumsfeld's Wars: The Arrogance of Power.* Lawrence: University of Kansas Press, 2008.

Huchthausen, Peter. *America's Splendid Little Wars: A Short History of U.S. Engagement from the Fall of Saigon to Baghdad.* New York: Penguin, 2003.

Jackson, Donna. *Jimmy Carter and the Horn of Africa: Cold War Policy in Ethiopia and Somalia.* Jefferson, NC: McFarland, 2007.

Johnson, Loch K. *The Threat on the Horizon: An Inside Account of America's Search for Security after the Cold War.* Oxford: Oxford University Press, 2011.

Johnson, Stuart E., and Martin C. Libicki, eds. *Dominant Battlespace Knowledge.* Washington, DC: National Defense University Press, 1995.

Joyce, James. *Ulysses.* London: Not So Noble Books, 2013.

Kagan, Frederick W. *Finding the Target: The Transformation of American Military Policy.* New York: Encounter Books, 1997.

Kagan, Robert, and William Kristol, eds. *Present Dangers: Crisis and Opportunity in American Foreign and Defense Policy.* New York: Encounter Books, 2000.

Kempe, Frederick. *Divorcing the Dictator: America's Bungled Affair with Noriega.* London: Putnam's, 1990.

Kitfield, James. *War and Destiny: How the Bush Revolution in Foreign and Military Affairs Redefined American Power.* Washington, DC: Potomac Books, 2007.

Knott, Stephen. *Secret and Sanctioned: Covert Operations and the American Presidency.* New York: Oxford University Press, 1996.

Locher, James. *Victory on the Potomac: The Goldwater–Nichols Act Unifies the Pentagon.* College Station: Texas A&M University Press, 2002.

Lock-Pullan, Richard. *US Intervention Policy and Army Innovation: From Vietnam to Iraq.* New York: Routledge, 2006.

Lowenthal, Mark M. *Intelligence: From Secrets to Policy*. Los Angeles: Sage, 2012.

Mahle, Melissa Boyle. *Denial and Deception: An Insider's View of the CIA from Iran Contra to 9/11*. New York: Nations Books, 2004.

Mandelbaum, Michael. *Mission Failure: America and the World in the Post–Cold War World*. New York: Oxford University Press, 2016.

Mann, James. *Rise of the Vulcans: History of Bush's War Cabinet*. New York: Penguin, 2004.

McChrystal, Stanley. *My Share of the Task*. London: Penguin, 2013.

McDonnell, Janet A. *Adopting to a Changing Environment: The Defense Intelligence Agency in the 1990s*. Washington, DC: Historical Office, Defense Intelligence Agency, 2013.

———. *Defense Intelligence Coming of Age: The Office of the Undersecretary of Defense for Intelligence 2002–2012*. Washington, DC: Historical Office, Defense Intelligence Agency, 2014.

Meacham, Jon. *Destiny and Power: The American Odyssey of George Herbert Walker Bush*. New York: Random House, 2015.

Metz, Steven, ed. *Revising the Two MTW Force Shaping Paradigm*. Carlisle, PA: Strategic Studies Institute, 2001.

Miles, Anne Daugherty. *The Creation of the National Imagery and Mapping Agency: Congress's Role as Overseer*. Washington, DC: Joint Military Intelligence College, 2002.

Nation, Craig R. *A History of the War in the Balkans*. Carlisle, PA: Strategic Studies Institute, 2015.

Nelson, Michael, and Barbara A. Perry. *41: Inside the Presidency of George H. W. Bush*. Ithaca, NY: Cornell University Press, 2014.

Odom, William E. *On Internal War: American and Soviet Approaches to Third World Clients and Insurgents*. Durham, NC: Duke University Press, 1991.

Olmstead, Kathryn S. *Challenging the Secret Government: The Post-Watergate Investigations of the CIA and FBI*. Chapel Hill: University of North Carolina Press, 1996.

Panetta, Leon, and Jim Newton. *Worthy Fights: A Memoir of Leadership in War and Peace*. New York: Penguin, 2015.

Paul, Christopher, Isaac R. Porche III, and Elliott Axelband. *The Other Quiet Professionals: Lessons for Future Cyber Professionals from the Evolution of Special Forces*. Santa Monica, CA: RAND, 2014.

Phillips, David L. *Liberating Kosovo: Coercive Diplomacy and U.S. Intervention*. Cambridge, MA: MIT Press, 2012.

Prados, John. *Lost Crusader: The Secret Wars of CIA Director William Colby*. New York: Oxford University Press, 2003.

———. *Vietnam: The History of an Unwinnable War*. Lawrence: University of Kansas Press, 2009.

Priest, Dana. *The Mission: Waging War and Keeping Peace with America's Military*. New York: Norton, 2003.

Rumsfeld, Donald. *Known and Unknown, a Memoir*. New York: Sentinel, 2011.

Scahill, Jeremy. *Dirty Wars: The World Is a Battlefield*. New York: Nation Books, 2013.

Schroen, Gary. *First In: An Insider's Account of How the CIA Spearheaded the War on Terror in Afghanistan*. New York: Ballantine Books, 2005.

Schwarzkopf, Norman H. *It Doesn't Take a Hero*. New York: Bantam Books, 1992.

Scott, Paul James M., ed. *After the End: Making U.S. Foreign Policy in the Post–Cold War World*. Durham, NC: Duke University Press, 2000.

Shackley, Ted, with Richard A. Finney. *Spymaster: My Life in the CIA*. Dulles, VA: Potomac Books, 2005.

Shelton, Hugh. *Without Hesitation: The Odyssey of an American Warrior*. New York: St. Martin's Press, 2010.

Sims, Jennifer E., and Burton Gerber, eds. *Transforming U.S. Intelligence*. Washington, DC: Georgetown University Press, 2005.

Smist, Frank J. *Congress Oversees the United States Intelligence Community 1947–1989*. Knoxville: University of Tennessee Press, 1990.

Snider, L. Britt. *The Agency and the Hill: CIA's Relationship with Congress, 1946–2004*. Washington, DC: CIA Center for the Study of Intelligence, 2008.

Strachan, Hew. *Clausewitz's On War: A Biography*. London: Grove Atlantic, 2007.

Sulick, Michael J. *American Spies: Espionage against the United States from the Cold War to the Present*. Washington, DC: Georgetown University Press, 2013.

Swain, Richard M. *Lucky War: Third Army in Desert Storm*. Fort Leavenworth, KS: US Army Command and General Staff College Press, 1991.

Tenet, George. *At the Center of the Storm: My Years at the CIA*. New York: Harper Collins E-Book, 2007.

Tyler, Patrick. *A World of Trouble: The White House and the Middle East—from the Cold War to the War on Terror*. New York: Farrar, Straus and Giroux, 2009.

Vistica, Gregory. *Fall from Glory: The Men Who Sank the U.S Navy*. New York: Simon and Schuster, 1997.

Warner, Michael. *The Rise and Fall of Intelligence: An International Security History*. Washington, DC: Georgetown University Press, 2014.

Wentz, Larry, ed. *Lessons from Bosnia: The IFOR Experience*. Washington, DC: US Department of Defense, 1997.

Wood, Lamont. *Datapoint: The Lost Story of the Texans Who Invented the Personal Computer Revolution*. Englewood, CO: Hugo House, 2010.

Woods, Randall B. *Shadow Warrior: William Egan Colby and the CIA*. New York: Basic Books, 2013.

Zegart, Amy. *Spying Blind: The CIA, the FBI, and the Origins of 9/11*. Princeton, NJ: Princeton University Press, 1999.

Articles

"The 1992 Campaign: On the Trail; Poll Gives Perot a Clear Lead." *New York Times*, June 11, 1992. At http://www.nytimes.com/1992/06/11/us/the-1992-campaign-on-the-trail-poll-gives-perot-a-clear-lead.html.

"2000 Republican Party Platform." July 31, 2000. American Presidency Project. At http://www.presidency.ucsb.edu/ws/?pid=25849

"*Achille Lauro* Hijacking Ends" (October 8, 1985). *This Day in History*, History Channel, n.d. At http://www.history.com/this-day-in-history/achille-lauro-hijacking-ends. Accessed March 18, 2016.

Adams, Gordon, and Shoon Murray. "An Introduction to Mission Creep." In *Mission*

Creep: The Militarization of US Foreign Policy, edited by Gordon Adams and Shoon Murray, 3–21. Washington, DC: Georgetown University Press, 2014.

"Al Gore 2000 on the Issues." N.d. At http://www.4president.us/issues/gore2000/gore-2000foreignpolicy.htm. Accessed February 26, 2016.

Allen, Gregory J. "The Feasibility of Implementing Videoconferencing Systems aboard Afloat Naval Units." Calhoun, Naval Postgraduate School, March 1990. At http://calhoun.nps.edu/bitstream/handle/10945/30671/90Mar_Allen.pdf?sequence=1.

Apple, R. W., Jr. "The 1994 Campaign: In Oklahoma's Senate Race, Both Candidates Are Running against Clinton." *New York Times,* October 5, 1994. At http://www.nytimes.com/1994/10/ 05/us/1994-campaign-oklahoma-s-senate-race-both-candidates-are-running-against-clinton.html?pagewanted=all.

Barry, John. "The Collapse of Les Aspin." *Newsweek,* December 26, 1993. At http://www.newsweek.com/collapse-les-aspin-190744.

"Body Believed to Be CIA Agent and Hostage Is Found in Lebanon." *New York Times,* December 27, 1991. At http://www.nytimes.com/1991/12/27/world/body-believed-to-be-cia-agent-and-hostage-is-found-in-lebanon.html.

Boyd, Gerald M. "Reagan Retracts Gates Nomination to Head the C.I.A." *New York Times,* March 3, 1987. At http://www.nytimes.com/1987/03/03/world/reagan-retracts-gates-nomination-to-head-the-cia.html.

"A Brief History of Vice President Al Gore's National Partnership for Reinventing Government during the Administration of President Bill Clinton, 1993–2001." National Performance Review, n.d. At http://govinfo.library.unt.edu/npr/whoweare/historyof-npr.html. Accessed June 26, 2016.

Campbell, James E. "The Curious and Close Presidential Campaign of 2000." In *America's Choice 2000,* edited by William Crotty, 115–37. Boulder, CO: Westview Press, 2001.

"Central America, 1981–93." Office of the Historian, Milestones 1981–1988, n.d. At https://history.state.gov/milestones/1981-1988/central-america. Accessed March 18, 2016.

"CIA Holds Annual Memorial Ceremony to Honor Fallen Colleagues." CIA, News & Information, May 22, 2012. At https://www.cia.gov/news-information/press-releases-statements/2012-press-releasese-statements/2012-memorial-ceremony.html.

Cooper, Jeffrey. "Dominant Battlespace Awareness and Future Warfare." In *Dominant Battlespace Knowledge,* edited by Stuart E. Johnson and Martin C. Libicki, 39–46. Washington, DC: National Defense University Press, 1995.

"Creating the National Imagery and Mapping Agency." CIA, Library, n.d. At http://www.foia.cia.gov/sites/default/files/DOC_0000619983.pdf. Accessed February 9, 2016.

"DCI Statement on the Belgrade Chinese Embassy Bombing." CIA, News & Information, n.d. At https://www.cia.gov/news-information/speeches-testimony/1999/dci_speech_072299.html. Accessed February 24, 2016.

Eikenberry, Karl. "The Militarization of US Foreign Policy." *American Foreign Policy Interests,* February 2013. At https://www.ncafp.org/2016/wp-content/uploads/2013/02/Amb.-Eikenberry-Mil-USFP.pdf.

"Election of 2008." American Presidency Project, n.d. At http://www.presidency.ucsb.edu/showelection.php?year=2008. Accessed March 7, 2016.

"The Evolution and Relevance of Joint Intelligence Centers." CIA, n.d. At https://www.cia.gov/library/center-for-the-study-of-intelligence/csi-publications/csi-studies/studies/vol49no1/html_files/the_evolution_6.html Accessed April 20, 2018.

"Feds: CIA Boss Had History of Bad Behavior." Associated Press, February 25, 2009. At http://www.nbcnews.com/id/29391260/ns/us_news-crime_and_courts/t/feds-cia-boss-had-history-bad-behavior/#.V3Kfd1d-t8.

Fiorina, Morris, Samuel Abrams, and Jeremy Pope. "The 2000 Presidential Election: Can Retrospective Voting Be Saved?" *British Journal of Political Science* 33 (2003): 163–87. At http://www.uvm.edu/~dguber/POLS234/articles/fiorina.pdf.

"Flashback: April 26, 1999: CIA Headquarters Named George Bush Center for Intelligence." CIA, News & Information, 2014. At https://www.cia.gov/news-information/featured-story-archive/2014-featured-story-archive/flashback-cia-headquarters-named-george-bush-center-for-intelligence.html.

FitzSimonds, James R. "Intelligence and the Revolution in Military Affairs." In *U.S. Intelligence at the Crossroads: Agendas for Reform,* edited by Roy Godson, Ernest R. May, and Gary Schmit, 265–87. Washington, DC: Brassey's, 1995.

Fritz, Sara, and William J. Eaton. "Congress Authorizes Gulf War: Historic Act: The Vote in Both Houses, Supporting Bush and Freeing Troops to Attack Iraq, Is Decisive and Bipartisan. It Is the Strongest Move since Tonkin Gulf." *Los Angeles Times,* January 13, 1991. At http://articles.latimes.com/1991-01-13/news/mn-374_1_persian-gulf.

Gallup. "Presidential Approval Ratings—Gallup Historical Statistics and Trends." N.d. At http://www.gallup.com/poll/116677/presidential-approval-ratings-gallup-historical-statistics-trends.aspx. Accessed January 28, 2016.

Garamone, Jim. "Rumsfeld Attacks Pentagon Bureaucracy, Vows Changes." American Foreign Press Service, September 10, 2001. At http://archive.defense.gov/news/newsarticle.aspx?id=44916.

Garfinkel, Michelle. "The Economic Consequences of Reducing Military Spending." *Federal Reserve Bank of St. Louis Review* 72, no. 6 (November–December 1990): 47–58.

Gellman, Barton. "Secret Unit Expands Rumsfeld's Domain." *Washington Post,* January 23, 2005.

Gerber, Burton. "Managing HUMINT: The Need for a New Approach." In *Transforming U.S. Intelligence,* edited by Jennifer E. Sims and Burton Gerber, 180–97. Washington, DC: Georgetown University Press, 2005.

Gordon, Michael R. "Cheney Gives Plan to Reduce Forces by 25% in 5 Years." *New York Times,* June 20, 1990. At http://www.nytimes.com/1990/06/20/us/cheney-gives-plan-to-reduce-forces-by-25-in-5-years.html?pagewanted=all.

Gorman, Paul F. "Preparing for Low-Intensity Conflict: Four Fundamentals." In *Essays on Strategy.* Washington, DC: National Defense University Press, 1988. At http://usacac.army.mil/cac2/csi/docs/Gorman/06_Retired/01_Retired_1985_90/30_88_NDUPreparing_LowIntensityConflict_Four%20Fundamentals_Aug.pdf.

Hamilton, Lee. "Dialogue: Last Word on the October Surprise? Case Closed." *New York*

Times, January 24, 1993. At http://www.nytimes.com/1993/01/24/opinion/dialogue-last-word-on-the-october-surprise-case-closed.html.

Hastedt, Glen. "Intelligence Failure and Terrorism: The Attack on the Marines in Beirut." *Journal of Conflict Studies* 8, no. 2 (1988): 7–22.

Heard, Alex. "The Schwarzkopf File." *New York Times,* August 11, 1991. At http://www. nytimes.com/1991 /08/11/magazine/the-schwarzkopf-filet.html.

Hevesi, Dennis. "Wesley McDonald, Who Planned for Grenada, Dies at 84." *New York Times,* February 23, 2009. At http://www.nytimes.com/2009/02/23/us/23mcdonald. html?_r=0.

Holmes, Steven A. "The 2000 Campaign: Foreign Policy; Gore Assails Bush on Plan to Recall U.S. Balkan Force." *New York Times,* October 22, 2000. At http://www. nytimes.com/2000/10/22/world/2000-campaign-foreign-policy-gore-assails-bush-plan-recall-us-balkan-force.html.

Holsti, Ole R. "Of Chasms and Convergences: Attitudes and Beliefs of Civilians and Military Elites at the Start of a New Millennium." In *Soldiers and Civilians: The Civil–Military Gap and American National Security,* edited by Peter D. Feaver and Richard H. Kohn, 15–100. Cambridge, MA: Belfer Center for Science and International Affairs-John F. Kennedy School, Harvard University, 2001.

Ignatius, David. "How the CIA Came Unglued." *Washington Post,* May 12, 2006. At http://www.washingtonpost.com/wp-dyn/content/article/2006/05/11/ AR2006051101947.html.

Jehl, Douglas. "2 CIA Reports Offer Warnings on Iraq's Path." *New York Times,* December 7, 2004. At http://www.nytimes.com/2004/12/07/international/middleeast/07intell.

Jones, David C. "Why the Joint Chiefs of Staff Must Change." *Presidential Studies Quarterly* 12, no. 2 (Spring 1982): 138–49.

Judis, John. "The Case for Abolishing the CIA." *New Republic Online,* December 20, 2005. At http://carnegieendowment.org/2005/12/20/case-for-abolishing-cia.

Kessler, Glenn. "Cutting the Defense Budget." *Washington Post,* January 25, 2011. At http://voices.washingtonpost.com/fact-checker/2011/01/cutting_the_defense_budget.html.

Kibbe, Jennifer. "The Military, the CIA, and America's Shadow Wars." In *Mission Creep: The Militarization of US Foreign Policy,* edited by Gordon Adams and Shoon Murray, 210–34. Washington, DC: Georgetown University Press, 2014.

Klaidman, Daniel. "Broken Furniture at the CIA." *Newsweek,* November 28, 2004. At http://www.newsweek.com/broken-furniture-cia-124599.

Kocieniewski, David. "Challenger to Toricelli Attacks Curbs on the CIA." *New York Times,* September 17, 2002. At http://www.nytimes.com/2002/09/17/nyregion/challenger-to-toricelli-attacks-curbs-on-the-cia.html.

Langer, Emily. "Ike Skelton, Congressman, Who Led House Armed Services Committee, Dies at 81." *Washington Post,* October 29, 2013. At https://www.washingtonpost. com/politics/ike-skelton-congressman-who-led-house-armed-services-committee-dies-at-81/2013/10/29/ba8ae458-40ad-11e3-9c8b-e8deeb3c755b_story.html.

"Lieutenant General Brent Scowcroft." US Air Force, current as of July 15, 1975. At http://www.af.mil/AboutUs/Biographies/Display/tabid/225/Article/104997/lieutenant-general-brent-scowcroft.aspx. Accessed April 2, 2018.

"Lieutenant General Buster C. Glosson." US Air Force, current as of October 1993. At http://www.af.mil/AboutUs/Biographies/Display/tabid/225/Article/106980/ lieutenant-general-buster-c-glosson.aspx. Accessed April 10, 2016.

Lockwood, Stuart. "That's Me in the Picture: Stuart Lockwood with Saddam Hussein, 24 August 1990 Baghdad, Iraq." *Guardian*, June 5, 2015. At http://www.theguardian.com/artanddesign/2015/jun/05/thats-me-picture-stuart-lockwood-saddam-hussein-iraq.

Loeb, Vernon. "After Action Report." *Washington Post*, February 27, 2000. At https://www.washingtonpost.com/archive/lifestyle/magazine/2000/02/27/after-action-report/3c474a43-ea21-4bf5-afc5–02820b8579e5/.

———. "Rumsfeld's Man on the Intelligence Front." *Washington Post*, February 10, 2003.

———. "Warlords, Peacekeepers, and Spies." *Washington Post*, February 27, 2000. At http://www.somaliawatch.org/archivejuly/000927601.htm.

"A Look Back . . . the National Security Act of 1947." CIA, News & Information, July 7, 2008. At https://www.cia.gov/news-information/featured-story-archive/2008-featured-story-archive/national-security-act-of-1947.html.

Markon, Jerry. "Former Top CIA Official Sentenced to 37 Months." *Washington Post*, February 27, 2009. At http://www.washingtonpost.com/wp-dyn/content/article/2009/02/26/AR2009022601742.html.

"McCain Defends '100 Years in Iraq' Statement." CNN.com, February 15, 2008. At http://www.cnn.com/2008/POLITICS/02/14/mccain.king/.

"Military Affairs/History." CIA, n.d. At https://www.cia.gov/offices-of-cia/military-affairs/history.html. Accessed November 18, 2012.

Miller, Greg. "CIA Director John Brennan Considering Sweeping Organizational Changes." *Washington Post*, November 19, 2014. At https://www.washingtonpost.com/world/national-security/cia-director-john-brennan-considering-sweeping-organizational-changes/2014/11/19/fa85b320-6ffb-11e4-ad12-3734c461eab6_story.html.

———. "CIA Expanding Presence in Afghanistan." *Los Angeles Times*, September 20, 2009. At http://articles.latimes.com/2009/sep/20/world/fg-afghan-intel20.

———. "DIA to Send Hundreds More Spies Overseas." *Washington Post*, December 1, 2012. At https://www.washingtonpost.com/world/national-security/dia-to-send-hundreds-more-spies-overseas/2012/12/01/97463e4e-399b-11e2-b01f-5f55b193f58f_story.html.

———. "Pentagon's Plans for a Spy Service to Rival the CIA Have Been Pared Back." *Washington Post*, November 1, 2014. At https://www.washingtonpost.com/world/national-security/pentagons-plans-for-a-spy-service-to-rival-the-cia-have-been-pared-back/2014/11/01/1871bb92-6118-11e4-8b9e-2ccdac31a031_story.html.

———. "Secret Report Raises Alarms on Intelligence Blind Spots because of AQ Focus."

Washington Post, March 20, 2013. At https://www.washingtonpost.com/world/
national-security/secret-report-raises-alarms-on-intelligence-blind-spots-because-of-
aq-focus/2013/03/20/1f8f1834-90d6-11e2-9cfd-36d6c9b5d7ad_story.html?hpid=z1.

———. "Senate Moves to Block Pentagon Plans to Increase Number of Spies Overseas." *Washington Post,* December 10, 2012. At http://articles.washingtonpost.
com/2012-12-10/world/35745387_1_defense-clandestine-service-pentagon-dia.

Miller, Mark Crispin. "Operation Desert Sham." *New York Times,* June 24, 1992. At
http://www.nytimes.com/1992/06/24/opinion/operation-desert-sham.html.

Mitchell, John L., and Nora Zamichow. "CIA Head Speaks in L.A. to Counter
Crack Claims." *Los Angeles Times,* November 16, 1996. At http://articles.latimes.
com/1996-11-16/news/mn-65300_1_cia-crack-cocaine.

Moore, Molly. "Schwarzkopf: War Intelligence Flawed; General Reports to Congress on
Desert Storm." *Washington Post,* June 13, 1991.

Mullen, Michael. Speech given at Kansas State University, March 2010. At http://
www.cfr.org/defense-strategy/admiral-mullens-speech-military-strategy-kansas
-state-university-march-2010/p21590.

Murray, Shoon, and Anthony Quainton. "Combatant Commanders, Ambassadorial
Authority, and the Conduct of Diplomacy." In *Mission Creep: The Militarization of
US Foreign Policy,* edited by Gordon Adams and Shoon Murray, 166–90. Washington, DC: Georgetown University Press, 2014.Myers, Steven Lee. "Chinese Embassy
Bombing: A Wide Net of Blame." *New York Times,* April 17, 2000. At http://www.
nytimes.com/2000/04/17/world/chinese-embassy-bombing-a-wide-net-of-blame.
html?pagewanted=all.

Oakley, David. "Partners or Competitors? The Evolution of the Department of Defense/
Central Intelligence Agency Relationship since Desert Storm and Its Prospects for
the Future." Joint Special Operations University, May 2014. At http://jsou.libguides.
com/ld.php?content_id=2876951.

———. "Taming the Rogue Elephant?" *American Intelligence Journal* 26, no. 2 (2008–
2009): 61–67.

Ogden, Pete. "Who Is Stephen Cambone?" Center for American Progress, July 20,
2004. At https://www.americanprogress.org/issues/security/news/2004/07/20/941/
who-is-stephen-cambone/.

Pellegrini, Frank. "Defense: Rumsfeld's Lonely, Losing Battle." *Time,* August 9, 2001. At
http://content.time.com/time/nation/article/0,8599,170605,00.html.

Perkins, David D. "Counterintelligence and HUMINT." In *Lessons from Bosnia: The
IFOR Experience,* edited by Larry Wentz, 225–54. Washington, DC: US Department of Defense, 1997.

Perle, Richard. "Iraq: Saddam Unbound." In *Present Dangers: Crisis and Opportunity in
American Foreign and Defense Policy,* edited by Robert Kagan and William Kristol,
99–110. New York: Encounter Books, 2000.

Pincus, Walter. "Defense Procurement Problems Won't Go Away." *Washington Post,* May
2, 2012.

———. "Secret Agency Reportedly Salted Away $1-Billion Fund: Finances: The

National Reconnaissance Office Did Nothing Illegal, but CIA Director Orders a Restructuring." *Los Angeles Times,* September 24, 1995. At http://articles.latimes.com/1995-09-24/news/mn-49643_1_national-reconnaissance-office.

Pincus, Walter, and Dana Priest. "Bush Orders the CIA to Hire More Spies." *Washington Post,* November 23, 2004. At http://www.washingtonpost.com/wp-dyn/articles/A8650-2004Nov23.html.

Powers, Thomas. "The Rise and Fall of Richard Helms: Survival and Sudden Death in the CIA." *Rolling Stone,* December 16, 1976. At http://www.rollingstone.com/culture/features/the-rise-and-fall-of-richard-helms-19761216?page=3.

Prados, John. "The Navy's Biggest Betrayal." *Naval History Magazine* 24, no. 3 (June 2010). At http://www.usni.org/magazines/navalhistory/2010-06/navys-biggest-betrayal.

Raum, Tom. "CIA Recruiting Drive Paying Off." Associated Press, January 17, 2000. At http://fas.org/sgp/news/2000/01/ap011700.html.

"Remembering CIA's Heroes: William F. Buckley." CIA, News & Information, n.d. At https://www.cia.gov/news-information/featured-story-archive/2015-featured-story-archive/william-buckley.html. Accessed February 10, 2017.

Richter, Paul. "For the Military, Bush Is Not Yet All That He Can Be." *Los Angeles Times,* February 10, 2001. At http://articles.latimes.com/2001/feb/10/news/mn-23691.

"Robert Gates: Government Official (1943–)." *Biography,* n.d. At http://www.biography.com/people/robert-gates-40993#early-career. Accessed April 3, 2018.

Rosenbaum, David E. "Les Aspin, 56, Dies: Member of Congress and Defense Chief." *New York Times,* May 22, 1995. At http://www.nytimes.com/1995/05/22/obituaries/les-aspin-56-dies-member-of-congress-and-defense-chief.html?pagewanted=all.

Rosenberg, Scott. "Panama and Noriega: 'Our SOB.'" Emory University, 2007. At http://history.emory.edu/home/documents/endeavors/volume1/Scotts.pdf.

Rosenthal, Andrew, and Michael R. Gordon. "A Failed Coup: The Bush Team and Noriega." *New York Times,* October 8, 1989. At http://www.nytimes.com/1989/10/08/world/failed-coup-bush-team-noriega-special-report-panama-crisis-disarray-hindered.html?pagewanted=all.

Safire, William. "Is Peace Bullish?" *New York Times,* June 8, 1989.

Schafer, Suzanne M. "Desert Storm General Volunteers for Lower Rank Retirement." Associated Press, July 7, 1994. At http://www.apnewsarchive.com/1994/Desert-Storm-General-Volunteers-for-Lower-Rank-Retirement/id-633995e095fc5db2694d3e47711c8b03.

Schmitt, Eric. "General Is Scolded in Ethics Inquiry." *New York Times,* December 4, 1993. At http://www.nytimes.com/1993/12/04/us/general-is-scolded-in-ethics-inquiry.html.

———. "Pentagon Sends Its Spies to Join Fight on Terror." *New York Times,* January 24, 2005. At http://www.nytimes.com/2005/01/24/politics/pentagon-sends-its-spies-to-join-fight-on-terror.html.

———. "War in the Gulf: Commanders; Top Brass in Gulf: Profiles in Uniformed Authority." *New York Times,* February 12, 1991. At http://www.nytimes.com/1991/02/12/world/war-in-the-gulf-commanders-top-brass-in-gulf-profiles-in-uniformed-authority.html?pagewanted=all.

Schraeder, Peter J. "From Ally to Orphan: Understanding U.S. Policy toward Somalia after the Cold War." In *After the End: Making U.S. Foreign Policy in the PostCold War World,* edited by Paul James M. Scott. 330–57. Durham, NC: D uke University Press, 2000.

Schudel, Matt. "William E. Odom, 75; Military Adviser to 2 Administrations." *Washington Post,* May 31, 2008. At http://www.washingtonpost.com/wp-dyn/content/article/2008/05/31/AR2008053102193.html.

Sciolino, Elaine. "Change at the Pentagon: Man in the News—Bobby Ray Inman; an Operator for the CIA." *New York Times,* December 17, 1993. At http://www.nytimes.com/1993/12/17/us/change-pentagon-man-bobby-ray-inman-operator-for-pentagon.html?pagewanted=all.

Shachtman, Noah. "Rumsfeld's Intel Chief: Iraq War 'Greatest Decision of the Century.'" *Wired,* July 2012. At http://www.wired.com/2012/07/cambone-iraq/.

Shenon, Phillip. "Noriega Indicted by U.S. for Link to Illegal Drugs." *New York Times,* February 6, 1988. At http://www.nytimes.com/1988/02/06/world/noriega-indicted-by-us-for-links-to-illegal-drugs.html?_r=0.

Shogan, Robert. "Centrist Ally Calls Clinton 'Old Democrat.'" *Los Angeles Times,* December 7, 1994. at http://articles.latimes.com/1994-12-07/news/mn-5990_1_leadership-council.

Sia, Richard H. P. "Embattled Les Aspin Steps Down." *Baltimore Sun,* December 16, 1993. At http://articles.baltimoresun.com/1993-12-16/news/1993350006_1_les-aspin-clinton-oval.

Sims, Jennifer. "More Military Spies: Why the CIA Is Applauding the Pentagon's Intelligence Grab." *Foreign Affairs,* May 18, 2012. At https://www.foreignaffairs.com/articles/2012-05-18/more-military-spies.

Snider, L. Britt. "Sharing Secrets with Lawmakers: Congress as a User of Intelligence." In *Intelligence and the National Security Strategist: Enduring Issues and Challenges,* edited by Roger Z. George and Robert D. Kline, 85–102. New York: Rowman and Littlefield, 2006.

"Soldiers Rammed by the Soviets Not in the Wrong, U.S. Says." *Pittsburgh Press,* July 17, 1985. At https://news.google.com/newspapers?nid=1144&dat=19850717&id=1NQbAAAAIBAJ&sjid=CWMEAAAAIBAJ&pg=4947,203827&hl=en.

Steele, Robert David. "The National Security Act of 1992." *American Intelligence Journal,* Winter–Spring 1992, 31–37.

"Text: President Bush Addresses the Nation." *Washington Post,* September 20, 2001. At http://www.washingtonpost.com/wp-srv/nation/specials/attacked/transcripts/bush-address_092001.html.

Troxell, John F. "Sizing the Force for the 21st Century." In *Revising the Two MTW Force Shaping Paradigm,* edited by Steven Metz, 7–40. Carlisle, PA: Strategic Studies Institute, 2001.

Tyson, Ann Scott. "Gates Warns of Militarized Policy." *Washington Post,* July 16, 2008. At http://www.washingtonpost.com/wp-dyn/content/article/2008/07/15/AR2008071502777.html.

"US Expands Its Sanctions against Panama." *New York Times,* September 13, 1989. At http://www.nytimes.com/1989/09/13/world/us-expands-its-sanctions-against-panama.html.

"U.S. Intelligence Official Acknowledges Missed Arab Spring Signs." *Los Angeles Times,* July 19, 2012. At http://latimesblogs.latimes.com/world_now/2012/07/us-intelligence-official-acknowledges-missed-signs-ahead-of-arab-spring-.html.

"U.S. Major Killed by Soviet Sentry: Accused of Photographing E. German Military Installation." UPI. *Los Angeles Times,* March 25, 1985. At http://articles.latimes.com/1985-03-25/news/mn-21307_1_soviet-union.

Wallace, Linda, and Mark Fazlollah. "The Man Whose Death Led to Warfare." *Philadelphia Inquirer,* December 22, 1989. At http://articles.philly.com/1989-12-22/news/26158426_1_jaime-paz-animal-science-panamanians.

Warner, Michael. "Central Intelligence: Origin and Evolution." In *Intelligence and the National Security Strategist: Enduring Issues and Challenges,* edited by Roger Z. George and Robert D. Kline, 41–56. New York: Rowman and Littlefield, 2006.

Weiner, Tim. "Rewiring the CIA for a Post-Cold-War World." *Rolling Stone,* June 27, 1991. At http://www.rollingstone.com/politics/news/rewiring-the-cia-for-a-post-cold-war-world-19910627.

Wentz, Larry. "Bosnia: Setting the Stage." In *Lessons from Bosnia: The IFOR Experience,* edited by Larry Wentz, 9–34. Washington, DC: National Defense University Press, 1997.

"Who Is Steve Cambone? A Look at Rumsfeld's Right-Hand Man." *Armed Forces Journal,* April 1, 2006. At http://www.armedforcesjournal.com/who-is-steve-cambone/.

Wines, Michael. "Washington at Work; after 30 Years in Shadows, a Spymaster Emerges." *New York Times,* November 20, 1990.

Zelikow, Philip. "A Personal Perspective: The Evolution of Intelligence Reform, 2002–2004." *Studies in Intelligence* 56, no. 3 (September 2012): 1–20.

Unpublished Materials

McCarty, Gregory C. "Congressional Oversight of Intelligence." PhD diss., Catholic University of America, 2009.

Urben, Heidi. "Civil–Military Relations in a Time of War." April 14, 2010.

INDEX

Central Imagery Office, 72, 102

Central Intelligence Agency (CIA): assistant deputy director of operations, 54–55; associate director of military affairs, 2; George H. W. Bush and, 63–65; Center for Study of Intelligence, 156; challenges of the post–Cold War world and budget reductions, 107–8; Chinese embassy bombing in Belgrade, 113; CIA/SOF relationship in Afghanistan and Iraq, 144–45; William Colby and the "Family Jewels" controversy, 56, 103; controversies over covert actions and, 137, 138; Counterterrorism Center, 1–2, 26, 144; crack cocaine allegations, 107; critical attacks on in the early 1990s, 103–4; Defense Clandestine Service and, 138; defense intelligence reform after the Gulf War and, 58; Ronald Dellums and, 56–57; John Deutch, 104–5, 106–7; Directorate of Intelligence, 44–45; Directorate of Operations (*see* Directorate of Operations); DoD/CIA relationship (*see* DoD/CIA relationship); drone technology and, 48, 113–14; entry into Afghanistan, 128; Robert Gates and intelligence reform, 66, 67, 68–74, 88, 89; Porter Goss and, 147, 148; Grenada invasion and, 15–16, 17; the Gulf War and, 32, 33, 38–40, 41, 44–45, 47, 50, 153–54 (*see also* Gulf War); Gulf War illness and, 57; Michael Hayden and, 148; human intelligence (*see* human intelligence); intelligence debate following the Gulf War and, 51, 52, 53–54, 57; intelligence reform and, 103, 139 (*see also* intelligence reform); Interagency Balkans Task Force, 111, 154; Joint Intelligence Task Force–Counterterrorism and, 130; Kosovo and, 113; militarization of, 7; mission in Iraq, 136; National Clandestine Service, 141; National Military Joint Intelligence Center and, 45; National Reconnais-

sance Office and, 72–73; National Security Act of 1947 and, 2–3, 152; National Security Directive 67 and, 5; national security drawdown in the 1990s and, 90, 91–92; Office of Military Affairs, 73, 75–76; organizational reform in the 1980s, 26; paramilitary operations and, 140–41, 202n48; recommendations in the 1980s for increasing support to military operations, 21; reinvestment in during the Clinton administration, 119; Donald Rumsfeld's pursuit of DoD independence from, 128–29, 133–38, 140, 145–46; Satellite Reconnaissance Program, 73; Somalia and, 154; Special Operations Command and, 26; "surging" of personnel to support military operations, 108; tactical operations and, 158, 207–8n24; Robert Torricelli and the Guatemala controversy, 105–6, 193n60; unconventional-warfare activities and the DoD, 136; US embassy bombing in Beirut and, 17

Centralized Management of Department of Defense Human Intelligence Operations, 93

Chalabi, Ahmad, 136

Charlie Wilson's War (film), 138

Checklist for the Future of Intelligence (Georgetown University), 117

Cheney, Richard: career overview and prioritizing of intelligence, 122–23; defense intelligence reform after the Gulf War and, 58; Robert Gates and, 67–68; Gulf War and, 39, 51; Gulf War blowback on intelligence and, 46, 48; Richard Haver and, 67–68, 121–22; national security drawdown in the 1990s and, 91; Panama invasion and, 30; Powell Doctrine of military ability to wage two midsize wars, 119; presidential election of 1992 and, 89; review of the DoD in 1992, 62; Donald Rumsfeld and, 121; as vice president, 121–23

Childs, Dan, 54

after the Gulf War and, 60; DoD
HUMINT reform in the early 1990s,
92–94; Grenada invasion and, 15;
Interagency Balkans Task Force, 111;
Lowell Jacoby and, 60; John Leide
and, 41; Remodeling Defense Initia-
tive and, 143; tactical and clandestine
HUMINT, 49; view of intelligence
support to the military, 54. *See also*
DoD human intelligence
Defense Intelligence Priorities Frame-
work, 191n21
Defense Management Review, 59
Defense Mapping Agency, 72, 102
Defense Planning Guidance of 1992,
196n102
Defense Planning Guidance of 2001, 124
Dellums, Ronald, 56–57
Democratic League of Kosovo, 112
Dempsey, Joan, 126
Department of Defense (DoD): *The 9/11
Commission Report* and, 139–40;
"areas of operation," 164n13; Les
Aspin and the Bottom-Up Review,
96–97; battle-damage assessments
controversy in the Gulf War, 38–40
(*see also* Gulf War); Beirut barracks
bombing and post-bombing reviews,
17–22, 18–22; centralization of imagery intelligence, 102; challenges of
the post–Cold War world and budget
reductions, 107–8; Richard Cheney's
1992 review of, 62; defense intelligence reform in the 1990s, 92–94;
DoD/CIA relationship (*see* DoD/
CIA relationship); *Final Report to
Congress on the Conduct of the Persian Gulf War,* 54; Robert Gates and,
148–49; Goldwater-Nichols Department of Defense Reorganization Act
and, 24–27, 31, 153; Grenada invasion and postinvasion reviews, 14–17;
Hart-Rudman Commission recommendations, 116; human intelligence
and, 48–49, 60 (*see also* DoD human
intelligence); intelligence reform after
the Gulf War, 58–60, 61; Intelligence

Reform and Terrorism Prevention
Act and, 139; David Jones's recommendations for unification, 13–14;
militarization of US foreign policy
and, 158–59; National Military Joint
Intelligence Center and, 45; National
Reconnaissance Office and, 72–73;
National Security Act of 1947 and,
2–3; national security drawdown in
the 1990s and, 90, 91, 92; overview
of interoperability failures, intelligence support, and calls for DoD
reform, 12–14, 21–22, 31; Panama
invasion and postinvasion reviews,
28–30, 31; "phasing model," 154–55,
169n52; Powell Doctrine and, 119;
reinvestment in during the Clinton
administration, 119; Remodeling
Defense Initiative, 142–43; response
to congressional bills on intelligence
reform in 1992, 87–88; response to
the Aspin-Brown Commission recommendations, 102; Donald Rumsfeld
and counterterrorism reform, 129–30;
Donald Rumsfeld's alienation of the
military by September 2001, 127–28;
Donald Rumsfeld's first tenure as
secretary of defense, 63, 64; Donald
Rumsfeld's pursuit of independence
from the CIA, 128–29, 133–38, 140,
145–46; Donald Rumsfeld's pursuit of
reform in, 123–25, 129; undersecretary of defense for intelligence, 131–33
Department of Defense Directive 5200-
37, 93
Department of Defense Reorganization
Act (1958), 25
Department of Defense Reorganization
Act (1986). *See* Goldwater-Nichols
Department of Defense Reorganization Act
Department of the Army, 53
deputy director of operations (DDO), 75
deputy director of the Central Intelligence
Agency, 98
deputy director of the Intelligence Community, 98

Hayward, Thomas, 40, 174–75n41
Helms, Jesse, 27, 28
Helms, Richard, 103, 137
Herspring, Dale, 128
Holbrooke, Richard, 112
Holt, Marjorie, 15–16
Horner, Charles, 42
House Armed Services Committee
   (HASC): David Jones's recommen-
   dations for DoD unification, 13–14;
   report on intelligence support in
   the Gulf War, 55–56; review of the
   Grenada invasion, 15–17; review of
   the US embassy bombing in Beirut,
   17–18, 19
House Permanent Select Committee on
   Intelligence (HPSCI): concerns over
   clandestine operations in the global
   war on terrorism, 136; defense intel-
   ligence reform after the Gulf War
   and, 58; hearings on the Chinese
   embassy bombing in Belgrade, 113;
   Intelligence Community in the 21st
   Century hearings and report, 99–101,
   102; Dave McCurdy and intelligence
   reform, 80, 82–83, 88; review of the
   Panama invasion, 29–30; Robert Torricelli and allegations against the CIA
   in Guatemala, 105–6
House Select Committee on Intelligence
   (Pike Committee), 56–57, 63, 65, 97
Howe, Jonathan T., 18
HPSCI. See House Permanent Select
   Committee on Intelligence
Hughes-Ryan Amendment, 136
Human Augmentation Teams, 135
human intelligence (HUMINT): Aspin-
   Brown Commission recommendations, 98–99; Balkans crisis and,
   111–12; Beirut barracks bombing
   and, 20, 21; John Deutch and, 106–7;
   director of the Central Intelligence
   Agency and the integration of, 141–
   42; Robert Gates's intelligence reform
   and, 69; Grenada invasion and, 15,
   16, 21; Gulf War weapons technologies and the need for intelligence sup-

port, 60–61; "Halloween Massacre"
   and reduction in, 15, 20; human
   rights and, 105–6, 107, 116–17;
   Intelligence Community in the 21st
   Century report on, 101; intelligence
   debate following the Gulf War and,
   51, 52, 53, 56; intelligence reform and
   the SSCI, 77–78; Intelligence Reorganization Act of 1992 on, 82; meanings of, 178n12; National Human
   Intelligence Tasking Center, 71–72;
   National Security Act of 1992 on, 83;
   Remodeling Defense Initiative and,
   142, 143; shortcomings in the Gulf
   War, 32, 33, 48–50; Somalia and,
   110–11, 154; tactical HUMINT, 16,
   49, 134–35, 158; trade-offs with the
   DoD/CIA relationship and, 157–58.
   See also clandestine human intelligence; DoD human intelligence
human rights: HUMINT and, 105–6,
   107, 116–17
HUMINT. See human intelligence
Hurwitz, Marty, 59
Hussein, Saddam, 33–34, 57, 146

IAA. See Intelligence Authorization Act
Ikle, Harold, 15, 16
imagery intelligence, 72, 102
Imagery Intelligence Directorate, 73
Inman, Bobby Ray: career overview,
   20–21; Robert Gates and, 66, 67,
   183nn15, 16; head of the Advisory
   Panel on Overseas Security, 20, 21;
   officers mentored by, 40, 47–48; SCSI
   hearings on intelligence reform and,
   78–79, 83; on trade-offs with the
   DoD/CIA relationship, 157–58; John
   Walker spy case and, 47
Inman Panel, 20–21
Inman Standards, 21
intelligence: Beirut barracks bombing
   and, 18–21; Richard Cheney and
   the prioritizing of, 122–23; Grenada
   invasion and, 15–17; Gulf War and,
   31–32, 33, 38–39, 40–45, 46–61,
   189n92 (see also Gulf War);